THE
WALKING
DEAD

ROBERT KIRKMAN'S
THE
WALKING
DEAD
INVASION

JAY BONANSINGA

PAN BOOKS

First published 2015 by Thomas Dunne Books,
an imprint of St Martin's Press

First published in the UK 2016 by Pan Books
an imprint of Pan Macmillan
20 New Wharf Road, London N1 9RR
Associated companies throughout the world
www.panmacmillan.com

ISBN 978-1-4472-7576-3

1 3 5 7 9 8 6 4 2

A CIP catalogue record for this book is available from the British Library.

Printed and bound by CPI Group (UK) Ltd, Croydon, CR0 4YY

For James J. Wilson, a fellow bad boy taken too soon

ACKNOWLEDGMENTS

Muchas gracias to Robert Kirkman for crafting the Rosetta stone—the greatest horror comic ever written—and giving me the gig of a lifetime. Also, a shout-out to the fans and the amazing staff of the Walker Stalker Convention—you make a humble writer feel like a rock star. Special thanks to David Alpert, Andy Cohen, Jeff Siegel, Brendan Deneen, Nicole Sohl, Lee Ann Wyatt, T. Q. Jefferson, Cris Macht, Ian Vacek, Shawn Kirkham, Sean Mackiewicz, Dan Murray, Matt Candler, Mike McCarthy, Bryan Kett, and Steven and Lena Olsen of A Little Shop of Comics, Scotch Plains, New Jersey. An extra special thanks to the role model for Lilly Caul, my wife and best friend (and muse), Jill Norton: You are the love of my life.

PART 1

The Behavior
of Sheep

May the Lord destroy all the tyrants of the church. Amen.

—Michael Servetus

ONE

"Please, for the love of Christ, STOP THAT INFERNAL BELLYACHING FOR ONE BLESSED MINUTE!!" The tall man behind the steering wheel struggles to keep the battered Escalade on the road and maintain his speed without clipping another jackknifed semi or cluster of dead things milling about the edges of the two-lane. His voice is hoarse from all the yelling. It feels as though every muscle in his body is on fire. He has blood in his eyes from an oozing wound along the left side of his scalp. "I told you, we're gonna getcha medical attention come sunup—soon as we clear this dad-blasted herd!"

"Just sayin' . . . ain't doin' too good, Rev. . . . Think one of my lungs is punctured!" The young man in the backseat—one of two passengers in the SUV—leans his head against the broken rear window as the vehicle rumbles past another cluster of ragged, dark figures dragging along the road's gravel shoulder, fighting over something dark and wet.

Stephen Pembry looks away from the window, blinking at the pain, wheezing miserably, wiping tears. A pile of bloody cloths torn from his shirttail litters the seat next to him. A gaping jagged hole in the glass blows a slipstream of wind through the dark backseat, stirring the rags and tossing the young man's blood-matted hair. "Can't breathe right—can't get a good breath, Rev—I mean, the point is, we don't find a doctor soon, I'm gonna be uppa creek without a paddle."

"You think I ain't aware of that?!" The big preacher grips the steering wheel tighter, his huge, gnarled hands going ashen white. His broad shoulders—still clad in a black, battle-tattered church coat—hunch over the dash, the green lights of the instruments illuminating a long, deeply lined, chiseled face. He has the face of an aging gunslinger, pocked and creased by many hard miles. "Okay . . . look . . . I'm sorry I got cross with ya. Listen, Brother. We're almost to the state line. Sun'll be up soon, and we'll find help. I promise. Just hang in there."

"Please make it soon, Rev," Stephen Pembry murmurs around a hacking cough. He holds himself as though his guts are about to spill out. He gazes out at the moving shadows behind the trees. The preacher has put at least two hundred miles between them and Woodbury, and yet signs of the super-herd still riddle the countryside.

Behind the wheel, Reverend Jeremiah Garlitz glances up into the hairline fractures of the rearview mirror. "Brother Reese?" He scans the shadows of the backseats, studies the other twenty-something young man slumped against the opposite broken window. "How you holding out, son? You okay? Talk to me. You still with us?"

The boyish face of Reese Lee Hawthorne becomes visible for just an instant as they pass the distant orange glow of a fire, either a farm or a forest or a small survivor community, all of it going up in flames, a mile-long conflagration that spews snowflakes of ash up into the atmosphere. For a moment, in the flickering light, Reese looks as though he's unconscious, either asleep or blacked out. All at once he blinks his eyes open and convulses in his seat as though electrocuted. "Oh—I was just—oh Lord—I was having a wing-dinger of a dream." He tries to get his bearings. "I'm okay, I'm good . . . bleeding's stopped. . . . But sweet Jesus that was one nasty dream."

"Keep talking, son."

No response.

"Tell us about the dream."

Still no reply.

They drive in silence for a spell. Through the gore-smudged windshield, Jeremiah can see his headlight beams illuminating the rushing white lines of leprous asphalt, mile after mile of wreckage-strewn road churning under them, a never-ending landscape of The End, a desolate wasteland of rural decay after almost two years of the plague. Skeletal trees on either side of the highway blur in the preacher's burning, teary gaze. His own ribs pang intermittently with each twist of his midsection, taking his breath away—maybe a fracture, maybe worse, his wounds sustained in the tumultuous confrontation between his minions and the people of Woodbury.

He assumes Lilly Caul and her followers all perished in that same vast mob of walkers that had wrought such havoc on the town, barreling through barricades, overturning cars, burrowing into homes and buildings, eviscerating the innocent and guilty alike, and ruining Jeremiah's plans to stage his glorious ritual. Was the Good Lord offended by Jeremiah's grand scheme?

"Talk to me, Brother Reese." Jeremiah smiles at the reflection of the haggard young man in his rearview. "Why don't you tell us about the nightmare. After all . . . got a captive audience here, right?"

For another moment, the awkward silence continues, the white noise of the wind and the drumming of the tires providing a hypnotic soundtrack to their misery. After a long, girding breath, the young man in the backseat finally begins murmuring in a soft, scratchy voice: "I don't know if it'll make any kinda sense . . . but we was back in Woodbury, and we was . . . we was about to end it all and go to paradise together as planned."

A pause.

"Uh-huh. . . ." Jeremiah nods encouragingly. In the mirror, he can see Stephen trying to ignore his wounds and listen. "Go on, Reese. It's okay."

The young man shrugs. "Well . . . it was one of them dreams you have once in a while, you know . . . so vivid, it's like you can reach out and touch it? We was in that racetrack arena—it was *just* like it was last night, matter of fact—and we was all set to perform the ritual." He looks down and swallows hard, either from the pain or the reverence for such a glorious moment, or maybe both.

"Me and Anthony, we was bringing in the sacred drinks, comin' down one of them passageways toward the infield, and we could see the arc light at the end of the tunnel, and we could hear your voice getting louder and louder, saying something about how these offerings represent the flesh and blood of your only son, sacrificed so that we may live in eternal peace . . . and then . . . and then . . . we get to the arena, and you're standing there at the podium, and all our brothers and sisters are lined up in front of you, in front of the bleachers, fixin' to drink the sacred drink that's gonna send all of us to Glory."

He pauses for a moment to get himself back from the edge, his eyes glittering with horror and anguish. He takes another deep breath.

Jeremiah watches him closely in the rearview. "Go on, son."

"So, this here's the point where it gets a little dicey." He sniffs and winces at a sharp pang in his side. Amidst the chaos of Woodbury's ruination, the Escalade had overturned, and the men were banged up pretty severely. Several vertebrae in Reese's spine had dislocated. Now he stuffs the pain down his throat. "One by one, they start takin' sips of whatever was in them Dixie cups—"

"My guess?" Jeremiah interrupts, his tone turning bitter and rueful. "That old hillbilly Bob, he replaced the liquid with water. I'm sure he's pushing up daisies himself by now, though. Or maybe he's turned, along with the rest of them people. Including that Jezebel of a liar, Lilly Caul." Jeremiah snorts. "I know it ain't exactly a Christian thing to say, but them people got what they deserved. Busybodies . . . cowards. *Heathens*, all of them. I say good riddance to bad rubbish."

Another beat of tense silence stretches, and then Reese continues in his feeble monotone: "Anyway . . . what happened then, in the dream . . . I can hardly . . . it's so terrible I can hardly describe it."

"Then *don't*," Stephen chimes in from the shadows across the seat, the wind flagging his long hair. In the darkness, his narrow, ferret-like features, smudged with caked-on blood and gore, make him look practically Dickensian, like a chimney sweep left in a chimney too long.

Jeremiah lets out a sigh. "Let the young man speak, Stephen."

"I know it's just a dream, but it was so real," Reese insists. "All our people, most of them gone now, they each took a sip, and I saw their faces darken like shades had come down over windows. Their eyes shut. Their heads bowed. And then . . . and then . . ." He can barely bring himself to say it. "They each . . . *turned*." He fights his tears. "One by one, all them good folks I grew up with . . . Wade, Colby, Emma, Brother Joseph, little Mary Jean . . . their eyes popped open and they wasn't human no more . . . they were walkers. I saw their eyes in the dream . . . white, milky, shiny . . . like fish eyes. I tried to scream and run but then I saw . . . I saw . . ."

He abruptly goes silent again. Jeremiah shoots another glance at the mirror. It's too dark in the backseat area to see the expression on the kid's face. Jeremiah glances over his shoulder. "You okay?"

A jittery little nod. "Yessir."

Jeremiah turns back to the road ahead. "Go on. You can tell us what you saw."

"I don't think I want to go there."

Jeremiah sighs. "Son, sometimes the worse things just shrivel up when you talk 'em out."

"I don't think so."

"Stop acting like a baby—"

"Reverend—"

"JUST TELL US WHAT YOU SAW IN THE GODDAMN DREAM!!" Jeremiah flinches at a stabbing pain in his chest touched off by the force of his outburst. He licks his lips and breathes deeply for a moment.

In the back, Reese Lee Hawthorne trembles, wiping his mouth nervously. He exchanges a glance with Stephen, who looks down and says nothing. Reese looks at the back of the preacher's head. "I'm sorry, Rev, I'm sorry." He swallows a gulp of air. "What I saw was, I saw *you* . . . in the dream I saw *you*."

"You saw me?"

"Yessir."

"And . . . ?"

"You was *different*."

"Different—you mean *turned*?"

"No sir, not turned . . . you was just . . . *different*."

Jeremiah chews the inside of his cheek, thinking it over as he drives. "How so, Reese?"

"It's kinda hard to describe but you wasn't human anymore, your face . . . it had changed . . . it had turned into . . . I don't even know how to say it."

"Just spit it out, son."

"I don't—"

"It was a gall-darned dream, Reese. I ain't gonna hold it against you."

After a long pause, Reese says, "You was a goat."

Jeremiah goes still. Stephen Pembry sits up, his eyes shifting. Jeremiah lets out a little puff of air that's part chuckle, part incredulous grunt, but he can't form any kind of response.

"Or you was a goat-*man*," Reese goes on. "Something like that. Reverend, it was just some crazy fever dream that don't mean nothin'!"

Jeremiah takes another look at the reflection of the backseat in the rearview, his gaze latching on to Reese's shadow-draped face.

Reese gives a very uncomfortable shrug. "Looking back on it, I don't even think it was you. . . . I guess it was the devil. . . . It sure as shit wasn't human. . . . It was the devil in my dream. Half man, half goat . . . with them big curved horns, yellow eyes . . . and when I laid my own eyes on him in the dream, I realized . . ."

He stops himself.

Jeremiah looks at the mirror. "You realized what?"

Very softly now: "I realized that Satan was running things now." His raspy voice, raked with the fear, is so low as to be barely a whisper. "And we was in hell." He shudders slightly. "I realized this is the afterlife we're in now." He closes his eyes. "This is hell, and nobody even noticed the changeover."

On the other side of the backseat, Stephen Pembry braces himself, waiting for the inevitable explosion from the man behind the wheel, but all he hears is a series of low, breathy sounds coming from the front seat. At first, Stephen thinks the preacher is hyperventilating, maybe going into some kind of cardiac arrest or seizure. Chills stream down Stephen's arms and legs, the cold terror constricting his throat, when he realizes with great dismay that the huffing, wheezy noises are the beginnings of laughter.

Jeremiah is laughing.

All at once, the preacher tosses his head back and lets out a chortle—a full-bodied guffaw that takes both young men completely aback—and the laughter builds. The preacher shakes his head in hilarity, slams his hands down on the steering wheel, hoots and cackles and snorts with great, lusty abandon—as if he'd just heard the funniest joke imaginable. He's just begun to double over with uncontrolled hysterics when he hears a noise and looks up.

The two men in back cry out as the Escalade's headlights illuminate a battalion of tattered figures shuffling directly into their path.

Jeremiah tries to swerve out of the way, but he's going too fast and there are far too many of the dead.

Anybody who has struck a walker with a moving vehicle will tell you the worst part is the sound. While it's undeniable that witnessing such a horrible sight is no easy thing, and the stench that engulfs one's conveyance is unbearable, it's the *noise* that lives in the memory—a series of greasy crunching sounds that brings to mind the *thunk* of an axe through cords of rotting, termite-infested wood. The horrible symphony continues as the dead are ground to paste beneath the moving chassis and wheels—a quick series of dull pops and cracks as mortified organs and bladders are squashed, bones turned to kindling and skulls burst open and flattened—mercifully bringing an end to the torturous journey of each monster.

This hellish noise is the first thing that registers with the two young men in the backseat of that battered, late-model Cadillac Escalade.

Both Stephen Pembry and Reese Lee Hawthorne let out great yawps of shock and revulsion, holding on to the seat-backs with viselike grips as the SUV bucks, shudders, and fishtails across the slimy detritus. Most of the unsuspecting cadavers go down like dominoes, pulverized by the three tons of careening Detroit metal. Some of the excess flesh and hurling appendages tumble across the hood, leaving ghastly leech-trails of rancid blood and fluids on the windshield. Some of the body parts go pinwheeling into the air, arcing across the night sky.

The preacher remains silent and hunched, his jaw set, his eyes fixed on the road. His muscle-bound arms wrestle with the jiggering steering wheel as the massive vehicle goes into a skid. The engine revs and keens as it reacts to the loss of traction, the squeal of the huge steel-belted radials adding to the din. Jeremiah is yanking the wheel back the other way, turning into the skid as best he can in order to avoid spinning out of control, when he notices that something has gotten lodged in the gaping hole in his side window.

The disembodied head of a walker, only inches away from his left ear, its rictus of teeth chattering softly, has gotten caught on the jagged maw of broken glass, and now the thing ratchets and gnashes its blackened incisors at the preacher, fixing its silver diode eyes on him. The sight of it is so grisly, so awful, and yet so surreal—the creaking jaws snapping at him with the hollow, autonomic force of a ventriloquist's dummy—that Jeremiah lets out another involuntary chortle, this one akin to a laugh, but darker, angrier, edgier, tinged with insanity.

He jerks away from the window, registering over the space of a single instant the fact that the reanimated cranium was torn from its upper body upon impact with the SUV, and now, still intact, continues to go about its business of seeking live flesh, forever seeking, forever masticating, swallowing, and consuming, and never finding nourishment.

"LOOK OUT!!"

The scream comes from the flickering darkness of the rear seats, and in all the excitement, Jeremiah can't identify the source—whether it's Stephen or Reese—but the issue is moot, because the preacher essentially mistakes the meaning of the cry. In the split second during which his hand shoots out and fishes through the contents of the passenger seat—rifling through the maps, candy wrappers, rope, and tools, frantically searching for the 9-millimeter Glock—he assumes that the warning cry is an admonishment to look out for the snapping jaws of the amputated head. He finally gets his hand around the grip of the Glock and wastes no time swinging it up in one fluid motion toward the window and squeezing off a single point-blank blast into the brow ridge of the grotesque face skewered there. The head comes apart in a blossom of pink mist, splitting melonlike and sending splatter into Jeremiah's hair before being launched into the wind. The vacuum left behind in the broken window throbs noisily.

Less than ten seconds have transpired since the initial impact, but now Jeremiah sees the true reason that one of the men in back has howled such a warning. It has nothing to do with the reanimated head. What they're screaming about back there—the thing Jeremiah is supposed to look out for—is now looming on the opposite side of the highway, coming up quick on their right, closing in as they continue to skid out of control on the spoor of dead things.

Jeremiah feels gravity shift as he swerves in order to avoid the mangled wreckage of a VW Bug, scuds across the gravel shoulder, then plunges down a steep embankment into the dark unknown of a wooded grove. Pine boughs and foliage scrape and slap at the windshield as the vehicle bangs and clamors down the rocky slope. The voices in the back rise into frenzied ululations.

Jeremiah feels the land level out, and he manages to keep control of the vehicle long enough to find purchase in the mud. He slams down the accelerator and the Escalade lurches forward under its own power.

The massive grille and gigantic tires grind through the thickets, cobbling over deadfalls, mowing down wild undergrowth and tearing through scrub as though it were smoke. For seemingly endless minutes, the bumpy ride threatens to compress Jeremiah's spine and rupture his spleen. In the blurry image of the rearview, he gets a brief glimpse of the two injured young men holding on to the seat-backs for fear of bouncing out of the vehicle. The front end hits a log, and the impact nearly cracks Jeremiah's back molars.

For another minute or so, they career willy-nilly through the trees.

When they burst out of the brush in an explosion of dirt, leaves, and particulate, Jeremiah sees that they've inadvertently come upon another unidentified two-lane road. He slams on the brakes, causing the men in back to head-butt the seat-backs.

Jeremiah sits there for a second, taking deep breaths and getting air back in his lungs. He looks around. The men in back let out collective moans, settling back into their seats, holding themselves. The engine idles noisily, a rattling sound introduced to the low rumble, probably a bearing knocked loose in the improvised off-road adventure.

"Well now," the preacher says softly. "That's one way to take a shortcut."

Silence from the backseat, the humor lost on the two young disciples.

Above them, the black, opaque sky is just beginning to lighten with a purple predawn glow. In the dull, phosphorescent light, Jeremiah can see enough detail now to realize that they've landed on an access road, and the woods have given way to wetlands. To the east, he can see the road winding through a fogbound, soupy backwater—probably the edge of the Okefenokee Swamp—and to the west, a rust-pocked sign says "State Road 441—3 mi." No sign of roamers in either direction.

"Judging from that sign up there," Jeremiah says, "I believe we just crossed the Florida state line and didn't even know it."

He puts the vehicle in gear, carefully makes a U-turn, and starts down the road in a westerly direction. His original plan—to try and find refuge in one of the larger towns along the North Florida citrus belt, such as Lake City or Gainesville—still seems viable, despite the fact that the engine continues to ping and complain. Something has come loose during the plunge through the woods. Jeremiah doesn't like the sound of it. They need to find a place to stop soon, look under the hood, get their wounds looked at and dressed, maybe find some provisions and fuel.

"Hey! *Look!*" Reese speaks up from the shadows of the rear seats, pointing off to the southwest. "At the end of that lot."

Jeremiah drives another hundred yards or so and then brings the Escalade to a stop on the gravel shoulder. He kills the engine, and silence crashes down on the Escalade's interior. Nobody says anything at first; they just stare at the roadside sign in the middle distance. It's one of those cheap, translucent, white-fiberglass jobs, set on wheels, with the big removable plastic letters—common in the rural U.S. outside everything from flea markets to tent revivals—this one still bearing the letters:

C-A-L-V-A-R-Y B-A-P- -I-S-T C-H-U-R-C-H
A-L-L W-E- -C-O-M
S-U-N-D-A-Y 9 - & - 11

Through the spindly cypress trees and columns of pines that line the two-lane, Jeremiah can see the luminous white gravel of a deserted parking lot. The long, narrow lot leads to the front of a slumped frame building, its broken stained glass windows partially boarded, its steeple caved in on one side and scorched as though devastated from the sky in a bombing raid. Jeremiah stares at the edifice. The huge steel cross at the top of the steeple—which is covered with a patina of rust—has come loose from its moorings.

It now lies upside down, dangling by the remaining threads of its rotted hardware.

Jeremiah stares. He gets very still, gazing up at that ruined, upended cross—the sign of satanic influence—but the symbolism of an upside-down cross is only the beginning. Jeremiah realizes that this may very well be a sign that they've been left behind, and this is the Rapture, and the world is their purgatory now. They must deal with what remains, like junkyard dogs, like vermin scouring a sinking ship. They must destroy or be destroyed.

"Remind me," Jeremiah says at last, almost under his breath, not taking his eyes off the building in the distance. One of the windows in the rear has a dull yellow incandescent glow behind it, the chimney spewing a thin wisp of smoke up into the lightening sky. "How much ammunition did y'all manage to scavenge before we left Woodbury?"

In the rear seats, the two young men give each other a quick look.

Reese says, "I got one of them thirty-three-round mags for the Glock, and a box of two dozen .380s for the other pistol, and that's it."

"That's more than I got," Stephen grouses. "All I managed to grab ammo-wise was what's in the Mossberg, which I think is like eight rounds, six maybe."

Jeremiah picks his Glock up from the seat, counting the number of times he's fired since they left Woodbury. He's got six rounds left. "All right, gentlemen . . . I want you to bring all of it, all the hardware, locked and loaded." He opens the door. "And look alive."

The other two men get out of the vehicle and join the preacher in the golden light of dawn. Something is wrong. Reese notices his hands shaking as he injects the fresh magazine into the hilt of his pistol. "Rev, I don't understand," he says finally. "Why we loading up for bear? I doubt there's anything in there but scared church people. What are we doing?"

The preacher has already started toward the derelict church, his Glock gripped tightly in his huge hand, dangling at his side like a calling card. "This here's the Rapture, boys," he murmurs casually, as though informing them it's Presidents' Day. "There ain't no such thing as 'church' anymore. It's all up for grabs."

The two young men glance at each other for a moment before hurrying to catch up with the preacher.

TWO

They approach the property from the rear, through a grove of sickly eucalyptus trees that mark the outer edges of the church's lot. Jeremiah can smell the cloying stench of menthol and ammonia in the air as he creeps across the weed-whiskered gravel, careful not to make too much noise when his big boots crunch on the pea stones. The light in the chapel's rear window has dwindled with the advent of the morning sun, and the roar of crickets has faded. Now the silence lies like a pall over the area, making Jeremiah's heart throb in his ears.

He pauses behind a tree about twenty-five feet away from the lighted window.

With a few quick hand signals, the preacher rouses the two younger men, who are hiding behind a nearby oak. Stephen limps as he moves out from behind cover, carrying the pistol-grip shotgun against his solar plexus like a vestigial appendage. Reese moves in behind his friend, wide-eyed and jumpy, flinching at twinges of pain. These two are not exactly the crème de la crème of the world's new survivor class, Jeremiah realizes, nor are they the greatest disciples imaginable for a spiritual leader such as himself. But perhaps, the preacher should see these young men as they truly are: clay to be molded in this new world, this hell on earth. As Jeremiah's old man used to say, quoting Thessalonians 5:1, *"The day of the Lord will come like a thief in the night, and while people are saying, Peace and safety, destruction will come on them suddenly, as labor pains on a pregnant woman, and they will not escape."*

Jeremiah issues another signal, stabbing a finger at the rear of the building.

One by one, the three men move in toward the small, wood-sided annex off the rear of the chapel—Jeremiah in the lead, his pistol gripped in both hands, muzzle downward. The closer they get, and the more the sun dawns over the horizon, the more they realize something isn't right. The windows of the rear building—the rectory or the deacon's quarters, maybe—are lined in aluminum foil. The screen door has been ripped off its spindle, and the inner door has been nailed shut and crisscrossed with lumber. The stench of walkers permeates the air, and it gets stronger as they approach.

Jeremiah reaches the building first, and he gently stands with his back against the boarded door, signaling to the others with a finger to his lips.

They approach as quietly as possible, stepping lightly over the trash and dead leaves that are skittering across the back deck on the morning breeze. Stephen stands on one side of the preacher, Reese on the other, both keeping weapons at the ready. The preacher reaches down to his scuffed Wellington boot and pulls a twelve-inch Randall knife from the inner lining. He carefully wedges the point under one of the boards near the door's latch and yanks.

The door proves stubborn. Jeremiah pries at it repeatedly with the knife—making more racket than he cares to, but he has no choice; they would make even more noise if they tried to break through one of the windows. The nails give slightly, the rusty squeal sounding amplified in the hushed air of dawn. He has no idea what they're about to find inside this building, but he's fairly certain now that both humans as well as walkers inhabit this place.

Walkers don't build fires; and the average survivor with access to soap and water doesn't usually smell like death warmed over.

The door finally gives, and the two younger men move in closer, guns up now.

They enter one at a time.

They find themselves in an empty room, illuminated by dim, yellow, incandescent light and smelling of stale smoke and BO. Jeremiah slowly crosses the floor, his heavy boots making the floorboards creak. He makes note of the small potbelly stove still radiating the heat of dying embers, the braided rug stained with old blood, the solitary cot in one corner, the rolltop desk littered with tea bags, chafing dishes, candy wrappers, gossip magazines, empty MD 40-40 bottles, and crumpled cigarette packs.

He goes over to the desk and looks down at a display of playing cards arranged in the classic solitaire pattern. It looks like somebody—very likely a single person—was here only a moment ago and left in a hurry. A noise from behind an inner door suddenly yanks at Jeremiah's attention. He whirls. Reese and Stephen both stand across the room, gazing sheepishly back at their leader.

Again, Jeremiah puts a forefinger to his lips, giving them the *shush* sign.

The two men wait by the door, eyes aglow with nervous tension. On the other side of the door, shuffling noises build—the telltale, languid dragging of clumsy feet. There's also the reek of mortified flesh as acrid as methane, and it's getting stronger. Jeremiah recognizes the noises as well as the odors—a number of undead trapped in an enclosed space—and he turns and points to Stephen's shotgun.

A few silent hand gestures later, Stephen understands that he's supposed to blow the lock off the door and Reese is supposed to back them both up. Neither young man is very happy about this plan. Stephen looks ashen, and Reese is drenched in sweat, both of them nursing severe wounds and perhaps even internal bleeding. Neither seems very gung ho about fighting off an undetermined number of biters. But Jeremiah is an irresistible leader, the mere look in his eyes enough to quell any dissension in the ranks. He holds three fingers up. He begins to count down.

Three, two . . .

A pale blue hand covered with mold bursts through a weak spot in the lumber.

Nothing in reality ever seems to play out the way Stephen Pembry imagines it will. As a sickly, skinny kid growing up in Macon, Georgia, he lived the life of a pint-sized Walter Mitty—always rehearsing his heroic exploits standing up to bullies, saving fair maidens from evildoers, and generally being a badass. But life on the playground can quickly short-circuit your fantasies, and many black eyes later, Stephen turned to God and free weights to build up his resistance to the real world. He was never going to be Superman, but he would always be able to defend himself.

Unfortunately, the devil has a way of throwing curves at a person, and ever since the plague broke out, Stephen Pembry has constantly been thwarted. Like the time he got that woman killed in Augusta, or the time he dropped that fresh clip of ammo down the sewer grating and got chewed out for days by Brother Jeremiah. Even now, Stephen feels the world around him quickly gaining an advantage.

He trips on his backward-shuffling feet and falls to the floor. The pain in his ribs explodes, the injury jostled by the impact. The Mossberg goes spinning. At the same time, another pair of hands have thrust their way through the busted slats of the door, and Jeremiah has pulled something from his boot. Stephen watches as the dull gleam of a Buck knife streaks through the air. A butcher trimming a stubborn ham hock couldn't have amputated the gray, fleshy extremities faster or more decisively. Jeremiah drives the blade through tissue and cartilage, sawing through bone.

Hands flop to the floor as neatly as knotted limbs being pruned.

Stephen watches. He tries to sit up. His gorge clenches and burns and threatens to upchuck the paltry contents of his stomach. Things are moving quickly now. Reanimated hands are flopping around Stephen like fish on a boat's deck, slowly growing still as the electrical impulses from reanimated central nervous systems drain out. Stephen's vision blurs, his mind swimming, dizziness gripping him as his wounded lungs labor to get air.

Jeremiah has already scooped the fallen shotgun from the floor, pumping shells into its breech with a single jerk of his arm as he turns back to the door. Stephen manages to lever himself back up to a standing position, kicking the ghastly hands out of the way. Jeremiah slams a work boot into the door, and the door implodes, revealing the interior of the dark chapel.

Stephen gets a fleeting glimpse of the sanctuary before the first blast shatters the tableau.

Once a quaint little nave of burnished pine pews, maroon carpet, and stained glass panels depicting scenes of the Resurrection, the chapel now resembles an abattoir from the ninth circle of hell. The dead number in the dozens—maybe as many as forty or fifty—most of them chained to the pews with makeshift tethers of rope and electrical cord. They react to the light of the outer room as if Jeremiah had just turned over a rock and exposed a colony of vermin.

Insensate faces jerk toward the noise, their metallic eyes reflecting movement. Most of the parishioners sport their Sunday best—off-the-rack woolen suits and bargain-basement sundresses, fancy hats and wilted corsages—and the sight of their formal garb seizes Stephen's heart. Most of the dead appear to have once been African-American, although the lividity and gray rigor mortis of death have homogenized and camouflaged their original ethnicity. Stranger still, in that terrible instant before the first flash of the 12-gauge, Stephen sees that somebody apparently tried to minister to these beings after they reanimated.

Hymnals, their bindings cracked, lie open in front of each captive like dead birds. Morsels of food, pieces of roadkill, or unidentifiable human remains are scattered in the pews next to each being. Candles still burn in the sanctuary on advent stands at the front of the room on the modest little altar. Somewhere the buzz of a live microphone drones. The air smells of mortified sewage perfumed with acrid disinfectant.

It almost appears as though an outside party has tried in vain to keep the daily services going.

Stephen gets one final glance at Jeremiah before the air lights up, and the look on the preacher's face is horrifying: a mixture of sorrow, rage, loss, madness, and regret—the look of a man confronting the merciless abyss. Then the shooting starts.

The first blast flashes and takes the closest walker down in a puff of cranial tissue, the shell ripping through skull and taking a chink out of the lintel above the door. Three subsequent blasts boom in the flickering gloom, making Stephen's ears ring and vanquishing the other three creatures who had apparently managed to slip free of their bonds. Already covered with blowback, his anguished face stippled and spattered, Jeremiah now moves deeper into the chapel and starts in on the others.

It takes only a few minutes—the air flashing like a fireworks display—as Jeremiah goes from pew to pew, either vaporizing skulls or thrusting his Randall knife through putrefied nasal cavities before the parishioners even get a chance to bite at the air. Stephen staggers toward the open doorway to get a better view, and he notices Reese just inside the chapel entrance, crouched on the floor, gaping in horror at the proceedings.

Jeremiah has the strangest look on his face now as he finishes off the last of the monsters with hard, quick slashes of the knife. The Mossberg has been emptied, eight shells of tactical shot peppering the walls behind heaps of moldering flesh. Completely slimy with blood, his eyes burning with inscrutable emotions, the preacher looks almost beatific as he dispatches the last reanimated corpse.

For one terrible moment, watching all this from the doorway, Stephen Pembry thinks of a man having an orgasm. The preacher lets out a voluptuous sigh of relief as he impales the skull of an elderly woman in a frilly dress made of ruffles and chintz. The crone sags against the back of her pew. She was once somebody's mother, somebody's neighbor. She may have once baked cookies for her grandchildren, served her famous bread pudding at ice cream socials, and laid to rest her beloved husband of forty-seven years in the kudzu-lined cemetery out behind the rectory.

The preacher pauses to catch his breath. Staring down at the woman, he starts to silently pray. His head is bowed, his lips moving, when all at once he abruptly stops and looks up and narrows his eyes. His head cocks to one side as he listens closely to something in another part of the building. At last, he fixes his gaze on Reese and says softly, "You hear that?"

Reese manages a slow shake of his head.

The preacher looks up at the railings of the choir loft twenty feet above them. He reaches for his knife, pulling the bloodstained instrument from his belt. Then he signals for his men to follow.

They find the woman in the second-floor bathroom, just down a narrow passageway from the choir loft. A portly African-American gal in a filthy gingham mourning dress, ancient tennis shoes, and a hairnet, she huddles inside a stall, shivering with terror as the men enter the ladies' room. Jeremiah kicks open the stall door and sees the woman's enormous derriere sticking out from behind the commode. "Come on outta there, ma'am," Jeremiah says softly but firmly, as though addressing a family pet.

The woman twists around and pokes a small .38 caliber police special in his face. "Back off, motherfucker! I'll use it, I swear!"

"Whoa!—WHOA!" Jeremiah raises both hands, eyebrows rising as Reese and Stephen move in behind him with muzzles up and ready. "Let's all take a breath now. . . . All right . . . no cause to go all O.K. Corral on each other."

"Them people down there," the woman says, and then stops herself, her expression faltering. Her gun lowers. She slumps, a single tear tracking down her plump face, making a leech trail across her ashy brown cheek. "Them people . . . they was . . . they was my family . . . they was all in my choir and they . . . they needed to go . . . I know that. . . . I just didn't have the heart."

Jeremiah holsters his knife inside his boot, and kneels beside her. "Take a deep breath, Sister."

The woman starts to sob. She drops her gun. Her head lolls forward and her tears and saliva drip into the toilet. "Oh Lordy . . . Lordy . . . what a life."

"It's all right now." The preacher reaches out, puts an arm around her. Reese and Stephen back off, lowering their weapons. "It's all right, Sister." He pats her tenderly. "Let it out."

"I don't know what I was thinking." She sobs, shaking her head. "Keepin' them in there like that." Drool loops off her chin. She pulls a handkerchief from her moist cleavage and dabs her face. "I played organ for them sometimes. . . . Other times I would read the Bible through the PA system." She snorts and blows her nose. "Like it was doing any good. I didn't have the heart to put them outta their misery." She sniffs, dabs her bloodshot eyes. "I don't know what the Good Lord wants anymore."

Jeremiah smiles. "Look at me, Sister. What's your name, if I may ask."

"Norma." She swallows hard and looks up through her tears at him. "Norma Sutters, sir."

"You know what the Good Lord wants from you, Norma?"

"No sir."

"He wants you to survive."

She swallows and nods, and then gives him a heartbreaking look. "Yessir."

"C'mere, Sister."

Jeremiah leans in and puts his big arms around her, and she hugs him back, and they stay like that for quite some time, the woman clinging to the preacher like a child waiting for a bad dream to fade.

"We lost our pastor early on," the woman says, taking another sip of Mad Dog from an unlabeled bottle and wincing at the burn. "Brother Maywell shot him in the head and buried him out behind the sacristy." She sits in the back room at her desk, a tattered woolen blanket wrapped around her significant girth. Her face glistens with agony. The pale morning light seeps through the seams of the boarded windows. "Lord, Lord, Lord . . . what a time we in right now."

"How did all them folks down there die?" Jeremiah sits back pensively in a desk chair, the bones of the chair creaking with his weight. His head throbs. The bandage the woman applied to his scalp a few minutes ago is too tight. Behind him, Stephen sits on the edge of the windowsill, listening intently, gauze wrapped around his fractured ribs. He wheezes slightly. On the other side of the room, Reese shivers in a folding chair, his forehead crisscrossed with Band-Aids. The woman has already proven to be a gold mine of resources. In addition to medical supplies and first aid kits, she has stashes of canned goods, batteries, candles, dry clothes, bedding, liquor, cigarettes, tools, reading material, an extra box of .38 caliber rounds for the police special, and three sealed boxes of newly printed hymnals that will never be opened, and never be sung.

The woman hangs her head. "It only takes one," she says softly.

"Pardon?"

She looks up at the preacher. "Before this whole tribulation started up, I was a damn teetotaler. Drinking had gotten the better of me so I quit. 'It only takes one drink,' they used to say at them meetings." She shakes her head slowly and looks down, the immensity of her grief making her shoulders slump and her lower lip tremble again. "Even after the outbreak, we kept on with the services. Even after Reverend Helms passed. We kept on. We just figured . . . that's what you do."

She pauses.

Jeremiah leans forward on his swivel chair. "Go on, Sister."

She breathes in a pained breath. "One day, one of our regulars, a family, they brought in a kid with them to our Sunday service. Kid had been bit." She pauses, swallows the urge to weep. "Guess they thought the Lord would take care of things. It only takes one . . . know what I'm sayin'? It took less than a week for it to spread. The screaming—y'all should have heard it. I locked them all in the chapel;

it was all that I could think of doing. Before long, I was the last one . . . holed up in this dirty-ass office, all by my lonesome, listening to the scratching and clawing." Pause. "I guess you get so you don't hear it no more."

Reese speaks up from across the room. "Why didn't you just get on outta here, pack up and leave?"

She chuckles ruefully. "I don't know if y'all have noticed, but a person's odds ain't too good out there all alone."

Silence.

Jeremiah smiles at her. "Well, you ain't all alone no more."

The woman gives Jeremiah a look. "You is a big one, ain't ya?"

"Yes, ma'am."

"Heard them callin' ya 'Brother' and 'Rev'—you a preacher, too?"

"Yes, ma'am, guilty as charged." He sniffs, tries to put the tumult of the past few days into words. "I had a grand vision once, and the Good Lord decided it didn't measure up, and He left us all behind."

She cocks her head at him. "You one of them Rapture preachers?"

"Right at this moment, I don't rightly know *what* I am."

She shudders. "You sure seemed to know what you were doing down there in that chapel."

"I'm sorry you had to see that."

She chews on the inside of her cheek, thinking, pondering. She gives Jeremiah a strange look. "Can I trust y'all?"

Jeremiah looks at the others, then looks back at the zaftig choir mistress. "Yes, ma'am, you can trust us . . . you got my word on that."

The black woman purses her lips. "Reason I ask . . . I might know a way we can improve on our situation a little bit." She looks around the room at each man. "It's a long shot, but if y'all are up to it . . . we just might make it."

She takes their silence as a sign of mild interest, so she explains further.

THREE

It takes them the rest of that day to find enough fuel to get them where they need to go. They pack a wheelbarrow and three large satchels with supplies, including a twenty-five-gallon container of gasoline from the toolshed behind the building. By the time the light in the southwestern sky has begun to soften, fading from pale gray to pink over the coastal backwaters of the panhandle, they're ready.

They slip outside through the rectory's side door and creep single file along the edge of the property.

Jeremiah takes the lead, periodically glancing over his shoulder for any sign of the herd that had crossed the highway around the state line. He carries his Glock with a full magazine. Crickets roar, and the dusky air gets clammy and cool on the back of Norma's neck as she follows them toward the abandoned Escalade.

They hurriedly climb in, stowing their provisions in the rear cargo bay. Jeremiah kicks the engine on, and Norma settles down in the passenger seat next to him, unfolding a dog-eared map. "They usually stick pretty close to the ocean," she says, almost to herself, calculating the mileage between them and the gulf. "Probably should start our search down around Perry or Crawfordville."

She senses movement ahead of them, through the windshield, on the road, and glances up in time to see a couple ragged shadows emerging from the woods about a hundred yards away, drawn to the noise of their engine. The garbled growls can be heard above the drone of crickets, the smell like a faint trace of garbage on the breeze.

Norma feels a slight hitch of chills in her solar plexus. Considering the fact that the world has been infested with these things for almost two years now, she still hasn't seen that many of them out in the open like this. She feels like Rip Van Winkle—as though she's been asleep inside that church for a hundred years—and now the light and space of the outdoors is making her dizzy.

The preacher gooses the accelerator, and the Escalade lurches away.

Norma sinks into her seat as they roar down the road, swerving to avoid the half a dozen or so walkers now skulking out of the woods and blocking their path. They sideswipe one of the creatures, tearing a chunk out of its shoulder and the side of its face, spattering gore up across the glass of her window.

"You get used to it, sis," the preacher mutters after Norma flinches.

The woman takes deep breaths, smooths her dress across her wide belly, and tries to avoid looking at the splatter outside her window: flecks of bone chips, a long smudge of black bile. "I ain't sure a person could *ever* get used to this crazy-ass shit," she comments.

Night falls, and the darkness deepens behind the trees on either side of the road. Most of the streetlights in this part of the country have gone the way of the Internet and broadcast television, so the road gets darker and darker as they head south toward the steaming thickets and festering swamps of the coastal lowlands.

The going is slow. Most of the two-lane is crowded with rusted-out wreckage and the carcasses of cars and trucks so old now that the weeds and switch grass have begun to grow up through the metal endoskeletons. The two young men in the backseat breathe heavily, thickly, half asleep, while the preacher drives and softly hums gospel hymns. They had passed around the beef jerky and grape Kool-Aid a few minutes ago—their standard supper fare while on the run—and now their bellies growl and their eyelids droop with exhaustion.

Sitting in the shotgun seat, her plump, tawny hands folded nervously in her lap, Norma is still trying to wrap her brain around this good old boy preacher who calls himself Brother Jeremiah. On one hand, he seems trustworthy enough—friendly, a good listener, courteous, and capable of single-handedly taking out an entire chapelful of reanimated corpses—but on the other, he seems like a walking time bomb, a human hair trigger that could go off at any moment.

The sad fact is, Norma Sutters doesn't have a large array of options. Staying hunkered down in that claustrophobic rectory for the rest of her life, listening to the drooling groans of the dead in the next room while she drained the last of her Mad Dog supply, was quickly beginning to lose its charm. Watching the preacher clean house back there with that big hunting knife had given Norma a strange sort of charge—a cathartic release—but now it's starting to worry her a little bit. If this dude is capable of such violence, God only knows what he's capable of doing to a plump little sister-girl from Macon with flat feet and no living relatives. But Norma also knows that she would never be able to find the caravan on her own. She really has no choice but to go along with these scruffy-ass men and hope for the best.

Fortunately, Norma has grown accustomed to taking risks. Born poor and fatherless in the Pleasant Hill area of South Macon, the youngest in a family of six kids, she quit school her sophomore year in order to support her family after her mama passed. She played organ in bars and taverns, sang the blues in horrible places, and took a lot of shit from men who thought they were better than her. Maybe that's why she never hooked up with anybody. She saw men at their worst—drunk, abusive, arrogant, getting thrown out of clubs, throwing their weight around, acting like babies. Her faith got her through those years, and led her to a job as assistant choir director at Calvary Baptist in Jasper, Florida. This was where she had hoped to find men at their best: God-fearing men, decent men, faithful men. No such luck. Here the men were just as bad, but now the shenanigans were coated with a slimy veneer of hypocrisy.

Miles Littleton was the exception. Who would have thought a twenty-three year old former meth-head from Atlanta—a convicted car thief who had gotten clean in rehab and gotten right with the Lord at Calvary Baptist—would restore Norma's faith in men? Miles was the little brother whom Norma Sutters had always wished for, and their relationship had blossomed in those quiet months before the Turn, a friendship both platonic and healing.

Unfortunately, after the outbreak had taken everything to hell on a horse, Miles had started raving to Norma about this magical caravan that he had heard about from Pastor Helms. Norma hadn't believed a word of it—Reverend Helms had been known to tip a few now and again—and after the walkers had gotten to the minister, there was nobody left to confirm these tall tales. But young Miles had been such a believer that he had finally decided to set out in his beat-up muscle car to find the Travelers. Norma had always believed that one day he would return to save her.

But that day had never come.

Now she is putting all her chips down on the hopes that Miles hadn't been crazy and he's still alive and the caravan is real.

"That sign back there . . . said 'Cross City 12 Miles.'" Norma glances up from the map and gazes out the side window at the stewing darkness of Dixie County, Florida. "I got a feeling we're getting close."

The vast patchwork of wetlands passes in a blur on either side of them, the land oozing a low blanket of methane, as gray as mold and clinging to the shadows of pine thickets and gullies like dirty lace. The air smells briny and rotten with dead fish. Every few miles they pass the ruins of a small town or a wreckage-strewn trailer park. No signs of survivors in these parts, though, only the occasional silhouette of an upright corpse shambling through the trees, its eyes like twin yellow reflectors in the darkness.

"We can't just keep burning gas all night," Stephen says from the backseat, his voice all cranked up with pain and panic. "And we can't just go on feelings."

"We're in the right ballpark," Norma persists. "Believe me, gonna be hard to miss 'em."

"Do we know exactly what we're looking for, though?" Jeremiah grips the steering wheel with his huge hands, his jaw working over-time on a piece of gum, snapping and chewing compulsively as he drives. "For instance, how many vehicles they got in this convoy?"

"No idea . . . but it's quite a few, I can tell ya that for sure."

"That's pretty general."

"They'll be easy to spot," Norma says, gazing out at the darkness. "Our best bet is to just to follow the coast. They like to keep close to the water."

"Why is that?"

She shrugs. "According to Miles, they keep their eyes peeled for ships . . . or any possible way they might get their asses the hell outta this place. Most of the big boats around here been destroyed in the hurricane that hit a couple years ago, so it's a long shot they're gonna find anything."

Reese speaks up from the back. "Why didn't this Miles dude come back for you?"

Norma glances down at the floor mats. "We had a little bit of a falling-out." She wipes her mouth. "It was my fault, and I ain't too proud of it."

After a pause, Reese says, "But why didn't you try and find these people yourself?"

She glances over her shoulder at him. "Travel alone in this god-awful back country crawling with dead folks?"

Silence returns to the Escalade's dark interior as they all chew on the prospects of being alone and isolated in a forestful of walkers.

They're about to give up the search when they start to climb a gentle slope—at first so gradual it's almost unnoticeable—up the side of a vast malodorous landfill. The barren, trash-strewn scrubland to their left reaches across miles of sandy berms, all the way down to the de-serted, ghostly boardwalks that wind their way along the beaches. The sky has begun to bruise pink with predawn light, and the preacher has just started to say something when Norma sees the first faint streaks of red dots on the distant haze.

"Wait! Wait!" She points a plump finger down at the far dunes of ashen white sand winding along the coast, the surface so pocked and windswept it resembles the dark side of the moon. "There!—See 'em?!"

"Where?" The preacher cranes his neck, slowing the vehicle down to a crawl. "I don't see a thing."

"About a half mile up yonder, see?" The woman is positively vibrating with excitement. "Whole slew of 'em! See the taillights?"

Jeremiah Garlitz takes in a deep, cleansing breath as he finally sees the caravan chugging along the coastal road. In the predawn light, it looks like a ribbon of burning embers throwing gouts of smoke in its wake. "Yes, ma'am, I surely do!" Jeremiah's big, barrel-shaped chest puffs with relief. "Whaddaya think of that, boys?"

The two young men in the rear seats lean forward, transfixed by the sight, each of them rapt and silent as they gaze at the convoy.

"Give 'em a blast on your horn!" Norma Sutters wrings her hands anxiously. "Don't let them get away!"

Jeremiah smiles to himself. In his former life, he used to be fascinated by wildlife shows on television. He would record them on the VCR in the back of his trailer for later viewing, and he would watch them between revival meetings late at night for hours on end before turning in. He remembers one episode in particular, on the behavior of sheep versus the behavior of wolves. He remembers the flock mentality: the sheep moving almost as one, a school of helpless fish, easily managed by a single sheepdog. He remembers the instinct of the wolf—stealthy, solitary, patient—as it creeps up on the flock.

He shoots a glance across the dark interior at the heavyset little woman. "I got a better idea."

Father Patrick Liam Murphy, ordained Catholic priest and former head of Jacksonville's Most Holy Redeemer Parish, doesn't see the unexpected obstruction in the middle of the road until it's almost too late. The problem is, the slender, silver-haired priest has diarrhea of the mouth—perhaps an occupational hazard for someone charged with sermonizing, counseling, and easing fevered brows.

He sits behind the wheel of his rumbling Winnebago, relentlessly chewing the ear off his protégé, James Frazier, who's slumped in the cab's passenger seat, struggling to pay attention. "May I remind you, Jimmy, that there are two distinct versions of Christ, and the one of whom you speak now, in your insolent and narrow perspective, is the one we call the 'historic' Jesus, who lived and breathed and walked the earth a couple of millennia ago, but also the one who is merely the vessel for the second version, the one that matters, the one who is the absolute true son of—"

"LOOK OUT!"

James Frazier, an angular man of thirty-three, blond-whiskered and dressed in ragged denim, sits up with a start, eyes wide and fixed on something he sees through the massive windshield. Father Murphy jerks the wheel and stands on the brakes. The contents of the RV shift in the back, water bottles, canned goods, tools, and weapons tumbling off their shelves and cubbies. Both men slam forward as the trailer skids to a sudden halt.

The priest flops back in his seat, blinking, breathless. In his side mirror, he sees the long line of vehicles behind him—pickup trucks, RVs, four-wheelers, and a few sedans—forming a chain reaction of lurching skids, the members of the caravan screeching to a stop, one by one, in a billowing cloud of carbon monoxide.

"Dear Lord, what's this?" The priest sucks in a breath, still gripping his steering wheel, as he tries to focus on the figure standing blithely in their path less than twenty yards ahead of them.

The man is tall, Caucasian, dressed in a tattered black suit, and has one of his big muddy Wellington boots propped up on the front fender of a fancy Cadillac SUV—the big black kind often used by shadowy government types—which is currently parked and idling in the middle of the road. The strangest part of this tableau is that the man is smiling. Even from this distance, the man aims his big Ultra Brite grin at the convoy's lead vehicle as though preparing to sell a new line of Fuller Brushes.

James goes for his .38, which is stuffed down one cowboy boot.

"Go easy, Jimmy. Go easy, son." The priest takes a deep breath, waving off the weapon. Approaching sixty, Father Murphy still wears his collar underneath a worn Notre Dame sweatshirt, his hangdog face deeply lined and whiskered with a ruddy beard. His pouchy eyes radiate a certain kindness, along with the swollen lividness of a lifelong drunk. "This appears to be a group of the living, and there's no reason to believe they're not friendly."

James shoves the short-barreled pistol under his belt. "You stay here, Father, I'll go—"

The priest puts his hand up. "No, no . . . Jimmy, *I'll* go. You tell Leland to keep his cool, and tell the rest of the group to stay in their vehicles."

The younger man reaches for his walkie-talkie as the priest climbs out of the cab.

Over the next thirty seconds—the amount of time it takes the scrawny beanpole of a priest to climb out the cab door, struggle down the running board steps, and scuffle across twenty feet of pavement in his ancient Florsheims—a chemical reaction occurs. Unseen, subtle, undetectable to anyone other than the two gentlemen coming to face each other in the middle of the asphalt two-lane, it bubbles up within the priest unexpectedly, unbidden, and as powerful as an electrical charge passing through his brain. He instantly dislikes this fellow.

"Morning, Padre," the man standing in the middle of the road says with a gleam of neighborly congeniality in his deep-set eyes. The priest can see others behind the tinted glass of the Escalade—a woman, a couple of men, their moods and demeanors unknown. Their hands are hidden, their spines rigid, their muscles coiled.

"Hello there." Father Murphy forces a smile. He stands ramrod-straight, his rheumatic joints aching, his hands curled into fists at his side. He can feel the eyes and ears of his people on the back of his neck. They need fresh souls and strong backs to help with the maintenance and fuel runs and heavy lifting involved in keeping the caravan moving. At the same time, they must be careful. A few bad apples have passed through the group in recent months and have threatened its very existence. "Something we can help you with, sir?" the priest says to the stranger.

The thousand-kilowatt smile brightens. The man shoots his threadbare cuffs as though beginning a sales meeting. "Didn't want to sneak up on you back there." He sniffs and casually spits. "You never know who you're going to run into out here in the wilds of walker country. You folks seem to have it down to a science. Traveling in that little cavalcade of yours, always moving, safety in numbers, no moss growing on y'all. It's sheer genius, you ask me."

"Thank you, son." The priest keeps his artificial smile plastered to his face. "That's a honey of a vehicle you got there."

"I thank you for that."

"That a Caddy?"

"Yessir. Two thousand and seven Escalade XL, runs like a top."

"Looks like it's been in some rough scrapes."

"Yessir, it surely has."

The priest nods pensively. "What can we do for you, son? You seem like a man . . . has something on his mind."

"Name's Garlitz. Jeremiah Garlitz. Fellow shaman and holy soldier like yourself."

The priest feels a twinge of anger. "Always good to meet a fellow minister."

"Had a church down in Jacksonville, then lit out after the Turn, tried to keep it up." He jabs a thumb at the battered SUV behind him. "Now all that's left of the Pentecostal People of God is them two good old boys in there . . . along with a real nice lady from a church up to Jasper."

"Uh-huh." Father Murphy scratches his chin. He knows what's coming and he doesn't like it one bit. It doesn't feel right. "What can we help you with? We got a little extra biodiesel, if that would be something you'd be interested in. Maybe some bottled water?"

The big preacher pours on the charm. "That's mighty kind of you. These are difficult times. Them walkers out there are often the least of our problems. You gotta be real careful. I wouldn't expect you to just take in any old stray you find along the road." His expansive expression softens, his eyes filling with sadness and humility. "Father, we are good, hardworking, God-fearing people who need a place of refuge . . . need medical treatment, food, and the safety of fellowship. Never occurred to us that solace might be found in a moving target like the one you got here."

The daylight has dawned enough now for Father Murphy to clearly see the young men and the woman hunkered in the Escalade, nervously waiting. The priest swallows, licks his dry, chapped lips. "I'm gonna ask if the folks in the Caddy could maybe go ahead and show their hands."

The preacher turns and gives them a nod. One by one, the people in the SUV hold up their hands, revealing that they are unarmed.

The priest nods. "I appreciate that. Now may I ask the number and type of weapons you might be carrying?"

The preacher grins. "It ain't much. Got a couple of nines and a shotgun. Lady's got a snubby. Not much left over in the way of ammo, I'm afraid."

Father Murphy nods and starts to say, "Fair enough, and now if I might ask you to—"

Out of nowhere, a number of unexpected noises and quick movements in the priest's peripheral vision interrupt his spiel and make him flinch as though a bomb has just gone off. A figure from behind him approaches at a dead run, arms pumping excitedly, voice caterwauling: "FOR THE LOVE OF CHRIST, IT'S HER, I TOLD THEM IT WAS HER—I JUST KNEW IT—!!"

The young African-American boy in the flopping braids and ragged hoodie charges toward Jeremiah's Escalade. The preacher jerks back, reaching for his knife, taken completely by surprise.

"It's okay, he's one of ours!" Father Murphy calls out, shooting his hands up in a conciliatory gesture. "It's all right, he's harmless!"

Behind Jeremiah, the SUV's side door bursts open, and Norma Sutters struggles out. Her face aglow with emotion, her eyes wet as she spots the kid, she opens her plump arms. "I'll be damned if you ain't a sight!"

The young man plunges into Norma's softness and musky odors.

"I thought you was dead for sure," he murmurs, his face pressed into the crook of her neck. The woman hugs him back, stroking his head with maternal tenderness. The young man begins to softly weep.

Norma shushes him and strokes him and mutters soothing words. "I ain't dead yet, child. . . . Still in one piece, still the cranky-ass old bitch you left in Jasper."

The young man sobs into her neck. "I missed you so damn much, I thought of going back, but I didn't, but I should have, I'm a chick-enshit, that's all, too scared, too proud, and you said I'd be back with my tail between my legs, I just . . . I just didn't . . ."

Norma shushes him and strokes his braided hair. "That's enough now, everything's gonna be okay, that's enough now, child." She glances over at Jeremiah. She gives the preacher a furtive look. "What's the deal, Preacher Man? We stayin' with these folks or what?!"

Jeremiah looks at Father Murphy, and the old Irishman shrugs and then smiles. "Looks like you're already part of the family."

The transaction is seamless. Within minutes, the two groups come together, pool their resources, and Jeremiah and company begin to build goodwill, getting to know the other members of Father Murphy's traveling caravan. By noon that day, the procession has pulled back onto the road, continuing its endless looping journey across the panhandle as though the preacher and his people had always been part of the group.

Nearly a week passes without incident. They travel mostly during daylight hours, resting their bodies and machines at night within the confines of caves and clearings. Jeremiah makes a special point to introduce himself to each and every member of the caravan. There are thirty-three in all, commandeering fifteen vehicles, including six full RVs and three heavy-duty trucks. There are four children under the age of twelve, five married couples, and a few senior citizens.

They have an impressive array of weaponry (much of it scavenged from Camp Blanding, a deserted military base outside Jacksonville); and they have enough canned goods to last another six months if rationed carefully.

The alpha dogs are mostly good old boys from central Florida—blue-collar tradesmen with dirt under their fingernails and sun-reddened faces—and Jeremiah instantly ingratiates himself with these hillbilly types. He speaks their language—God, guns, and whiskey—and he further solidifies his place in the pecking order by pitching in with vehicle maintenance; the preacher once worked as a grease monkey in a service station as a teen, and the skills serve him well here. Reese and Stephen also show their willingness to get their hands dirty by going along on numerous side trips and detours to obtain the raw materials for cooking up more fuel.

Up until now, the members of the caravan have been able to keep the engines running with a combination of crude biodiesel (which they produce in a modified still in the rear of the lone flatbed truck) and the precious last gallons of standing gasoline in the storage tankers and underground reservoirs of abandoned gas stations and marinas across northern Florida. Jeremiah marvels at the amount of cooking oil still sitting in worm-eaten roadside diners and deserted restaurants along the way. But the pickings are getting slimmer and slimmer, and a grim reality is creeping into the demeanor of the caravan. Nobody is making more oil or canned goods or tires or spare parts or gasoline or any other durable good you can name, and that's the elephant in the room. The sand is running out the bottom of the hourglass. Everybody senses it, feels it, and ruminates on it without ever really talking about it.

Each morning, well before dawn, as the caravan fires back up and the vehicles rumble away from the night's bivouac, Jeremiah ponders this grim reality. Driving the Escalade in the tail position, engulfed in clouds of exhaust and dust as the convoy snakes its way through swampy coastal backwaters and walker-ridden fishing villages, Jeremiah gets a lot of thinking done. These are *indeed* the end-times, the glorious terrors of the Rapture, and these hapless bedouins are the poor souls who have been left behind. If God wants Jeremiah to remain, to scuttle across festering hellscapes, eking out a meager existence, starving and wasting away until it all turns to dust, so be it. He will take advantage of this tumultuous time. He will be the one-eyed king in the land of the blind. He will prosper.

Then everything changes one evening at a deserted KOA camp a couple miles east of Panama City.

Opportunity presents itself at just past 8:00 that night in the form of a rustling sound off in the adjacent woods, very faint at first but loud enough to register on Jeremiah's ear as he takes his customary walk along the periphery of the camp. He has gotten into the habit of taking solitary evening strolls around the circled vehicles in order to keep tabs on the mood of his fellow travelers. It also doesn't hurt to press the flesh, say hello to his new comrades, and do a little public relations work.

On this night, the forest is separated from the ring of cars and trucks and campers by an ancient split-rail fence fortified at some point in the past—perhaps by stubborn KOA customers hunkering down after the early days of the Turn—with a ribbon of tangled, rusty concertina wire, which lines the fence all the way around the ten-acre site. At a few junctures, gates are visible between the larger posts, most of them padlocked. Jeremiah pauses in the dusky light, the sunset now nearly faded to darkness, most of the travelers retired to their campers and bed rolls.

His heart thumps as the noise of a few roamers shambling nearby gives birth to an idea, fully formed, unspooling in his brain.

FOUR

Jeremiah snaps his fingers in the darkness, standing just inside the northwest corner of the compound, the drone of crickets so loud it nearly drowns out the snapping sound. He knows the risks here. He knows he's walking a delicate tightrope. There are so many variables that could go wrong. If he was caught, it would be the end of his reign on this earth, and at this point, he doubts very highly he would be welcomed with open arms by St. Peter and his posse at the pearly gates.

He snaps again and again, and soon he hears the unwieldy footsteps shuffling closer and closer. He can see their shadows now. Three of them—two males and a female of indeterminate ages—dragging through the undergrowth. Heads lolling slightly, mouths working fiercely, they make their trademark noise as they close in—a sort of buzz-saw growling that emanates from the deepest pits of their insatiable gorges.

The stench rises. Jeremiah pulls a bandanna from his back pocket and quickly wraps it around the lower part of his face—bank-robber style—and keeps softly snapping his fingers. Summoning them. Beckoning to them. The smell is so strong now, it's as though the preacher has stuck his head in an oven filled with roasting shit. He reaches down and opens the gate.

Timing is critical here. Like baboons in a cage, the creatures can start to get noisy if aroused. And even if they remain fairly docile and silent, their odor *alone* could easily draw a fellow caravan member out of a trailer. Snapping out a brisk rhythm with his thumb and forefinger, Jeremiah starts backing away from the fence, discreetly ushering the monsters through the gap.

They stay bunched together—the three of them—as they enter the northeast corner of the compound. One of the males is missing his left eye, a ragged pouch of arteries and pulp dangling down. The female looks as though she had been in her eighties before she turned—her flaccid, wrinkled flesh dangling now on her bones like turkey wattle. Each of their mouths churn and gnaw at the air, their feral jaws looking as though they could easily tear into metal. Collectively the three of them smell of graves under a compost heap.

Jeremiah quickly and quietly leads them toward the rear door of Father Murphy's RV.

The final part of phase one proves the trickiest. Jeremiah reaches the trailer first, with about fifty feet between him and the walkers— which is not much; at the rate the creatures are shambling toward him, the distance will be crossed in less than a minute. He carefully, silently, stealthily tries to open the rear door without making a sound.

"Dang it," Jeremiah whispers under his breath when he realizes the door is locked. The Catholic bastard is probably in there masturbating to kiddie porn. The walkers close in, reeking and groaning softly, their shuffling footsteps growing louder and louder. Jeremiah reaches down to his Wellington and draws the Randall knife, and then hurriedly pries at the seam between the screen door lock and the trailer's jamb.

A soft click signals the breach as the walkers get close enough to raise hackles on the back of Jeremiah's neck. He turns and opens the trailer door, letting a dull bruise of incandescent light spill out across the darkness. Snoring sounds come from the shadows of the trailer.

The monsters swarm toward the door, the lamplight reflecting off their nickel-plated eyes.

Jeremiah stands behind the door, his hand on the grip of his nine-millimeter just in case one of them goes for his throat. Luckily, they seem drawn to the odors of living flesh and noises inside the RV, and one by one they lurch toward the doorway. Jeremiah watches from the shadows behind the screen as each creature stumbles on the metal stairs, then cobbles crablike up the slight incline and into the trailer. When the last one has vanished inside the shadows of Father Murphy's lair, Jeremiah quickly closes the aluminum door behind them with a faint but satisfying metallic click.

Now phase two begins as Jeremiah hurriedly backs away from the trailer.

This is the part Jeremiah relishes the most: the acting part. He once heard of an actual psychological disorder categorized and catalogued in the Diagnostic and Statistical Manual called Munchausen Syndrome by Proxy. The condition involves behavior patterns in which caregivers, often nannies and nurses, induce health problems in those under their care merely so the patient can be rescued. Thinking about it brings a wry smile to the lips of the preacher as he crouches in the shadows and waits for the screaming to start.

Father Patrick Liam Murphy stirs from a strange recurring dream, a nightmare he has been having for the last year that involves being buried alive.

He sits up suddenly on his sweat-damp portable cot, which is shoved against the RV's front fire wall. Heart hammering in his chest, he sees shadows moving on either side of him, smells the rancid rot, and hears the buzz-saw growling. He rolls off the cot just in time to avoid a clawlike hand about to grab his nightshirt.

The priest lets out a bellowing howl of shock and surprise and smashes into an aluminum cupboard, which teeters and falls with a resounding crash, spilling bowls and cups and utensils and bottles of butane across the floor. He realizes far too late that he's trapped, alone in his trailer with three monsters, that his gun is on the other side of the room, and that he left a lantern on the bedside table burning when he drifted off after his nightly pint of cheap whiskey.

The impact of the falling cupboard causes the lamp to tip and fall on one of the creatures, the kerosene instantly catching the thing's pant leg on fire. The air crackles and fills with hellish odors as the priest moves on instinct now. Rolling away from another cold, dead hand slashing down at him, he crawls toward the cab and suddenly finds a long, metal barbecue fork that has fallen off a nearby shelf.

Something grabs his leg, and cold gooseflesh spreads across the bare skin of his ankle for a single instant before he reacts. He jerks his leg back before the female can get her slimy incisors into his flesh, and he howls again and says something garbled and inarticulate to his One Dear Lord and Savior.

Then Father Murphy plunges the fork into the eye socket of the female, the tines sinking into the pulpy meat of the dead occipital. Black matter bubbles and oozes around the hilt of the fork as the female instantly sags and collapses to the floor, her desiccated body now as still as a sack of laundry. The priest twists around and madly crawls toward the front cab enclosure, still unharmed, still unbitten.

Behind him, in the flickering light of the fire, the two males freeze at the sound of footsteps. A figure appears outside the back door. "PADRE!" An all-too familiar-voice—to the priest, a voice like fingernails clawing across slate. "PADRE, I'M COMING!"

The door bangs open with the force of a huge Wellington boot kicking it in.

A big man in a black suit fills the doorway. The two male walkers stagger, clawing at the air, the fire sparking and climbing up the leg of the older one. Reverend Jeremiah Garlitz raises his 9-millimeter pistol and squeezes off two shots in quick succession at point-blank range. The blasts take off the tops of the creatures' skulls, sending pink mist spraying against the inner walls of the RV.

The monsters collapse, the flames exploding in a blossom of sparks.

"Are you okay?!" Jeremiah scans the dark living space for the priest. He sees the flames creeping across the floor. "Talk to me, Padre!" Jeremiah removes his coat and pats out the fire. "Padre?!—WHERE ARE YOU?"

From behind the fallen cot, the Irishman lets out a meek little chuckle. "That was . . . interesting."

"Thank Christ!" The big preacher rushes over to the upended cot. He kneels by his fallen comrade. Jeremiah's eyes already shimmer with emotion as he cradles the priest's head. "Are you bit?"

"Don't think so." Father Murphy tries to move but his arthritic joints are frozen, seized up with pain. He needs a drink. He pats his arms, his midsection, feels his neck. He looks at his hand. No blood. "I think I got lucky this time, if you can call this lucky."

Outside the trailer, the sounds of voices and footsteps fill the air.

"Don't try to move," Jeremiah says. "We're gonna get you help, you're gonna be fine."

"Why are you looking at me like that?" A bolt of panic travels down the priest's spine. "What are you doing? Why are you—?"

"You're gonna be fine. You're a tough old cuss, gonna outlive us all."

Father Murphy feels the cold steel of a Glock's muzzle under his ear. "What are you doing? Why in God's name are you holding your—"

The sudden and unexpected blast is the last thing Father Patrick Murphy hears.

The priest's skull erupts, the bullet passing through his brain and blowing back wet splatter in Jeremiah's face. The big man flinches. The bullet chews a hole in the RV's ceiling, puffing fiberglass and metal shards in a tuft of filaments. The explosion makes Jeremiah's ears ring, almost drowning out the footsteps closing in from outside, several sets, each one hastening across the yard toward the priest's RV. Someone hollers Father Murphy's name.

Jeremiah springs into action. He shoves the priest's body to the floor, lurches across the enclosure, and grabs the shriveled remains of the old female. He drags the corpse by the nape over to the priest.

Within seconds, Jeremiah has clamped the walker's teeth down upon the priest's exposed ankle. Ragged incisors pierce the skin. Phase three. Quickly. Now. Working up tears is easy. With all the adrenaline sluicing through his body—the thrill of this impromptu coup d'etat—he spontaneously breaks into artificial sobs, his lungs heaving, genuine tears welling up, salt-sting burning his eyes.

A face appears in the rear doorway, the fair-haired young man named James. "Father?! FATHER MURPHY?!"

Jeremiah gazes up, the blood spatter on his face mingling like watercolors with his tears. "James, I'm sorry, he got—"

"Oh Jesus."

Jeremiah shakes his head and cradles the priest in his arms. "He got bit."

"How the fuck—?!"

"He begged me to put him down, and I didn't want to do it but he begged me and we prayed together."

"But how did—?!"

"I recited the last rites for him the best I could remember them."

"Oh Jesus." James Frazier climbs into the living chamber, choking on his shock and tears. "How the hell did they get in?"

Jeremiah lets out a raspy sigh of agony, bowing his head in an Academy Award–worthy performance. "Dear God, dear God . . . I just don't know."

"Oh Jesus, Jesus, sweet Jesus Christ our Lord," James babbles, and kneels and puts his hand on the dead priest. "Dear Lord, in this hour of . . . this hour of . . . of sorrow . . . please take his soul in the bosom of . . . your kingdom . . . and . . . and . . . deliver him . . . OH *JESUS!*"

The young man slumps to the floor, weeping convulsively, as Jeremiah tenderly strokes his shoulder. "It's okay. Let it out, son."

The crying carries out into the night and echoes up into the black sky.

The other caravan members—now gathering by the open doorway—stand paralyzed.

Not a single one of them is aware they are witnessing an epochal exchange of power.

For the rest of that night, and for most of the next day, Jeremiah helps the surviving members of the convoy deal with the tragic loss of their spiritual guide and moral compass. No one feels like driving, so they secure the periphery and place guards at key points around the site, and Jeremiah urges people to vent, to express themselves, to pray, and to remember their leader.

They bury the man in the southeast corner of the KOA camp, near a grove of pecan trees. James says a few words, and then a few other alpha dogs have their say, each one of them eventually breaking down and sobbing, unable to continue. The death of Father Murphy hits them hard. Jeremiah can see they need to let out the grief.

By sundown the next night, very few caravan members have wandered away from the makeshift grave site. Most linger over the loosely packed pile of earth, as though they are houseguests who refuse to leave a beloved relative's abode, praying, sharing stories of Father Murphy's generous spirit and acts of kindness and legacy of courage in the face of Armageddon. Some share flasks of cheap, stale moonshine . . . or home-rolled corn-silk cigarettes made from the local tobacco that still stubbornly grows in profusion in south Georgia and along the northern edges of the panhandle . . . or the same beef jerky that they've been sharing for weeks now, ever since they hit that deserted truck stop outside Jacksonville.

Jeremiah watches all this until he gets an idea right around sundown.

"Folks . . . if I may say something?" He rises to his full height at the edge of the burial mound. Still dressed in his black mourning suit and threadbare tie, he looks more than ever like a strange government man from another age—a revenue agent or an auditor come to take stock of the caravan's books. He holds a leather wine bota filled with the same awful whiskey he'd been sharing for hours with James Frazier, Norma Sutters, Leland Burress, and Miles Littleton. "I know it ain't my place to speak at such a solemn and important occasion such as this." He looks around the group with a humble, contrite expression. "I didn't know the Padre even remotely as well as y'all. I have no right to say anything on his behalf. All I want to say is, you measure a man *not* by what he makes in his life, you measure a man by what he leaves behind. And let me tell ya, old

Patrick L. Murphy left behind a whole mess of love, and one great big dream."

He pauses, and this is Jeremiah Garlitz's genius: the ability to hold an audience with well-chosen silence. He lets silence work like a river cleaves mountains, like a tiny sapling takes root and grows into an enormous redwood. He makes love with silence.

"Father Murphy left behind a dream of solace and succor in the face of the End Days . . . a beautiful dream amidst the beasts of hell . . . a dream of something more than survival. He left behind a dream of life. He wanted y'all to flourish. *Together.* Moving, always moving. Like a stream turns into a river and a river turns into the sea."

More silence. Some listeners begin to clear their throats, fight tears, and bow their heads. They need this. They need to release something, and the silence gives them permission. They listen so closely to the silence, Jeremiah feels as though he can hear their heartbeats.

"I don't know about y'all, but in my short sweet time with the Padre, I realized he knew something that I didn't. He knew the key to paradise—and no, I ain't talking about heaven right now. I'm talking about paradise on earth. Even amid these desecrated times, these horrible ruins, he held the key to paradise, and you know what that was? At the end of the day, do you know what paradise is?"

Another beat of dramatic silence as Jeremiah makes eye contact with each listener—dirty, plague-worn, terrified faces staring back at him, hungering for salvation and answers, eyes moist with sorrow.

"It's us. *Us!* With good treads on our tires and a few gallons of high test in our tanks." He raises his voice. "That's all Father Patrick Murphy ever wanted. For us to stay together, and stay on the move. That simple. That's what the Padre's paradise is . . . the *convoy*. On the move. Just as the ancient Israelites escaped from Egypt! The convoy! Just as the Hebrews wandered Canaan!" He lets out a triumphant shout: "THE CONVOY!"

Leland Burress, a heavyset former pipe fitter from Tallahassee who has been known to regularly vent about the Jews controlling the banking system, springs to his feet and makes a ham-hock-sized fist and cries out, "Damn straight!"

Jeremiah grins a beatific sort of grin full of humility and earnestness.

Across the makeshift burial site, a portly woman in a floral print sundress turns away, her lips pursed with disdain and incredulity.

Norma Sutters stands on the far edge of the pecan grove, listening with a sour look on her face, as the preacher finally gets to the point of his little impromptu sermon. The whole speech strikes Norma as not only inappropriate but also a little disturbing—the way the big man in the black suit coat has almost seamlessly taken over the ceremony, and the subtle tone of condescension in his voice as he blatantly tugs on the heartstrings. Norma Sutters knows all the signals. She has dealt with a rogues' gallery of hypocrites in her life. This guy is off the scale.

"You all right?" Miles whispers to her. The young man standing next to her in the hoodie and the tarnished bling from happier times furrows his brow. It's obvious from the look on his face he senses something as well, but he apparently can't quite articulate it.

She shushes him, putting a plump finger to her lips, indicating they should pay attention to what the preacher is saying.

"Friends, I humbly come to you today with a proposition," the preacher is now announcing to the group, letting out the stops on his big baritone, lifting his voice to the heavens, projecting with the skill of a backwoods Olivier, so that the far edges of the crowd can hear every breath, every dramatic pause. Most preachers are just naturally theatrical and vociferous, but there's something about this guy that Norma can't quite pin down. Something manipulative. And scary. "I have no right to stand in the shoes of our dearly departed Padre—no one does—but I will gladly, in tribute to his legacy, volunteer to step up. With your blessings, with your approval, with your help, I will gladly take the reins of this great community—this mobile fraternity of God-fearing Christians—if you'll have me, if you'll give me that honor."

Murmurs of approval ripple through the two dozen or so mourners still lingering there in the purple twilight and the dense shadows of crooked pecan boughs hanging over the grave site. Miles had secretly shared with Norma earlier that day his belief that Leland Burress would be the one to take over. Leland was a far more likely candidate to replace Father Murphy than some interloper with a Bible and a cross. Leland had started the convoy back around the early days of the outbreak. An independent gun shop owner from Jacksonville, Leland and his late wife had lived in a trailer park near the St. Johns River, and when people had started dying and coming back hungry for human flesh, Leland followed his instincts to move and keep moving.

A breeze blows the faint odor of rotting flesh across the musk of fallen pecan shells. Norma feels sick to her stomach as she shares a loaded glance with the young man standing next to her. "Mmmmm-hm . . . what a surprise," she mutters under her breath with wry disgust.

Across the bare ground of the freshly dug grave, the big preacher does what all salesmen do naturally—he goes for the close: "I don't expect y'all to accept me right off the bat, to trust me as much as y'all came to trust that dear, dear man we just put in the ground. I don't expect y'all to make a decision this important without giving it a lot of thought, without takin' a vote, without being *dang sure*."

One final dramatic pause. One final moment of eye contact with practically every listener, and then: "But I promise you this, and I assure you that this is the God's gospel truth: If y'all accept me as your leader, I *will* lead. I have been in the wilderness for nigh on to a year now, and I have survived, and I will do everything in my power to make sure *all* y'all survive, each and every last one of you, and I will pray to the Lord Almighty that He helps me make sure that all y'all prosper. Because y'all are God's children, and we will prevail!" A few shouts of approval mingle with his words. "WE! WILL! PREVAIL! TOGETHER! AS ONE!!"

Now the hollering drowns out his words and sets Norma's teeth on edge.

As the crowd gathers around the big man, a victory celebration breaks out, reminding Norma of the campaign headquarters of some two-bit politician. She signals to Miles, and the two disgruntled listeners discreetly slip away into the shadows beyond the pecan trees.

The Reverend Jeremiah Garlitz, flush with boisterous approbation, doesn't notice the hasty departure of his only two skeptics.

FIVE

The next morning, just before dawn, as the caravan sparks its engines in a series of rumbling reports and coughing blasts of carbon monoxide, Jeremiah assumes his newly acquired throne behind the wheel of the priest's battered RV, on the same shopworn pilot chair that the previous leader had planted his bony rear end for so many months. At first demurring at the offer to drive Father Murphy's beloved Winnebago, with its rattling portraits of the Pope and church-sponsored Little League teams, Jeremiah eventually reconsiders, coming to the conclusion that it might be an elegant little piece of symmetry.

Now Jeremiah proudly pulls onto the main road with the weight of the entire convoy behind him, an early morning mist coming down like gunmetal steel curtains in the gray dawn. The air has an acrid tang to it, like burned circuits, and the sky is so low and opaque it has the look of old charcoal, like something taken out of the ground. This part of Florida has a primordial feel to it, all mossy and moldy with a patina of furry age on every surface, every fence post, every mailbox and road sign and power line.

Reese and Stephen follow immediately behind the RV in the dented Escalade, each young man healing nicely with the benefit of the caravan's first aid and medical provisions. Behind the SUV come the fourteen other vehicles, each filled with plague-weary, shell-shocked former acolytes of the dead priest. The vote to make Jeremiah the new leader—simple "Yes" or "No" declarations on torn paper ballots gathered in Jeremiah's hat—had been almost unanimous, with the identities of the only two members of the caravan to dissent still unknown to Jeremiah.

He would keep a close eye on morale, and maybe one day he would ferret out the pair of Philistines who had the gall to vote against him.

The previous night, Jeremiah had explained to his newly acquired disciples that part of his new leadership platform would be to explore neighboring states rather than clinging to the coastline. He assures them there are more opportunities in Georgia, Alabama, and South Carolina to find untapped resources. What he does *not* tell his followers is that the seed of an idea has taken root in his brain. It was sparked by the secret removal of Father Murphy, and it has been growing ever since. It may be the greatest single inspiration to kindle within Jeremiah Garlitz since the conception of his apocalyptic church.

They cross the Georgia state line around 5:00 that afternoon. They reach the outskirts of Atlanta by midnight. Low on fuel, hungry, sore and exhausted from the long drive, they make camp in a clearing on a wooded hill not far from the same landscape across which Jeremiah and his followers had traversed on their fateful journey to Woodbury. Is there a silent clarion calling Jeremiah back to this godforsaken place? Was this Jeremiah's personal Gethsemane, the mysterious wooded hill on which Christ ate his last supper and was subsequently cornered and arrested by the Centurions?

That night, the big preacher calls Stephen, Reese, Leland, and James to his fire pit.

"Boys, it's high time we launch another fuel run." He announces this in the flickering light of the fire. "I want you four to light out around dawn, and take two vehicles so you can cover more ground." Jeremiah gives this order with confidence, his mantle of leadership already second nature to him. "Look for gas, diesel, even roadside dives that might still have fryers with oil on the premises."

The men disperse to prepare for their mission, and the preacher spends the rest of that night awake in the RV, guzzling cold instant

coffee, drawing sketches, making notes, and just generally strategiz-
ing on how to bring his grand idea to life . . . or *death*, he thinks with
amusement. The concept will make him as powerful as any post-
plague man has ever been—the true one-eyed king. He works almost all the way through sunrise, eventually falling into a deep sleep
on the RV's sofa bed, oblivious to the fact that a member of his new
tribe has been spying on him all night.

Outside the RV, the shadow of a plump African-American woman
lurks behind a skein of undergrowth less than thirty feet from the
trailer's rear bumper. She has been listening intently to everything—
including the occasional faint mutterings of the preacher talking to
himself, sometimes in the gibberish of ancient "tongues"—much of
it making little sense to her. All she knows, at this early stage, is that
this preacher, despite his natural charisma and oratory skills, is
clearly as mad as a hatter, and probably as dangerous as a poisonous snake.

Later that day, Jeremiah holds court in front of his RV, perched on
an old woven lawn chair, a small toddler named Melissa Thorndyke
curled like a pet cat on his lap, thumb in her mouth, sound asleep.
Completely relaxed behind the circle of vehicles and temporary
barricades, puffing a stale Dominican cigar, sipping instant tea, his
shirt collar open to reveal his hirsute upper chest, he's chatting with
the patriarchs of two separate families—Chester Gleason and Rory
Thorndyke, both men former laborers, meat-and-potatoes types, perfect specimens for Jeremiah's new army. In fact, Jeremiah is about to
kick off a motivational discussion of the walker horde and their purpose in the Rapture when he's interrupted by the voice of Stephen
Pembry.

"Brother Jeremiah!"

The big preacher jerks with a start, stricken silent before getting
out a single word of his litany, twisting around to gaze back over
his shoulder at the four men emerging from the adjacent woods.
Breathing hard, eyes hot and wide with urgency, they come from the

north. Stephen is first, his windbreaker zipped up to his throat, his stocking cap pulled down over his bandaged forehead. He wheezes profusely in his agitated state, his ragged breath coming out in raspy honks.

Behind him, the other men hustle to catch up, hauling huge plastic containers of fuel, their faces shimmering with sweat and excitement.

"Calm down, Brother," the big preacher admonishes while rising out of his chair and gently handing the slumbering child back to her father. He shoots a glance at Chester and Rory. "Why don't you fellas take the little girl back to her mama, give me a second to talk to these boys."

Each of the two patriarchs gives a nod and hastily trundles off toward the other side of the camp as Stephen Pembry approaches breathlessly. "You ain't gonna believe . . . what we just saw . . . about maybe ten miles from here. . . . They were . . . they were . . . huntin' for something. . . . "

The young man twinges, holding his tender rib cage, struggling to get air into his lungs. The others gather around the preacher. Holding up his huge hands, Jeremiah says, "Okay, calm the hell down, I can't understand a word you're sayin'. Take a damn breath!"

Stephen Pembry looks at Reese Lee Hawthorne, who is setting down his fuel container with a grunt, swallowing hard, licking his lips as though measuring his words. "They're still alive, Brother."

Gooseflesh breaks out on the preacher's thick neck and he fixes to ask them who the hell they're talking about, but he already knows.

It turns out to be quite a story, and Jeremiah listens intently to the whole thing in the privacy of his RV as the two original members of the Pentecostal People of God pace and hyperventilate through their blow-by-blow account of setting out at dawn that morning, zigzagging up the tobacco fields of south-central Georgia, searching for untapped gas stations, checking out farmhouses and barns, and just generally combing the countryside for whatever drops of fuel they might find.

For hours they searched in vain. Every truck stop, service station, farm implement store, and storage barn was either empty, picked over, or lousy with walkers. Finally they got lucky just south of Carlinville, not far from the very place in which they got pinned down many months ago—in that god-awful chapel, a festering hellhole Stephen and Reese will not soon forget.

It was there, about five miles south of the township limits, that they came across a dairy farm with a high chain-link fence somebody had erected in recent months to keep the walkers out. The buildings inside the fence looked deserted, decimated by fires, many of them scorched ruins. But out behind one of the empty barns were rows of aboveground fuel tanks that appeared to be untouched by flames.

For the next hour, they went from tank to tank, siphoning gasoline into their containers. They came to the conclusion that there must be thousands, maybe tens of thousands of gallons of pristine unleaded fuel in those tanks, enough gas to power the convoy for months. It was one of those rare, magnificent finds—a real headscratcher, which begs the question: *How the hell did everybody else miss this?*

In fact, they were so excited about their unexpected windfall that they nearly missed the two figures way off in the distance, moving along a high ridge of pines above a neighboring river.

"At first, I thought I was seeing things," Stephen Pembry says finally, pacing the short length of the RV's kitchen area. Outwardly serene, Jeremiah sits on the small sofa across the interior, his long legs crossed diffidently as he listens. He holds his cup of tea, but he hasn't taken a sip since they started. He is rapt, transfixed, galvanized—not by their story per se, but by the inherent providence beneath the surface of it. Fate wanted them to stumble upon these figures on this random hill. The emotion wells up in the preacher as he listens, a combination of rage, excitement, and something unnameable, something almost erotic. "There they were, just as plain as day," Stephen marvels. "I thought I was seeing ghosts. But I knew deep down I wasn't. I took a closer look with the binoculars just to confirm what I already knew."

Reese speaks up from the other side of the kitchen, where he's been nervously tapping a spatula on the edge of the tiny stove. "It was *Lilly Caul*, Brother . . . Lilly Caul and that young buck she was always hanging out with."

Jeremiah has a pleasant smile painted like clown-white on his face as he mutters softly, "Tommy Dupree."

"Right! Dupree . . . that's it . . . Tommy Dupree. He was the son of that fella, was helping us."

"Calvin." The preacher's voice is even, measured, almost tender. "Calvin Dupree."

"Calvin, right!" Reese cocks his head. "Didn't the kid blow him away?"

Stephen Pembry chimes in, "That's right, the little shit killed his own father."

Reese marvels, "If *they* made it outta that place alive . . . I wonder how many more of them did!"

"May I ask a silly question?" The big preacher carefully sets his drink on the side table. "Did either of you simpletons think of tracking these two?"

Reese and Stephen share a jittery glance. Reese stammers, "The thing of it is . . . we figured . . . the fuel was the most important thing . . . at that moment . . . considering the situation . . . and we could . . . we thought—"

"You *thought*?!" The preacher levers himself off the sofa and rises to his full height, which is formidable in any context, but especially in the tiny dollhouse of the RV's living area, his huge pompadour hairdo scraping the ceiling with the imposing posture of a golem. The preacher clenches his massive fists. "Who told you to *think*? Don't you realize what you let slip through your fingers?! *DO YOU NOT REALIZE WHAT THIS MEANS?!*" Each young man starts, wincing at the booming voice of the master orator. "I want you two numbskulls to get your asses back out to that abandoned dairy farm on the double, and I want you to fan out and search the area. Bring Leland's night vision goggles and enough provisions to keep you going for a while, because it may take days, weeks maybe, to find these people. But you *will* find them, or you might as well not come back. You understand? And when you do find them, I want you to keep your distance, follow them, keep an eye on them, and find out everything you can about how they survived that herd that over-turned our Caddy and nearly killed us. Do you understand? Tell me you understand. Each of you! I want to hear you say, 'I understand.' NOW! SAY IT!"

Almost in unison, their warbly, choked voices announce that they understand.

"Okay." The Reverend Jeremiah Garlitz lets out a pained sigh, smooths his hair back, stretches his neck, and gives a nod. "Now get outta my sight."

The two young men nearly stumble over each other in the process of departing.

Jeremiah turns away from the door and listens to the cheap alu-minum screen bang as the men make their exit. He takes in a deep breath and exhales slowly. He can feel his pulse racing. He hadn't bargained for this little turn of events, and at first it had merely ig-nited his bloodlust, his need for vengeance. These are the people who vanquished him from the Kingdom of Heaven. These folks ripped apart his dreams, shat on his destiny, kicked him out of the Garden. But the more he thinks about it, the more he realizes that this fortu-itous event is actually part of the grand scheme of things. The forces of darkness are aligning against him. He is the angel of light, the last Christian warrior of the Rapture. He will do far more than merely avenge the wrongs inflicted upon him by these people. With his masterpiece nearing fruition, his theories becoming reality, he will turn their minds to dust. He will grind their souls into the dirt and make their world a living hell.

He will take them apart and bury them alive and salt the earth for eternity.

"All right then," he murmurs to himself with a cheerful little smile. "Let's get to it."

Reese and Stephen spend the first part of their search in the fields out behind the dairy farm, and over those two days are forced to repel several waves of walkers drifting up from the deep woods along the river. At night, they camp on the high ground and use their infrareds. But they detect no signs of Lilly Caul or any of her people.

On the third day, they run low on ammo and retreat back to their truck, which is parked along Highway 19. They have enough food and water for maybe a week, but the dearth of ammo could easily bring their search to an ignominious end. They investigate the next town east—a ghost ship of a village once known as McCallister— and in a boarded smoke shop they find a drawer filled with cartons of Glaser 9mm safety slugs that fit Stephen's Glock.

The next day they decide to start circling Woodbury in an everincreasing diameter sweep—according to their paper map—keeping an eye on the adjacent tobacco fields, where many farmhouses and barns still stand in one piece, empty and rotting from the inside out, drowning in kudzu, but still full of treasures and refuge for wandering survivors. Reese thinks that Lilly and the kid might be hunkered down in one of the outbuildings.

Neither Reese nor Stephen gives a thought to the underground labyrinth—which had been discovered during their brief stay in Woodbury—until the fifth day, when Stephen sees something out of the ordinary along the tree line about a half a mile west of the town.

"Whoa! WHOA!" Stephen sits up straighter on the passenger side, pointing out the window at the blot of red that just blurred past them on their right. The day is overcast but bright, and the flat gray light penetrates the woods at least fifty yards or so on either side of them before the shadows of birches and pines swallow everything. The air smells of mildew and fetid earth. Rains are in the offing. "Slow down! GO BACK!"

Behind the wheel of the Escalade, Reese jerks nervously before applying the brakes. "What is it? You see something? What is it, Brother?"

"Back up!"

Reese stands on the brakes, sending both men lunging forward, causing a wet cloud of particulate to flume up from the rear of the SUV. The Escalade slams to a stop, the gears shrieking as Reese yanks the shift lever into reverse. The vehicle screams backward and screeches to a halt in front of a broken-down mile marker. "What did you see?" Reese demands as he peers out the window.

"There!" Stephen points. "About thirty or forty yards that way, right next to that huge oak—see it? It's like a red flag or marker—about twenty feet up! See it? Shit, man, open your eyes!"

Reese finally sees the flag. Barely visible in the shadows of tree boughs and power lines, it looks like a bandanna or red cloth one might see tied to the end of an especially long timber hanging off the back of a truck. "Oh my God . . . the tunnels." Reese's voice comes out low and breathless. "That's a marker. There's an opening right there."

Stephen looks at him. "I can't believe we forgot about the tunnels."

"That's how they survived the horde."

Stephen gives a thunderstruck nod. "And that's how they're getting in and out of town."

"Holy shit."

"Yeah . . ." Another exchange of feverish glances. "*Exactly.*"

They park the Escalade under the cover of foliage and wait for three days. Near the end of their rations, completely out of water, they huddle in the weeds a hundred yards upstream from the makeshift manhole and wait, and wait. They keep an eye on it at night with the goggles, and they stare at it for hours on end during the day—through rain and high winds and blazing sunlight and clouds of mosquitoes—and nothing stirs below the red flag. They have to ward off a few walkers every now and then—saving their ammo, caving in heads quietly with a small pickaxe and hammer—but for the most part the woods remain biter-free. On the morning of the fourth day of waiting, Stephen decides maybe it's time to go get help. His punctured lung is burning, panging with pain, making him wheeze furiously. Reese is no better—feverish from the stress, running a temperature, and getting dehydrated.

At last, just as they're packing up to leave, they detect motion through the trees around the lip of the hole: *An arm is thrusting up, grabbing turf for purchase.*

Reese goes still. He puts the binoculars to his eyes. His breath gets caught in his throat. Goose bumps ripple down his arms and back. Even at this great distance, through the telescopic lenses, Reese can identify the owner of this slender, freckled, wiry arm: the stalwart, inimitable, hazel-eyed woman who changed the course of his life.

SIX

Lilly Caul emerges from the hole with a grunt. She wears her Georgia Tech T-shirt and ripped jeans, her dishwater auburn hair tied back with a rubber band, her .22 caliber Ruger on her shapely hip, her Doc Martens planted firmly on the muddy ground as she twists around and helps a second person out of the subterranean portal.

David Stern, graying and arthritic despite his natural vigor, struggles to climb out of the manhole. Lilly offers him a hand but he stubbornly waves it off and maneuvers himself over the lip of the hole and onto the ground. He hauls himself to his feet and brushes the grit from his silk roadie jacket, his deep, cigarette-cured voice mingling with the shifting breezes. "Let's make this quick—I have a bad feeling about this one for some reason."

Lilly closes the hatch, camouflaging it with sticks and leaves, grumbling, "You always have a bad feeling. It's your default setting."

"You should be thankful for that." He tightens his gun belt with a sour grimace. "It keeps you on your toes."

"I prefer my fallen arches, thank you very much."

"You're starting to sound like my wife."

"I'll take that as a compliment," Lilly retorts, and gestures to the east, toward a clearing. "Let's get in and out, make this short and sweet. Agreed?"

"Agreed."

David Stern follows her as she marches down the trail toward the closest access road.

As she walks, she keeps one hand on her backpack and the other on the grip of her Ruger, which is thrust down a homemade holster tied to her belt. Barbara Stern did the leather stitching on the thing, and even burned the initials "LC" into the sheath—the monogram being more of a practical measure than a frivolous luxury: People in the tunnels were constantly taking the wrong guns from the rack near the exit steps. In the aftermath of the violent and surreal events of the last couple of months, Lilly has come to feel as if the tunnels are a prison, or at best a sort of limbo between two worlds. She relishes these times aboveground, however dangerous or brief they may be. Her claustrophobia is a constant dissonant thrum of tension beneath the surface of her subterranean life, and today, even the threat of rain can't dampen her enjoyment of this little field trip.

"Wait up, Lilly!" David Stern trots up behind her, breathing heavily. "It's not a race."

"Just want to make it back before nightfall."

"Where we headed first? Drugstore?"

Lilly waves the idea off like a bad smell. "That place is picked clean, even the basement—plus we can always get there through the side tunnels."

"You gonna make me guess?"

Lilly smiles to herself as she walks. "Thought we'd hit the guardhouse at the reservoir and the supermarket warehouse on the way over to lovers' leap."

"Lovers' leap? You want to go all the way out there?"

"That's right."

"Lilly, there's no fuel up there; there's nothing but bird shit and walkers."

Lilly shrugs as she lopes along the narrow dirt trail, her sensory organs dialed up high now, absorbing every noise in the isolated forest. "It won't take long."

David Stern rolls his eyes. "You're not fooling anybody, Lilly."

"What do you mean?"

"You just want to get another gander, don't you?"

"A what?"

"A look-see, a glimpse."

"David—"

"You're just torturing yourself, Lilly."

"I'm just trying to—"

"There's nothing anybody can do about Woodbury. We've been through this a million times."

"Wait!" She comes to an abrupt stop, David nearly colliding with her. "Hold on a second."

"What is it?" David glances over his shoulder, whispering now. He reaches for his axe, which dangles from a clasp on the side of his pack. "Walkers?"

She shakes her head, gazing around the immediate area, scanning the shadows, listening to the rustle of the breeze through the leaves. She thought she heard a twig snap, or perhaps a series of shuffling footsteps, behind them, in the middle distance, but she can't be sure.

"Humans?" David licks his lips and gazes again over his shoulder.

"I don't know. Just hearing things, I guess." She continues on.

David follows, his hand on his axe now. They walk for another mile or so without saying much to each other. When they get to the intersection of Country Club and Rosewood, they turn north.

The sensation of being followed never completely fades from the back of Lilly's mind.

By the time they reach the winding road that meanders up the side of Emory Hill along the eastern edge of Carrol Woods, a low cover of dark afternoon clouds have rolled in, and Lilly and David are exhausted and cranky. So far, they've found very little in the way of fuel—a few ounces from a generator at the reservoir guardhouse, and another liter or so in the tank of a wrecked minivan out on

Highway 18. Other than that, a few scraps of vending machine food and over-the-counter medication scavenged from the ruins of a truck stop on Interstate 85, and that's it. They've basically come up empty.

All of which makes the climb up that narrow two-lane a more arduous task than usual.

"Just let me do this and stop nagging me," Lilly grumbles as they finally reach the scenic pull-off that marks the crest of Emory Hill.

"Did I say you couldn't?" David Stern follows her, exhausted and spent. He has sweated through his silk jacket, and now he has it tied around his waist as he trudges along. His gray chest hair and sagging pectorals are visible through his stained sleeveless T. They had encountered a couple stray roamers about a mile back down the hill, and David cleaved in their skulls with the axe as casually as if he were chopping a few extra cords of firewood. Now he follows Lilly as she steps over a low guardrail and strides across a dirt clearing to the edge of a gravel precipice. "It's a free country," he mutters as he shrugs off his pack and sets it down.

"Hand me the binocs, would ya?"

He fishes in his pack, hands over the binoculars, and stands there waiting.

She puts the lenses to her eyes and gazes out across miles of farmland.

Woodbury can be seen in the binoculars' hazy, milky panorama, so far away that, even at 10x magnification, it looks like a quaint little toy village of dollhouses, a LEGO town, adorable but stained black and rotten with oily floodwaters undulating and oozing down its main drag and branching into every side street, alleyway, and cul-de-sac. Lilly adjusts the focus. The flood reveals itself to be an incomprehensible number of dead, shambling aimlessly, shoulder to shoulder, standing-room-only, ping-ponging around with the random madness of electrons. Woodbury is literally submerged in a sea of cadavers. The countless ragged corpses crowd every square foot of pavement, every doorway, every alcove, every yard, every parking lot, every knoll, and from this distance, the impenetrable quality of it—the sheer finality that radiates off the sight—makes Lilly's capillaries go cold, her solar plexus clenching suddenly with a massive wave of sorrow and despair so black and toxic that she drops the binoculars.

"You okay?" David looks up from his absent nail-biting. "What's the matter?"

Lilly has already started back down the sloping pavement of the turnoff.

David grabs the binoculars and hustles after her, calling out in the stillness, "Slow down!"

The sound of a small tin can rattling—a makeshift entryway bell—fills the dank air of the cluttered subterranean passageway.

"I'll be damned if that doesn't sound like our intrepid scouts returning to the fold." Bob Stookey, his dark, greasy locks pomaded back from his corrugated brow, his chambray denim shirt damp under the arms, looks up from his cup of coffee and sees the thin shaft of pale light shining down from the tunnel ceiling fifty feet away. It's almost dawn. "About freaking time."

"Thank God," Gloria Pyne says from the other side of the rickety wooden table, which was once a cable spool but is now one of the many items repurposed for the narrow stretch of brick-lined tunnel. Gloria has her trademark visor—emblazoned with the faded words "I'M WITH STUPID"—tilted to one side of her graying head, a stick of stale gum snapping nervously on one side of her mouth.

The cluttered tunnel is about the length of half a city block, maybe a little less, with intersecting tunnels at each end barricaded with brightly painted chain-link barriers, installed to keep the underground walkers—dubbed "moles" by Gloria—from invading the space. Once a section of the old antebellum Underground Railroad, the tunnel was transformed almost single-handedly by Bob Stookey into a barracks and living space for the surviving residents of Woodbury, Georgia. Now the air smells of both decay and disinfectant, mold and coffee freshly brewed on a hot plate. Cage lights dangle down, running off the power supplied by two propane-fueled generators situated aboveground, over the far end of the passage-way, their feed cable snaking down like octopus tentacles from the stalactite-lined ceiling.

Bob and Gloria push themselves away from the table and creep as silently as possible—not wanting to awaken the children—toward the main entrance portal. In a mirror aimed up at the opening, Bob can see Lilly's leg thrusting down toward the inner steps, and hears her raspy voice saying, "I never thought I would say this, but it's good to be back."

Lilly lowers herself down the footholds embedded in the mortar-lined tunnel wall.

"What in the Sam Hell took you so long?" Bob gives Lilly the once-over, inspecting her pack, her ammo belt, her muddy boots.

She gives him a look. "Don't ask."

"Lilly thinks walkers are stalkers now." David Stern's voice filters down as he lowers himself, gingerly maneuvering his sore, rheumatic limbs toward the tunnel floor. He lands with a grunt, the contents of his heavy pack rattling, and adds, "She's convinced we were being tracked by the dead."

"Nice of you two to drop by!" Barbara Stern's voice echoes. A middle-aged earth mother in a faded floral-print muumuu and wild gray locks approaches, her eyes shimmering with love and relief. "You had us worried sick, by the way."

"Don't start with me, Babs," David says, his own eyes filling with emotion, reaching for her. She grabs him and pulls him into a desperate embrace. He hugs her back, stroking her soft curves, murmuring, "I'm cranky and tired and in no mood to be chastised."

"Back home one second and already he's whining." Barbara clings to him. "Look at you. You've got sweat stains under your sweat stains."

"I love you, too, sweetheart."

"Walker stalkers?" Bob Stookey asks Lilly, giving her an incredulous smirk.

Lilly shrugs, wriggling out of her pack, dropping the ruck to the tunnel floor, the contents clanking. "*Something* was following us. If it wasn't walkers . . . I don't know who the hell it was, or why they were being so . . . what's the word?"

David chimes in from across the tunnel. "Furtive?"

Lilly nods. "Yeah, exactly."

Bob studies her, his grin fading. "You okay, Lilly-girl?"

"Yeah, peachy . . . Why?"

Now Bob gives *her* a shrug. "Just asking."

"Well, I'm fine."

Bob looks at the others. "Okay, people, let's give them some air. Gloria, can you go put another pot of hot water on? These folks look like they could use some coffee."

They sit in the lounge area and sip instant coffee and chat for nearly an hour about the possibility of a walker actually stalking someone. Bob assures Lilly that the dead have no tactical skills whatsoever. "Biters have the intellect of a snail," he proclaims at one point, after which David Stern wisecracks, "That's an insult to snails." Everybody roars at that one except Lilly. Bob can tell something's wrong, and he thinks he knows what it is.

During the conversation, Tommy Dupree, the oldest of the children, stirs in his sleeping bag on the other side of the tunnel. Amid the propane tanks, food crates, folding chairs, and bundles of electrical cords running down the walls like vines, the area directly above Tommy's sleeping pad is plastered with clippings and pages from various magazines salvaged from Woodbury's library, giving the area the look of a teenager's room on a submarine.

Roused by the sound of Lilly's voice, the gangly twelve-year-old jerks awake and scampers barefoot over to her table, hugging Lilly to the point of making David Stern wonder aloud if he's chopped liver. In recent weeks, the boy has latched on to Lilly—his mentor, his teacher, his big sister, and maybe, just maybe, much to Lilly's chagrin, his adopted mother—largely in compensation for the tumult that took his parents' lives.

At length, the adults finish their debate regarding walker behavior, the other kids start waking up, and Gloria and Barbara begin their day of shepherding a half dozen children under the age of eleven through their morning rituals of sponge bathing, eating instant oatmeal, playing card games, and complaining about the smell in the tunnels. David goes off to help Harold Staubach rewire one of the gennies, and Lilly is left alone with Bob.

Bob stares at her. "Something's wrong—I can see it in your eyes."

Lilly sips her coffee. "We went out, we didn't find much, and then we were followed by somebody. . . . End of story."

"You sure that's all?"

Lilly looks at him. "What do want me to say? Where are you going with this, Bob?"

"You saw something out there."

She lets out a pained sigh. "Bob, don't go down that road."

"Just be honest with me."

"Always."

For a moment, Bob burns his gaze into her eyes, the worry lines forming deep folds in his forehead under his dark pomaded hair, his kind, sad eyes buried in crow's-feet. Beneath his gruff, coarse exterior, the former army medic and reformed alcoholic is a tenderhearted, doting mother hen. "You looked, didn't you? You went and looked at the town again."

"Bob—"

"What did I tell you?"

"I just—"

"What good does it do right now?" He crosses his arms over his chest and lets out a puff of exasperation. "Lilly-girl . . . c'mere for a second." He gestures toward a dark corner of the tunnel. "C'mere, I want to talk to you."

Bob leads her past the folding tables of the dining area, past stacks of crates containing their supplies of canned goods and dry cereal, past the racks of weapons, past the hooks upon which winter coats and thrift-shop clothing hang, past the curtained-off bathroom facility (people do their business in a bucket, then empty it down a trough leading into the sewer), and finally over to an alcove of crates stacked in front of the Rust-Oleum-painted hurricane-fence barricade. The shadows deepen around them as the faint, breathy smell of the grave filters through the chain-link barrier. Bob speaks in an urgent whisper. "You're confusing these people, Lilly."

"Bob—"

"We can't keep talking about this. You can see for yourself. It's a foregone conclusion."

"Bob, these kids deserve to live as normal a life as possible, and that means getting Woodbury back. We can do it, if we all pitch in."

"It's too soon."

Lilly feels a twinge of anger. "The time is *now*, Bob. The horde has stabilized; it's not getting any bigger."

"Yeah, and it's not getting any smaller."

"Bob—"

"Put it to a vote, you don't believe me. Let everybody vote on it, kids too."

She sighs and looks over her shoulder at the others. Fifty feet away, the youngest kids are splashing and giggling inside the confines of a huge galvanized washtub. Gloria squats next to them in her threadbare Capri pants and high-top sneakers, helping the Slocum twins and Lucas Dupree take sponge baths with the last of the dishwashing liquid.

Gloria has taken it upon herself to be the interior decorator of the group, her latest creation visible in the dim light just beyond the washtub. The little makeshift lounge has pieces scavenged from Woodbury's Dew Drop Inn—bar stools, highboy tables, plastic flowers in tin cans, a dartboard, and even a poster that says, "BEER IS THE ANSWER. . . . BUT WHAT WAS THE QUESTION?"

Right now, Harold Staubach and the Sterns sit at one of these highboys, drinking instant coffee and fiddling with exposed wires and circuitry from one of the generator junction boxes. None of these people seems as restless or displaced as Lilly, as she softly murmurs now, almost to herself, "Bob, it's not legislation . . . it's not an act of Congress."

"What's wrong with taking a vote? Isn't that the way you always wanted to run the town?"

She looks at him and lets out another bitter sigh. "I don't want to get into this now."

"Are you saying you don't want to get into a discussion about taking Woodbury back or you don't want to get into a voting situation?"

"I mean, I don't want to go over this again."

"Why not?"

"Bob, these people have no idea what the implications of staying down here are."

"It's the lesser of two evils, Lilly."

"I don't see it that way. We had something good up there, or at least we saw glimmers of it."

"I ain't saying we didn't. All I'm saying is, this place is our best bet for now. It ain't gonna be forever. But for now, we got everything we need down here."

She exhales a derisive little breath. "We got food and water, electrical power, fucking beans and rice, but we really don't have anything."

"Lilly, come on."

"Anything that *matters*." She fixes her gaze on him. "We don't have light, air . . . the earth, the sky . . . freedom."

Bob shakes his head with mock dismay, a crooked little smile creasing his deeply lined features. "How can you say that? We got plenty of earth—just look around."

"Very funny, Bob. Maybe you should do stand-up comedy down here for the gang Fridays and Saturdays. You'll have a captive audience."

He cocks his head at her, his smile fading. "Is it the claustrophobia flarin' up again?"

Another anguished sigh from Lilly. She would take a bullet for this crusty old medic, she would die for him, but he makes her so goddamned crazy sometimes. "What are you asking me? You asking if I'm willing to put everybody else's life at stake because I get the shakes or a few headaches every once in a while?"

"I didn't say—"

"We can't stay down here indefinitely, Bob. You know that as well as I do."

He puts his big, grime-stained hand around her shoulder, his touch both tender and deferential. "Look, I'm not saying we stay down here till the twelfth of forever. I'm just saying we stay put until it gets a little less hairy up there. Right now it's Grand Central Station up there, and I don't want to lose any more people if I don't have to."

She gives him a hard look. "How do you know it's ever going to get any better?"

He removes his hand from her shoulder and doesn't say anything.

Lilly glances off toward the barricade. In the shadows next to the fencing, a single heavy-duty power cable snakes down from the ceiling and into a rectangular light fixture aimed down at a row of flowerpots on a shelf. Lilly's beloved petunias stick out of the potting soil in the purple glow, spindly, sickly, looking like wadded tissue paper. She has given up on her flowers. Now, each day, she watches them die. She mutters, "How do we know they're not going to be there a thousand years?" She looks at Bob. "Maybe this is the new normal."

He keeps looking at the floor, shrugging, not saying anything.

She stares at him. "All this aside . . . we're vulnerable down here, Bob. And it's not just the risk of walkers getting in. We're vulnerable to human attack."

Bob finally looks at her and gives her his patented sideways grin. His voice drops an octave, coming out with smug certainty: "Who the hell in their right mind would bother us down *here*?"

SEVEN

Two figures move through the woods, through thick drapes of foliage, the shafts of overcast daylight flickering down into their eyes as they scan the distant trees for any sign of their encampment.

They walk silently, stealthily, their pistols gripped tightly in their hands. They have silencers attached to the muzzles of their weapons but they're low on ammo and conserving their bullets. They carry secondary weapons—the younger man a machete stuffed down his belt, the older man a twelve-inch hunting knife in a sheath on his hip—each using his auxiliary weapon for both slashing thickets of foliage and impaling the skulls of errant walkers. They've been lucky these last few hours, running into very few roamers. The herd seems to have coalesced north of here, with only a few stragglers dragging along the back roads of southern Meriwether County.

"Look!" Reese Lee Hawthorne, his face shimmering with sweat, his clothes soaked through, speaks in a loud whisper, cautious about drawing too much attention. "Straight ahead—the other side of that clearing—see it?!"

The two young men come to a halt under a canopy of thick pine boughs. The late afternoon light undulates above them with bugs, the air smelling of wood-rot and forest musk. Stephen Pembry catches his breath and nods slowly. "Thank the Lord, thank the Good Lord."

Through the brambles he can see the temporary barricade of logs and chicken wire, and the dull silver gleam of Chester Gleason's

Airstream trailer. The circle of vehicles stretches at least a hundred yards in both directions—pickups, SUVs, stake trucks, and all manner of RVs—their battered exteriors camouflaged by the shadows of the deep woods. The two scouts give each other one last fleeting nod of excitement, and then lurch single file through the remaining grove of trees between them and the caravan.

They burst out of the forest and practically leap over the fence.

Reese runs with a limp, his hip panging with agony where he fell earlier that morning trying to cross a dry, rocky riverbed. Stephen wheezes furiously as he runs, his injured rib cage and punctured lung on fire. Their packs feel as though they weigh a thousand tons on their backs, and their eyes bug out with thirst and hunger as they stumble awkwardly toward the huge plastic water jug on the tailgate of the Thorndyke family camper. The noise of their arrival brings dozens of survivors out of their RVs or out from behind temporary latrines to see what all the commotion is about.

Stephen reaches the water jug first and drops to his knees, putting his parched mouth under the tap.

"Careful, Brother," Reese says, kneeling beside him, cupping his hands to catch the runoff dripping from the tap and Stephen's chin. "You don't want to puke it all up before it hits your gut!"

Stephen Pembry gulps the water and then has a coughing attack, dropping to his hands and knees, keeling over, hacking and wheezing into the grass. "Sweet Jesus," he gasps between coughing fits, his face livid with exertion. "Water has never tasted so good!"

The two men had run completely out of drinking water twelve hours earlier, and figured it was no big deal. They had all the evidence they needed to return to camp, and the caravan wasn't that far away, and besides, they were driving the Escalade, and as long as the main road was passable, they could be back home before suppertime. But as Stephen's father, Pastor Evan Pembry of the First Baptist Church of Murfreesboro, Kentucky, was fond of saying when he got in his cups or was trying to make a point about the capriciousness of life, "*Man plans and God has a big old laugh.*"

"You boys all right?" a voice intones cautiously behind Reese.

Stephen looks up, wiping his mouth and blinking, and sees Rory Thorndyke standing over him. The former bricklayer from Augusta, garbed in a stained wifebeater T-shirt, his tree-trunk arms emblazoned with naval tattoos and hard gristly muscles, holds his cherubic little three-year-old daughter in his arms while he gums a wad of Copenhagen. "Y'all look like you been hit by a truck."

"We'll live," Stephen mutters as he sits back in the grass and tries to catch his breath.

"You see the herd out there—the big one?" Rory wants to know, giving his little girl a bounce on his hip. For weeks now, the gathering hordes of walkers along the backwaters of southern Georgia have been a hot topic of conversation among the members of the convoy. It's bad enough that the infernal things had managed to get into their beloved Father Murphy's camper, but the fact that they seem to be coalescing like individual amoebas morphing into a larger and larger organism has everybody spooked.

Stephen shakes his head. "Nope . . . Other than the swarms that have settled down on some of the towns south of Atlanta, we didn't see no herd."

"Well, y'all better get your shit together, the preacher said he wanted to see you two the minute you got back."

Reese and Stephen share another loaded glance and then begin to brush themselves off and run fingers through their hair as though preparing for a court appearance.

"What in tarnation happened to your dad-blamed vehicle?" The preacher sits at the RV's dining table, his hat off, his huge hair greased back from his forehead. He is dressed in shirtsleeves, slacks, and his big Wellington boots, and he sits back against the bulwark, one boot propped up rakishly on the seat cushion as he plays with a child's toy. His enormous gnarled hands fiddle with the tiny propeller, turning it as though he's never seen a remote control helicopter before. This morbid fascination with toys—in fact, the mere *idea* of toys, and the existential *absurdity* of them in this day and age, as though the very *idea* of someone playing with toys now is an offense to God—practically crackles in his brain with a strange effervescence. His pappy didn't take kindly to the concept of *play*.

"Ran outta gas about ten, fifteen miles from here," Stephen reports from across the camper. He paces nervously and wheezes between sentences as he speaks. "Didn't bargain on all the driving around in circles."

"We'll get it back. I'll send Chester and Harlan out for it."

Stephen nods. "Appreciate it, Brother. Sorry about having to leave it."

"And you say the Caul woman and her party is now livin' in this tunnel like a bunch of sewer rats?"

"Not sure how many are down there—at least a half dozen or so adults. That Bob fella, Harold, and some ladies, a few kids maybe."

"Brother Staubach is with them?"

Jittery nods.

"Makes you wonder what kinda firepower they're packin' down there."

Reese looks at Stephen and gives a shrug. "Mostly small arms, looks like, and they don't seem to have a heck of a lot of ammo. I'm thinking they're pretty much running on fumes down there, even though they got gennies providing power and whatnot."

The preacher chews on this for a moment. "I thought for sure old Harold had met his maker during all that hubbub in Woodbury." He twirls the little plastic propeller. "Man is a traitor to his church."

"What are you fixing to do, Brother?" Reese wrings his hands as he sits on the flip-down love seat at the rear of the camper.

Jeremiah takes a deep breath as the rage turns in him, churning into something new, something ingenious and grand and almost biblical in nature. His great notion, his brilliant idea, smolders like a white-hot ember in the back of his brain. "Found this little gizmo in the back of Thorndyke's camper, was in a toy box, belonged to the previous owners—a few batteries that hadn't turned to dust, some other stuff, little gadgets and things."

It becomes obvious the other two men have no idea what Jeremiah is talking about.

Jeremiah holds the little olive drab–colored plastic helicopter aloft as though illustrating his point. " 'Then I saw heaven standing open, and there before me was a white horse, whose rider is called Truth.' "

The two younger men share a nervous, fleeting glance. Reese recognizes the quote from Revelations but hasn't a clue as to what it means in this context. The preacher gazes lovingly at the remote control chopper. " 'With justice he judges and makes war,' " he murmurs, his eyes getting far away. " 'For he is vengeance.' "

"Brother Jeremiah, are you—?"

" 'The cowardly, the unbelieving, the vile . . . they shall be consigned to the fiery lake of burning sulfur.' "

"Brother—?"

" 'They will be tormented day and night,' " Jeremiah recites dreamily, lost in his great plan, his brilliant idea. He can't hear the voice of the younger man. He hears imaginary screams, temples falling. He leans forward and carefully blows on the tiny rotor.

" 'They shall be in agony . . . day and night . . . forever and ever and ever.' "

The little propeller spins and spins.

Miles Littleton has heard enough. On his hands and knees under the window of the preacher's RV, his skinny form shielded from the eyes of other campers by a curtain of foliage and poplar trees, the young car thief has been listening to the conversation going on inside the camper for nearly a half an hour now, and with each passing minute he has gotten more and more disgusted.

Considering the fact that Miles has been in and out of jail for petty crimes for most of his life, he knows a con man when he hears one.

The trouble is, this bat-shit preacher seems to have won over most of the members of the caravan. In fact, there may be only one person around here other than Miles who has the bullshit detector turned on, and it's high time Miles went and talked to her about it.

He turns away from the RV and silently crawls through the trees.

He emerges on the other side of the clearing and then goes searching for Norma.

She'll know what to do.

PART 2

The End of the Whole Mess

"For then shall be great tribulation, such as was not seen since the beginning of the world . . . nor ever shall be seen again."
—Matthew 24:21

EIGHT

Days later, in the main sewer conduit beneath the outskirts of Wood-bury, Georgia, two figures splash through six inches of brackish muck, walking side by side in the darkness. The older of the two, a slender woman of wan complexion and auburn hair, wears a min-er's helmet she found in one of the maintenance offices in a neigh-boring water treatment plant. The single battery-operated light attached to the helmet sends a thin shaft of luminous yellow across the passageway in front of her, shimmering dully off the ancient terra-cotta tiles of the tunnel wall.

The younger of the two—a gangly boy of twelve dressed in a flan-nel shirt that's two sizes too big for him—trundles along beside the woman, cheerfully babbling, "I heard what you said to Bob the other day, and I totally agree with you, Lilly. I mean, I think we can and we *should* take Woodbury back from the slugs, and I know it's not up to me, but I'm like totally down with you on this, and I'll do what-ever I can do to help, you know what I mean?"

Lilly shoots a glance at the boy, but doesn't break her stride. "You were spying on us?"

He shrugs as he walks. "I wouldn't call it spying, I was just sort of—"

"You were pretending to be asleep."

"Sort of."

"You were eavesdropping."

"All right, yeah, I admit it, but the point is, I totally agree with you."

She shakes her head. "You heard the whole thing about me being claustrophobic?"

He nods. "I'm not sure what that means."

Lilly sighs. "It means—literally—a fear of enclosed spaces."

The boy walks and thinks for a moment. "That's kinda bad, huh, considering where we're living nowadays?"

"You think?"

"Lilly, can you keep a secret?"

"What do you mean?"

"There's something I want to show you."

"Right now? Down here?"

"Yeah."

"We don't have a lot of time, Tommy, we're supposed to be checking the culvert opening."

"It'll just take a—"

"Wait, hold on." Lilly slows down, detecting a troubling odor in the fusty, airless atmosphere of the sewer. Beneath the stench of human waste wafts a secondary stench—greasier, more acrid. "Just a second," she says, and stops.

The boy halts, and waits, and stares at her. "What is it? A slug?"

Lilly cocks her head and listens.

"Slug" is the boy's latest slang word for the reanimated dead. For weeks now, he has been using a seemingly infinite number of monikers for the creatures—stinkers, empties, geeks, rotters, shells, stiffs, carcasses, chewies, dicks, reekers, meat-flies, feeders, mofos—to the point that Lilly has lost count of all the nicknames. She believes it's a defense mechanism—a way for the twelve-year-old to objectify the monsters and minimize the horror of seeing human beings reduced to these repulsive parasitic *things*—so she goes along with it, trying in vain to keep up with the latest terminology. Right now, in fact, as she listens closely to the watery smacking noises coming from the shadows ahead of them, she thinks "slug" is a fairly accurate appellation for the sewer corpses she has been encountering underground lately.

"You hear that?" Lilly says finally.

"Yeah." The boy goes stone-still as the watery sounds rise into a tortured, raspy, moaning noise. "Sounds like it's coming from that side tunnel up there." He indicates a dark intersection of tunnels about fifty feet away, a workman's shovel leaning against the wall. They've traveled almost a mile west of their barracks, their position somewhere under Gable's Pond. In the thin beam of light from the miner's helmet, a series of ripples agitate the standing water.

Lilly pulls her .22 caliber Ruger and starts screwing on the suppressor attachment. "You stay here, and I'll go and—"

"No." The boy puts a hand on her arm. "Let me take care of it."

"Tommy—"

"I can do it." His chin juts with determination, his eyes blazing. His expression nearly breaks Lilly's heart. Newly orphaned, steeped in death and loss, the boy is a born survivor. "I'll be fine," he says. "Let me do it."

Lilly nods. "I'll be right behind you. Be careful. No hesitating."

"I'll be okay."

Lilly follows the boy through the mire, her gun at her side, her finger poised on the trigger pad. Tommy approaches the intersecting tunnels slowly. He carefully picks up the shovel.

Something moves around the corner, making little radiating ripples across the flooded floor. The boy silently sucks in a breath and raises the shovel. Lilly moves in behind him as he turns the corner.

Something shoots toward his leg, and cold fingers clutch his ankle.

The boy yelps and rears back, and Lilly gets a fleeting glimpse of the thing before the shovel comes down—a flash of the miner's light illuminating a pasty, bloated, fish-belly face, its slimy, piranha-like teeth clacking. The bottom of the creature's torso is missing, a spaghetti knot of entrails flagging off. The rot and months of being submerged in the swampy muck have inflated its upper half to twice its normal size, giving it the appearance of being artificial and rubbery, like a discarded doll.

Tommy Dupree slams the shovel down on the thing's sodden skull, the sound like wet celery snapping. The creature instantly sags, its cadaverous hand releasing the boy's ankle. Tommy strikes it again. The thing has already expired, its flattened head now sinking below water level, but Tommy keeps smashing the shovel down on its remains. Again and again . . . until Lilly grabs the implement and makes Tommy inhale with a gasp as though waking from a dream.

"Good job, good job . . . you did it." Lilly soothes the boy by patting him on the back and tousling his hair. "You killed that thing real good."

"Yeah . . . okay." The boy is breathing so hard he's about to hyperventilate. "Okay . . . um . . . yeah."

"You all right?" Lilly holsters her gun, takes the shovel, and leads the boy over to the opposite corner of the intersecting tunnels. "Look at me."

The boy looks at her. His eyes are red. He's still breathing hard. "I'm okay, Lilly."

"You sure?"

He nods. "Yep." He takes a deep breath, wipes his mouth, and looks as though he just woke up. "Can I show you something now?"

Lilly smiles at him. "Why not?"

An hour or so later, after leading Lilly down a mile of narrow passageway, the boy shines the light at the tunnel ceiling. "There it is!" he marvels, abruptly coming to a halt.

Lilly gazes up, her miner's light canting up at the leprous ceiling, where tendrils of roots and wormy gray icicles of calcium dangle down, whiskering the edges of a large drainage grate. A patina of grit and age cover the rusty underside of the grating, but it's apparent by a series of fresh scratches and gouge marks that somebody has forced it open in recent days. Lilly's heart beats a little faster.

"Okay, hold the light for a second," Tommy says. She does so as he scuttles up the ancient steps embedded in the masonry. He pushes open the grating with a grunt and shimmies up through the gap.

"You mind helping an old lady up?!" Lilly says. She sees nothing but darkness on the other side of the hatch as the pale face of Tommy Dupree stares down at her.

"Here, take my hand."

He helps her into the fetid atmosphere of a cavernous boiler room.

She rises to her feet and brushes herself off, gazing around at the shadowy convolutions of ductwork, furnaces, hot water heaters, and ancient plumbing like the tentacles of prehistoric beasts. The air smells of the centuries, a faint whiff of old rubber and overworked heating elements. Tommy leads her over to a staircase with rickety metal treads going up one flight.

Lilly aims her light at the top of the stairs and sees the word "SHOWROOM" stenciled across the backside of a latched metal door. Tommy reaches the door first, and pauses. He smiles at her.

"Get a load of this," he says. He opens the door as though ushering a guest into an exclusive club, and Lilly takes a single step into the room.

At first, she goes still, as though gobsmacked by the sheer scale of the place. It takes a long moment for the vast, spacious room filled with enormous shadowy objects to even register in her brain.

She slowly scans the showroom, which is arrayed with shiny new farm implements, the beam of her miner's light passing across the high-gloss Kelly green fenders of John Deere tractors, the gleaming candy apple red tusks of Case harvesters, the gigantic scoops of backhoes, the enormous blades of reapers, and the countless rows of riding mowers, diggers, transports, wagons, and attachments sitting in the dark like cadavers in a carpeted morgue. The high ceiling, at least fifty feet above the floor, houses massive gantries, inverted lighting long ago gone dark, the rustle of birds up in the ironwork like termites eating away at the place.

"Is this sweet or what?" the boy enthuses, striding across the showroom floor, his footsteps silent on the thick pile carpet. Lilly sees a massive company sign on a banner spanning the back wall: "CENTRAL MACHINERY SALES."

"Good God," she utters, taking a few more steps in toward the center of the room. She can smell the welcoming perfume of new upholstery, fresh lubricant, immaculate tire treads, and shimmering steel joints like jewels in elaborate settings. "How the hell did you find this?"

"I kind of accidentally found that opening in the basement," he explains with a sweeping gesture of his skinny arms, indicating the totality of the dark showroom, a modicum of pride in his voice as though explaining the genesis of a winning science fair project. "I was just wandering, and I noticed some parts of the ceiling were, like, dripping, like water draining or something. And then I realized that the drain was in the floor of a basement. C'mon."

He takes her by the hand and leads her across the showroom to a side door behind a cashier's desk. Lilly draws her pistol. They make their exit carefully, stepping through a malodorous vestibule into the overcast afternoon. Trash blows around their feet as they survey the grounds of Central Machinery Sales—the deserted parking lot, the security fence, the streetlights and power lines.

"Holy Christ, is that what I think it is?" Lilly nods toward a holding tank. The size of a Volkswagen Bug, the horizontal tank is rust-pocked and sun-faded, but the legend stamped on the side is still faintly visible: "F U E L."

"Is that full?" Lilly asks.

"I think so. C'mere." The boy crosses the gravel lot to the edge of the fuel tank, makes a fist, and pounds on the side. The ringing sound is flat, and accompanied by the slosh of fluid inside the reservoir. "Sounds like it's half full."

Lilly looks around. "Looks like the fence is still intact. And the place is walker-free?"

"Yep."

"Oh my God." She looks at the boy. "Oh . . . my . . . God."

"I know." He grins. "Whaddaya think?"

"Oh. My. God."

"Sweet, huh?"

She stares at him. "I'm not sure yet, but this place might just change everything."

"Reverend, with all due respect . . . you're leading us straight into Injun territory."

The voice comes from the rear of the Winnebago, the sound of it warbling as though coming through a tissue of liquid. James Frazier stands behind the pilot seat, bracing himself on the nearest cupboard as the vehicle clamors over rough road, rattling and thudding furiously, knocking dishes askew and sending books tumbling off shelves. Some of the preacher's remote control toys topple, sending plastic airplanes, model cars, transmitters, and batteries skittering across the floor. James cringes with each bump, his flannel shirt sweat-damp under the arms. He glances out the passenger window as the camper roars past a fence post on which a walker head has been impaled as some sort of warning, the pasty cadaverous face still openmouthed, still looking hungry, still gripped in agony for eternity.

"Trust, James! Trust in the Lord, and trust in your humble clergy!" Jeremiah buzzes with energy, despite the fact that his rosacea has returned with a vengeance this morning. Dressed in his trademark black frock coat, now bunched in the middle with a heavy bullet bandolier, he glances up at the rearview and takes in his square-jawed reflection: the rosy patches across his cheeks and chin, the moistness of his eyes, his prominent nose already broken out in darkened capillaries as though he were a skid-row juicer on his last bender. The skin disorder has a habit of breaking out when the preacher least expects it, often in times of great upheaval or stress. It also seems to be advancing. For years, it had only caused a faint swelling in his eyes and a reddening of the cheeks, as though he were blushing. But lately the condition brings on severe flushing, a burning in the eyes, and visible blood vessels. And today is shaping up to be the worst outbreak yet. It's been brewing ever since they left camp.

The caravan has been on the road for hours, following the preacher west, toward the state line, where scouts have seen signs of another super-herd brewing. The official purpose of the journey—the ostensible reason that Jeremiah has given to his followers—is reconnaissance: The preacher wants to gauge the threat level of this so-called ungodly swarm of monsters. But what very few people in the convoy know is that Jeremiah is returning to the scene of devastation that claimed the lives of his fellow parishioners almost a year earlier. He is returning to the river of blood, to ground zero, where dozens of his flock were devoured. And the real reason he's returning to this cursed territory is to execute the first few brushstrokes of his masterpiece.

A third voice behind James: "Relax, Jimmy, the good reverend knows what he's doing!"

In the rear of the cabin, around the L-shaped dining table, Reese Lee Hawthorne and Stephen Pembry are dressed in heavy leathers for battle, loading their weapons with knowing smiles, the smiles of disciples embarking on a great mission. Reese snaps a magazine into his Mossberg 12-gauge, then pumps the forearm slide, injecting a magazine. "We're gonna get in and get out," Reese proclaims. "Fast and hard, before anybody knows better."

James runs fingers nervously through his thick thatch of ginger-colored hair. "You don't understand. . . . Where we're headed, along the border, where the river meets the barrens . . . this is Scorpion territory."

Stephen Pembry looks up from his loading. "The motorcycle gang, you're talking about?"

"Exactly."

"What gang?" Reese snaps the slide and throws a look at Stephen. "What are you talking about?"

Stephen sighs. "Ragtag group of scuz-balls from Birmingham, banded together after the outbreak, formed a sort of tribe . . . fueled on crystal meth and fear along the Chattahoochee River."

"They're animals!" James gazes from man to man with a worried expression. "Believe me! You get within a mile of their territory, they will take you down and cook you on a spit for barbecue!"

"That's ridiculous," Stephen Pembry counters with a dismissive wave. "Urban legend."

"Have you ever met up with one of them guys?"

"No."

"Then you don't know what you're talking about."

"What makes you such an authority? Have *you* met up with one?"

After a brief pause, James lets out a sigh. "It doesn't matter whether I have or not . . . I'm telling you these dudes are bad fucking news."

Stephen shakes his head and slams a full magazine—the last eight bullets in his arsenal—into his Glock. "You ask me, I bet these biker boys are all bark and no bite."

James starts to say something else when the deep baritone voice from the front cuts him off.

"Why don't you boys ask one of these Scorpion fellas yourselves?!"

All heads snap up, gazes fixing themselves on the pilot seat.

The preacher leans forward in his contour seat, goosing the accelerator. The RV rumbles faster and faster, the distant chain-saw noises of motorcycle engines rising on the wind. Reese, Stephen, and James now quickly move toward the front of the camper to see just exactly what the preacher is talking about.

Through the massive windshield, the flatlands along the Chattahoochee spread in all directions under a bleak magnesium silver sky—an arid, sepia-toned wasteland of fallow fields, immolated farmhouses, and errant wreckage littering deserted dirt roads. On the convoy's flanks, kicking up clouds of dust and debris in the wind, a half dozen tricked-out motorcycles converge on the lead vehicle. The closer they get, the more clearly the details of their riders come into focus.

The closest biker looks huge, with greasy, long gray hair flagging under his World War I Kaiser helmet, his gigantic tree-trunk arms sleeved with tattoos. He has a sawed-off shotgun on his back, and wears a tattered leather vest, a necklace of fleshy objects banging against his barrel chest. The objects dangling on the necklace may or may not be human ears or fingers or pieces of a face or all of the above. His mirrored aviator glasses reflect the RV menacingly as the massive Harley approaches.

" 'Will the circle be unbroken!' " Jeremiah sings out joyfully, keeping a close eye on the progress of that first biker. The other five riders close in fast behind the first—most of them ragged, tattooed thugs in shades and war paraphernalia—their individual thunderheads of dust whirling up into the greasy sky. Some of the men reach for weapons, drawing from saddlebags and packs. Jeremiah carefully keeps the RV on course, zooming at top speed along the abandoned river road, his gaze locked on his side mirror and the reflection of the big leader with the gray hair. " 'By and by, Lord, by and by!' "

The first shot rings out, a loud pop and a ding sparking off the front quarter panel of the RV.

"Sweet Jesus!" Reese cries out. "Brother J—what's the plan here?!"

James screams at the top of his lungs: "I told you! I TOLD YOU!"

"Get on the two-way," the preacher calls out with surprising calm. "Tell Leland to bring the big Mack up to the front when we stop."

Reese scrambles to find the walkie-talkie, which has fallen off a shelf with the rest of the books and knickknacks and dishware.

" 'Will the circle be unbroken!' " the preacher croons off-key as he fixes his gaze on the side mirror. He can see the big man on the closest bike preparing to fire again, a few of the other bikers preparing to launch a salvo of buckshot into the RV's tires. The preacher continues rejoicing. " 'In the sky, Lord, in the sky!' "

Jeremiah yanks the wheel at the perfect moment, and the front corner of the massive RV slams into the closest rider, creating a dull thudding noise that reverberates through the bones of the vehicle and launches the enormous man with the gray hair into the air. The impact throws the massive Harley into the slipstream, end over end, until it comes down in front of two other riders who are coming up fast.

In his side mirror, Jeremiah sees the two riders, unable to successfully swerve out of the way, collide with the careening motorcycle, the collision a chain reaction of pinwheeling metal, exploding shards of fiberglass, screams, geysers of blood, and bodies catapulting through the air. The chorus of hysterical yelling from outside sounds muffled, indistinct, like wind whistle.

The other three bikers pull off to the east, while the rest of the convoy swerves right, one by one, each vehicle coming to an abrupt halt in a fog bank of dust. Jeremiah registers all this in a split second, his laser focus on the mirror. He lifts his boot off the foot-feed.

In the oblong reflection he can see the remaining three bikers circling around, skidding to a stop, the riders yelling at each other. One of the bikers pulls a pistol-grip shotgun. Jeremiah pumps the brakes, bringing the massive vehicle to a bumpy stop in a whirlwind of dust. More toys fall off their shelf in back, batteries rolling across the floor. Without hesitation, without a scintilla of wasted energy, Jeremiah slams the shift lever into reverse and stomps on the accelerator pedal.

The RV lurches.

The gravitational force throws the younger men forward, Reese slamming into the sink, Stephen and James holding on for dear life. The camper roars backward, the power plant screaming, the infrastructure rattling and threatening to crack apart. In Jeremiah's mirror, the three surviving bikers loom closer and closer, looking up with shocked expressions, scrambling to aim their weapons, trying to get off a few shots. As the massive RV bears down on them, they try to scatter. Jeremiah skillfully steers the rear end with its massive tow rig and steel ladder directly at the three fleeing bikers. The sound of horrified cries rings out.

The impact throws two out of three bikers skyward and pulverizes the abandoned Harleys.

The RV thumps as dust and debris and broken fiberglass rain down. Jeremiah slams on the brakes. A mangled chrome pipe clatters to the ground next to the RV's cab as the vehicle skids to a stop, a few other pieces of shrapnel falling for a few seconds, until finally, mercifully, silence descends on the barren landscape.

For a moment, the three men in the back of the RV are

thunderstruck, paralyzed, as the sound of dripping fluids and dwindling screams from outside fade beneath the wind. Jeremiah stretches like an old cat that was just sunning itself and now wants to investigate its food bowl.

"Everybody okay?" he inquires, twisting around in his seat to inspect his troops.

At first not a single one of them can utter a word of response. Finally Reese manages to say, "Yessir, fine and dandy."

"What just happened?" James Frazier looks at the others, his eyes ablaze. "What was—?"

"Progress, son." The preacher climbs out of his swivel seat, takes a deep breath, and squeezes his way through the camper's rear cabin. "And you know what they say about progress."

James is still holding on to the sink as though he thinks he might fall at any moment. "I'm . . . not sure . . . what you mean. What do they say about progress?"

The preacher pauses, smiles at the younger man, and gives him a wink. "You can't stop it."

Then Jeremiah turns and searches through a nylon rucksack for his machete.

NINE

"What in God's name is he doing now?" Norma has her plump hand to her lips, her fingertips shaking as she sits on the passenger side of Miles Littleton's muscle car, watching the aftermath of the preacher's gonzo attack on the motorcycle gang.

Through the window, in the gray overcast afternoon, about a hundred yards away, several caravan members are visible, standing reverentially around Jeremiah, as though waiting for him to preach, as he drives a machete through the skulls of fallen gang members. He does this rather quickly and forcefully. Wind gusts and blows detritus around his legs, flagging the tails of his coat.

"What the fuck is this dude's deal?" Miles wonders aloud. "And why are we still here?"

Miles Littleton continues to hold the steering wheel with white-knuckle intensity, even though the vintage hot rod is parked and idling on the side of the road about sixty or seventy yards away from the accident scene. The engine rumbles softly, as comforting to Miles as a mother's heartbeat. The car is his security blanket. Miles grew up in Detroit—before moving to Atlanta at age eleven with his divorced, heroin-addicted mom—but his years in the Motor City made him a believer in good old American-made production-line muscle. He had stolen many classics in his day, but the one he always *drove*— the one he lived in and pampered and doted on like the first girl he ever kissed—was the 1972, four-speed, 426 cubic inch Hemi-V8 Dodge Challenger.

In fact, he and Norma currently sit in the latest incarnation of this first love, a gas-guzzling two-door hardtop sedan in Plum Crazy purple metallic with a tricked-out four-barrel Magnum and glass packs, which Miles has managed to hold on to even amidst this impossible post-plague energy crisis.

"Give me a second," Norma says. "I just want to see what he does next."

In the distance, Jeremiah turns to the few surviving riders lying here and there, clinging to life, battered and bloody in the dirt. They look like fallen soldiers in some brutal desert war. Jeremiah motions to a large box truck idling nearby. Leland Burress sticks his head out the driver's window, giving a wave and then backing the huge vehicle up to the death scene. The preacher and his three young associates start lifting the victims onto makeshift stretchers. One by one, the three survivors are loaded into the truck's rear cargo hold.

"I promise you one thing," Miles comments bitterly as he watches. "He's not taking them guys to the emergency room."

Norma shakes her head. "But what in the wide world of sports does this have to do with them poor folks in that tunnel?"

"Nothing . . . The dude's obviously fuckin' nuts."

"I don't know." Norma chews on a fingernail. "I think he's nuts like a fox. I think he's got a master plan."

"Good for him. I still say we blow this place, get the fuck outta here. This ain't about us; it ain't our concern. Know what I mean?"

"I hear you, Junior, I just . . . I'd like to know exactly what this creepy-ass preacher's got up his sleeve."

"Why? What difference does it make?"

Norma watches the last of the injured bikers being loaded into the Mack truck. "I don't know. . . . Maybe we can do something about it."

"You're gonna go and get your ass killed."

Norma sighs. "Maybe." She looks at him. "Listen. I'll make you a deal."

Miles shakes his head. "Oh no. Don't be doing this shit to me."

"C'mon, I promise we'll get away from these people soon enough."

Miles wipes his mouth nervously. "Norma, you're gonna get *both* our asses killed."

"Just stick around another day or two, just until we figure out what he's doing."

"Norma—"

"I promise you, we'll take off—as soon as we figure it out."

In the hazy distance, behind a dust devil of whirling litter, the preacher marches back toward the RV, looking all proud and satisfied and imperial. He looks like a third world dictator to Miles—like a cracker version of Fidel Castro—and this makes Miles all the more nervous. Miles finally looks at Norma. "Okay, one more day and then we're gone with the motherfucking wind."

The portly little woman leans over and kisses the young man on the cheek.

Miles rolls his eyes as he kicks the Challenger back to life, the glass packs growling as he revs the enormous engine. He sees the preacher climbing back into his RV, and the camper's exhaust pipe spitting vapor.

The convoy starts rolling away, and Miles lets out a weary sigh as he follows from a distance.

The preacher leads the convoy west. Hours later, they find themselves descending a sloping access road toward a litter-strewn public beach along the Chattahoochee.

Jeremiah grips the steering wheel tighter now, the memories of his baptism of death percolating up through his central nervous system like a witches' brew of terror, grief, and sorrow. He feels the weight of the caravan behind him—the sedans, the SUVs, the trucks pounding the weathered pavement, sending tremors through the sandy earth—girding him, bolstering him, galvanizing him. He sees the silvery surface of the river across the horizon, materializing in ghostly ripples before his eyes.

He pulls the RV around a hairpin and then descends the narrow river road toward a state park whose name he has blocked out of his mind. He lost half his flock here eighteen months ago. He saw the spawn of the devil rising out of the waters to devour his innocent parishioners as they were born again in the bloody currents of the river.

He steers the RV toward the end of the road, to a deserted pier with ancient gray pilings and sun-blanched timbers. An enormous, oily-black crow explodes into flight off one of the newels at the end of the dock, the sound of its caw echoing up across the low, threatening, black sky, reaching Jeremiah's ears, sending gooseflesh down between his shoulder blades and raising the hackles on the back of his neck.

He parks, turns the engine off. He hears the rest of the convoy coming to a halt behind him—one by one, engines dying, silence ensuing.

Inside the RV, no one says a word. Two out of the three young men inside the camper were present that day a year and a half ago when the women of the church group were devoured in the river only moments after receiving the rites of communion from Jeremiah. Two out of the three saw the white-clad matrons of the flock screaming, flailing, splashing up arterial fluids into the air that day, turning the river as red as oxblood. The silence in the camper fills it with a sort of reverent tribute to that day.

"Brother Stephen, get Earl on the blower," Jeremiah says at last, unbuckling himself. "Tell him to back the Kenworth down to the river's edge."

"What are you—?" Stephen Pembry almost asks the question that's on everybody's mind but no one will ask. They have been given bits and pieces of the whole picture but have yet to be told what's going on. What in the name of God is the preacher up to?

On his way out of the cab, Jeremiah grabs the machete from beneath the seat and murmurs cryptically, "It will all be revealed in time, Brother."

He walks down the path, across the gravel lot, and out along the docks.

The fishy-smelling wind tosses Jeremiah's greasy black pompadour. Wrecked boats lie in the muck here and there. He gazes out across the surface of the river, and his stomach clenches. The water still looks greasy, a deep reddish orange, as vivid as arterial blood—although somewhere in the back of Jeremiah's rational mind he knows that the dark amber hue is due to the Georgia clay at the bottom of the silt-rich river bottom.

He hops off the end of the dock, landing in the marshy weeds.

His Wellingtons sink about half a foot into the silt. The cold travels up his legs, makes him shiver. He grips the machete and slogs into the deeper water. Something stirs around him. He can see objects moving now under the surface of the river, like the bulbous backs of tortoises rising up through the haze.

He splashes the edge of the machete on the surface of the water, which is now up to his waist. " 'Bringing in the sheaves, bringing in the sheaves,' " he croons in his basso profundo singing voice, a cross between an off-key Caruso and a sleepy Elvis. The hymn is from the 126th Psalm: "We shall come rejoicing, bringing in the sheaves."

Twenty-five feet away, the first slimy cranium rises out of the water with the lazy menace of a crocodile surfacing. The thing was once a woman—her age unknown, her long hair dangling in spidery strands like Spanish moss hanging off the smooth stony surface of a boulder. Her eyes are craters of maggoty white pulp, her flesh as bloated and puffy as an undercooked soufflé.

"Sister!" The preacher raises his hands in a welcoming gesture. "Praise the Lord, you're right on time!"

The thing in the water grinds its slimy teeth as other skulls surface around her, stirred by the sound of the preacher's singing, his voice calling his children home. There are dozens of them—both genders, in all imaginable states of decay, their monstrous faces fixed on the sound of Jeremiah's singing voice, their flesh as swollen as rotten seedpods about to burst.

" 'We shall come rejoicing,' " the preacher croons, " 'bringing in the sheaves!' "

The big man begins backing toward the riverbank. He sends a gentle wake through the bloody, rusty water as he beckons the walkers, a stringy mass of river moss clinging to his waist, trailing off into the currents. The fishy stench of the river mingles with the odor of mortified organs. The preacher claps his hands as though applauding, luring the monsters toward the waiting truck.

Jeremiah reaches the muddy bank and climbs out. He turns and bellows, "Earl, go ahead and open the rear door and lower the ramp!"

A squat, muscular, bald man in a denim jacket and sweatpants climbs out of the cab, hurries around to the rear of the trailer, and throws open the garage-style accordion door. Jeremiah reaches into his side pocket and pulls out a small novelty toy he found in the cache of trinkets in the Thorndykes' camper. Made of hard painted plastic, the little windup chattery teeth remind Jeremiah of his childhood a million years ago. He got one on Halloween once, and remembers now the sound it made when it hit the bottom of his candy bag. When he got home that night he got a whuppin' from his dad for going out on Satan's night, but he kept the chattery teeth in his drawer. Now he winds the stem of the Thorndykes' toy and thumbs the button. The chattery teeth begin clacking noisily, and a pair of tiny cartoon feet churn busily.

By this point, the monsters have reached the river's bank and have started dragging themselves up the slope, their mossy, skeletal arms outstretched, their mouths drooling dirty spindrift. Earl stands aside and watches with queasy awe as Jeremiah tosses the little toy on board the empty cargo trailer. The little toy buzzes and chatters and whirs loudly inside the enclosure, a beacon, the noise magnified by the corrugated steel of the trailer walls.

The walkers cock their heads toward the clatter as they stupidly lumber toward the trailer. When they get there, some of them manage almost accidentally to trundle up the walkway, others fall off the sides. Jeremiah watches with the pride of a father watching toddlers take their first steps as several of the creatures vanish inside the trailer, drawn to the clacking noise. The preacher's skin tingles and itches, his eyes burn, but he barely notices it now.

He is transported by the sight of the whole convoluted trap working so well. "That's enough for now!" he finally calls out when he's got five of them.

Earl hops up on the bumper rail and hooks the top of the door, pulling it down quickly and decisively.

The dull metallic thud rings out, bringing a smile to Jeremiah's lips.

"We owe it all to young Thomas here," Lilly Caul announces to the other tunnel dwellers after finishing her story of uncovering the treasures at Central Machinery Sales in Connersville, Georgia. Tommy stands beside her, trying to stifle the awkward little grin on his face, his hands in the pockets of his faded OshKosh dungarees. He nervously taps the heel of his hiking boot against the tunnel wall as he listens to Lilly. "He found this place on his own initiative." She gives him an appreciative glance. "He deserves all the credit."

The five other adults grin and nod, and Barbara Stern clucks her tongue approvingly at Tommy.

Seated on makeshift chairs around the makeshift table in the makeshift lounge, the elders have remained silent throughout most of Lilly's report. The air smells of coffee and black earth. The soft whir of aboveground generators vibrates the ceiling. At the other end of the tunnel, the children play quietly, reading books or fiddling with dolls. Barbara had asked Bethany Dupree to watch the little ones while the grown-ups have their talk, and now the third-grader hovers over the gaggle of tykes with the watchful eye of a mother hen.

At last, Bob Stookey winks at Tommy. "The young man is a regular Christopher Columbus."

Lilly grins at Bob. "And you thought he was loafing that day." She sits down at the table, and Bob pours her some fresh instant coffee. Lilly takes a sip and says, "My guess is, there's at least a thousand gallons of gas in that tank."

David Stern speaks up. "So what's the next step? I see the value of all this fuel, but how do you see the equipment entering into the equation? I mean, we're not exactly farming down here."

Lilly looks at Bob, and the glance they exchange is charged with emotion. "Bob and I disagree over what our focus should be right now."

Bob gives her a shrug. "I think we're all focused on the same damn thing, Lilly-girl—*survival*."

"Of course, Bob." Lilly takes a deep breath. "I guess we might as well throw it out there. Maybe take a vote."

Gloria Pyne looks around the table. Underneath the brim of her athletic visor, her expression furrows with confusion. The years have stolen some of Gloria's natural beauty, but beneath the deep lines, her blue eyes still glitter with vigor. "Am I missing something? What are we voting on?"

Barbara Stern sighs and wipes a wisp of curly gray hair from her face. "Let me take a wild guess: Lilly wants to take Woodbury back and Bob wants to stay put down here in the catacombs indefinitely."

For a moment, Lilly and Bob stare at each other, taken aback.

Harold Staubach grins, his bony ebony features filling with mirth, his dark eyes twinkling. He has his Banlon golf shirt buttoned up tight against his neck wattle—ever dapper, stubbornly genteel. "She's right, though, isn't she?"

David Stern clears his throat. "I've lived with it for almost thirty years—the woman is always right."

"David, shush."

Scattered chuckles fade quickly under the weight of the subject. Finally, Gloria Pyne looks at Lilly. "She *is* right, though, isn't she?"

Lilly lets out a pained sigh. "Look, I know it's basically an open secret that I want to take the town back. I see the pros and cons, believe me. It feels safe down here. I get that. But I don't think we've really thought through the long-term effects of living down here."

"Lilly, we've been over this—" Bob starts to object when he sees Barbara Stern raising a hand.

"Let the lady make her case, Bob."

"Thank you, Barbara." Lilly takes a deep breath. "Okay, first of all, you can't live under here indefinitely, no matter how good your ventilation is, or how clean your water from those underground springs is. Your muscles are eventually going to atrophy. Plus, it might seem like we're impervious to walker attacks, and maybe we are, but what about survivor attacks? Those two gennies up there are like red flags, like neon signs saying 'Attack *us*.'"

Bob motions toward Harold. "Lilly, I already told you, Harold and I are working on blimps for those generators, and we also got an exercise area in the works. And there's miles of tunnel down here we haven't even charted yet. We got tons of room—the kids could play *soccer* in some of these passageways. And we're working on better ventilation every day. Plus, you get tunnel fever, you can always go up top."

Lilly looks at him. "Bob, you have no idea what effect this is having on the kids."

"What are you talking about? They're fine."

"Fine?" She looks at Barbara. "Tell him how fine their skin is."

Barbara Stern looks at Bob. "Well, it's hard to tell if it's getting better or worse. I showed you the rash on Melissa's ankles, Bob, and Lucas has what looks like the beginnings of hives on his neck and back, and most of the kids are coughing and congested now, getting a lot more colds, it seems. I think it's the dampness, but *you're* the expert."

Bob takes a deep breath. "Okay. Look. We'll go out again this afternoon, hit that drugstore we passed up north on the last run we did. I'm thinking a little cortisone cream and Sudafed will do the trick."

"That's not the point, Bob." Lilly fixes her gaze on the older man's deep-set eyes, which are buried in wrinkles and leathery skin. Bob's face is a road map of hard days and nights—hard drinking, hard living. But behind his gaze is hard-won wisdom. Lilly can sense it; so can the others. "It's not just skin rashes and sniffles. It's quality of life. It's having the options that we only have aboveground. You know exactly what I'm talking about."

"Hold your horses for a second," Gloria pipes in again with passion glinting in her eyes.

" 'Quality of life' nowadays—if you'll excuse my French—means not getting our asses eaten. Period. It's like you said yourself, Lilly—we're safe down here. And I'm sorry, but somebody should acknowledge something else." She looks at Bob. "We're safe because of this man right here."

Bob proffers a weary smile. "I don't know about that, Glo. . . . I just got lucky snooping around one day."

She winks at him. "Whaddaya know . . . he's modest, too." She looks at the others. "Seriously, though." She looks at Lilly. "I'm with Bob on this. We're getting the ventilation working better and better every day. It's cool in the summer down here, and it's warm in the winter. We can get to the food sources when we have to, and we're almost to the point where we can filter the spring water."

Bob nods. "All true. Plus, think about this: We got modes of travel now that don't involve picking our way through hordes of walkers. We can get to most points within a ten-mile radius without even setting foot up top."

Lilly lets out an exasperated sigh. She feels as though she's not articulating her side of the argument well enough, not getting through to them. She remembers high school debate class, and how she always got too emotional trying to rally people to her side, how her emotions always stole her eloquence; and she acknowledges to herself now how those same emotions have almost gotten her killed in recent months.

Harold Staubach speaks up. "I have to say, for what it's worth . . . I'm leaning toward Bob and Gloria on this one." He looks down as though embarrassed to make eye contact with Lilly. "I guess I just don't see the upside of . . . going back . . . well . . . going back *up*."

Lilly shakes her head. She pushes herself away from the table and begins to pace. "You guys are not looking at the long term."

No one responds to this. Bob looks down. The silence weighs on them like a funereal pall. Lilly realizes the question she has posed—the imponderable question of whether there even *is* a long term—

torments them in their private thoughts and nightmares. She wipes back a wisp of hair that has fallen across her face, chews on her lip, thinks it over. She can hear the nervous tapping of Tommy's boot-heel on the wall behind her. She finally says, "Okay . . . fine. Let's put it to a vote. All those in favor of staying put, staying down here in the tunnels for . . . let's say the *foreseeable* future"—she looks around the table—"raise your hands."

Slowly, tentatively, Gloria raises her hand. Bob raises his. Harold Staubach throws a nervous glance at the Sterns, and then hesitantly raises his hand. Three votes for staying in the tunnels.

"Okay . . . cool." Lilly looks around the group. "All those in favor of working toward one day getting the town back, raise your hands."

Barbara and David Stern, with zero hesitation, each shoot a hand up.

Lilly nods at them and raises hers. "Who would have guessed . . . we got a tie on our hands."

"Hey!" Barbara Stern points at Tommy Dupree, who stands against the tunnel wall. The young man has his hand raised high, his ruddy, freckled face screwed up with indignation. Barbara grumbles, "What is he . . . chopped liver?"

Two separate supply runs are launched that afternoon, one underground and one at ground level.

The first, comprised of Bob Stookey and Gloria Pyne, disembarks shortly after noon. They follow a map that Bob had hand-copied from a 140-year-old plat survey, and they start out down the main conduit, squeezing through the east barricade and then turning south and proceeding down a side tunnel that up until now has been unexplored. Their target is the defunct mining company equipment that according to county surveys lies just beyond the river to the east. They believe all manner of supplies—including medicine—could very well still be stored there.

Meanwhile, Lilly and Tommy Dupree hike the three miles or so down the main tunnel to the Elkins Creek cave-in, dig their way through the drifts of dirt, and exit the underground near Pilson's Bridge, where scores of ruined walker bodies lie in disarray on the banks of the creek like Civil War casualties bleaching away to powder in the unforgiving sun. The wind and the light and the odors of rotting flesh amid the carpet of pine and pecan shells are so overpowering that Lilly and Tommy get dizzy as they creep through the shadows of the hardwood forest along the banks of the creek. They hike another mile or so until they come to Bob's secret fleet of vehicles parked under the canopy of great live oaks, camouflaged by nettings of foliage draped carefully over the SUVs and pickups. Bob and David Stern had risked their lives the previous week, amidst the building hordes, salvaging these vehicles from Woodbury and Carlinville.

Now Lilly and Tommy quickly and silently commandeer one of the SUVs: pulling off the shroud of leaves, finding the keys in the visor where Bob had left them, kicking the engine to life, and carefully pulling across the threshold and onto the access road that winds along Elkins Creek.

Fifteen minutes later, Lilly pulls down an entrance ramp onto the wreckage-strewn lanes of Highway 19 and heads south. Her plan is to try and reach Tifton or even Valdosta before nightfall—farther than they've ever traveled on a supply run—in order to search for a new source of propane, batteries, lightbulbs, and fuel that hasn't been picked over. She knows of a Home Depot down around Cordele. She makes note that the fuel gauge on the road-worn RAV4 is three-quarters full, and she explains to Tommy that they have to make sure that they don't go beyond the "point of no return." Tommy has never heard this expression, and it sounds ominous to him, but Lilly explains that it merely means they have to make sure they always have enough gas in the tank to get back home.

It's slow going for quite a while, the graveyard of wrecked cars and trucks petrified now by the turning of the seasons into leafy heaps, their kudzu-covered carcasses glued to the pavement in emulsified, pasty puddles. Weaving in and out of the wreckage, Lilly and Tommy idly talk about the future, hoping that there actually *is* a future.

Tommy starts reminiscing about his late mother and father, both of whom perished in the tumult that took Woodbury down last month. He speaks of them as heroes, forgiving them for their zealotry. Lilly is taken aback by the boy's maturity. Perhaps she's seeing a side effect of the plague. Maybe it weans a kid off childhood. Maybe it girds a person for the inevitable loss that will sooner or later touch every living human. The tragic events of the last few months seem to have made Tommy Dupree more comfortable in his skin, and this is thoroughly, endlessly fascinating to Lilly.

They drive and talk, and drive some more, and talk about the afterlife, and God, and the apocalypse, and the possible causes of the plague, and everything else under the sun that Tommy can think of. They pass at least a half a dozen gas stations that lie in ruins, the pumps overturned, the offices ransacked, the storage tanks as dry as coffins. They talk some more.

They talk for so long, and the conversation is so interesting to Lilly, that she does something she'd have thought she would never do in a million years.

She forgets about the fuel gauge.

TEN

The battered RAV4 skids to a stop, kicking up a whirlwind of dust, the g-force slamming Tommy into the dash, his shoulder belt preventing him from breaking his nose. He jerks back in the seat, blinking convulsively. The silence shrieks. Lilly holds on to the steering wheel with a death grip, staring straight ahead, taking deep breaths.

"What—? What happened?" Tommy looks at her. "What is it?"

"I can't believe it."

"What?"

"I can't believe what I just did."

"What—? Tell me! *What?!*"

"The point of no—" She starts to explain, but all at once she gets distracted by her surroundings: the thick woods on either side of the highway, the overturned bus in the culvert a few hundred yards up the road. Things are reacting all around them to the introduction of an alien car into the poisonous ecosystem—trees are shivering in the deeper woods, noises drifting on the breeze, smells wafting. Lilly can't believe what she's done.

Tommy cranes his neck in order to see the gas gauge. The needle is a hair above "E." "Oh shit . . . *shit.*"

He glances out the windshield. In the gray middle distance, behind columns of diseased pines, shadows stir. In the opposite lane, something crawls out from under a wreck, a pasty white cadaver with half its face missing. A hundred yards farther up the road, a pair of ragged reanimated corpses in bloodstained hospital smocks shuffle slowly out from behind a faded, torn billboard for the Florida Commission on Tourism showing a bikini-clad siren on a sun-drenched beach and the words "When you got it bad, we got it good."

Lilly pounds angrily on the steering wheel. "Fuck!—Fuck!—FUCK!"

"Okay, so, we got a little bit of gas left, right? Don't we?!"

Lilly stops banging in the wheel and gazes down into her lap with equal parts despair, rage, shame, and terror. "What was I thinking? How could I have been so fucking stupid?! Stupid! STUPID!!"

"But we got a little bit left, right?"

She wipes her mouth, tries to gather her thoughts. In her peripheral vision, she can detect shadowy figures shambling out of the woods, slowly but steadily moving toward them. The sky roils with dark clouds, a storm threatening. The smell of black decay filters through the vents. "Not enough to get back, Tommy. That's the main problem. We don't have enough to get back because we went way beyond the—"

"But maybe we should turn around and head back anyway and see how far we get."

Lilly sees three walkers in her rearview, closing the distance. They hobble robotically toward the RAV4 with arms outstretched—two males and a female, each of them very old, both in age and state of decay, perhaps former residents of a nursing home—working their black teeth with the fervor of piranhas, chewing at the air with feral hunger. They make the flesh on the back of Lilly's neck bristle. "I'm not sure that's going to get us anywhere."

"We can't just sit here."

"Hold on." Lilly opens the map case next to her, quickly fishing through the loose candy wrappers and garage door remotes. She grabs a lighter, a pocketknife, a flashlight, and a box of .22 caliber 36-grain bullets for the Ruger. "Grab the backpacks!"

"We're getting out?!"

"Just do it, Tommy! Don't ask any questions, just do what I say!"

He twists around and grabs their rucksacks from the backseat, then hands Lilly's over. She stuffs the items from the map case into it, checks the box of ammunition, pulls her Ruger pistol, checks the magazine. "Look under your seat, should be a crowbar under there— grab it!"

The boy finds the crowbar.

"And open the glove box!" Lilly orders.

Tommy flips the panel down. "What am I looking for?"

"Maps—any maps you see in there, grab them!"

The boy does so as Lilly glances back up at the rearview and sees the three dead senior citizens closing in on them. The creatures approach the SUV with heads cocked, mouths drooling black bile, eyes geeked open like silver reflectors. Lilly yanks the shift lever down into reverse. "Hold on, Tommy!" she cries.

She kicks the accelerator, and the engine howls. The steel-belted radials spin wildly for a moment on the sandy pavement, then find purchase and the SUV lurches backward. The walkers loom in the mirror for a single instant, their eyes getting big right before the impact.

The SUV shudders as the muffled sounds of wet bones and cartilage crunching travels under them, making them momentarily lose traction on the grease of dead remains. The RAV4 fishtails furiously as it continues to back away from the gore-soaked pavement.

A moment later, Lilly slams down the brake pedal and brings the careering SUV to a noisy halt.

"HOLD ON!"

She jerks it into drive and rockets forward. By this point, the pair of billboard lurkers have traversed out across the shoulder and lumbered onto the highway, and are now shuffling directly toward them—smack-dab in the middle of their lane—oblivious to the 3,500 pounds of Japanese steel rushing toward them.

The impact throws one of the creatures into the air with the force of a catapult and rips the other one in two, sending half its torso into the woods on a comet tail of glistening red entrails and the other half thumping under the chassis of the speeding SUV, grinding it into bonemeal. Lilly keeps the foot pedal pinned, the steering wheel steady. The RAV4 charges away from the scene.

"What now?!—What now, Lilly?!" The boy twists in his seat, gazing out the rear window at the carnage receding into the distance.

"Grab everything you brought with you! Pack, machete, water, the other pistol!"

The boy scrambles to gather up his things and secure them in the pack on his belt. The SUV rumbles over a series of potholes as Lilly steers it toward suitable cover. "We'll ditch the car in a safe place, hide it somewhere, and try to find some gas!"

She follows the highway around a bend, past a deserted industrial park, and down a sloping hill into a valley of long-neglected farm fields—now completely overgrown and gone to seed—before she realizes that the RAV4 has burned the last drops of fuel in its tank.

They roll into a rest area on fumes, and then have to get out and push the vehicle by hand around the back of one of the buildings.

By the time they light out on foot, heading south, the afternoon has already started to give way to evening.

"Easy does it, hotshot!" Norma Sutters braces herself against the car's passenger door as Miles Littleton careens down Georgia State Road 520 just west of Albany. He weaves the muscle car in and out of the slew of abandoned vehicles as though skiing down an Olympic slalom course, barely avoiding the corners, nearly sideswiping every other wreck. He drives with the practiced ease of a veteran wheelman, a street kid whose DNA has been recombined with axle grease and carbon monoxide. He wears a tricolored Bob Marley beret on his tight dark curls, and his long-lashed eyes fix themselves on the white lines clocking under the car as though they are the flash of a hypnotist's watch. His gold tooth glistens. He's in a hurry.

"You said to step on it," he mutters almost to himself. "I'm stepping on it."

"I didn't say get us killed." Norma gazes through the windshield for a moment, noticing a cluster of walkers up ahead, milling about the gravel shoulder. They look like commuters waiting for a train that will never come. Miles steers the car straight for them. Norma closes her eyes. "Lordy, Junior, don't do this to me again!"

She feels a thump, as though the car has just cobbled over a bump, and she opens her eyes.

The outside of the passenger window has turned deep red in the backwash of blood tossed up by the impact. Particles of brain matter and hair and tissue run horizontally across the glass, blowing off the side of the car in the slipstream. Miles is giggling. Norma glances in the side mirror and sees the human remains receding into the distance behind them, the walkers sideswiped by the Challenger now reduced to gruesome body parts and headless torsos strewn across the shoulder.

She throws him a look. "Can we just concentrate on finding these people?"

"I say fuck these people. I say we just boogie on outta this part of the world!"

"Miles, we been over this a million times—"

"I don't want no part of this crazy-ass shit," he grumbles. "Bat-shit fucking preachers waging holy wars and shit—fuck it! That don't have nothing to do with me. You neither! What that motherfucker is planning with them toys and shit—it ain't just crazy, it's fucking *evil*. I say we find an island somewhere, roll some fatties, and stay high for the rest of our natural lives."

"I thought you was a Christian!" She aims her scornful gaze at her surrogate son. "We can't just turn a blind eye to this shit, Miles."

"How the fuck we gonna find these people in the first place?"

"We'll find 'em—don't you worry." She taps her finger on the crumpled road map in her lap. "Just stay on this road until we get to 29, then head south. They gotta be somewhere around that Wood-bury place."

"They're in a motherfucking tunnel, girlfriend, they're below-ground—remember? How the fuck you expect to find them in a motherfucking tunnel?! You're the one's gonna get us killed."

"We'll find them. They gotta come up for air every once in a while."

"I ain't even sure I got enough go-juice to make it all the way down there."

"I thought you told me you had enough of them tanks in the trunk to make it to the coast and back two times over. You lying to me, boy?"

"Didn't plan on taking that side trip up the Chattahoochee with that motherfucker."

Norma lets out a weary sigh and rings her plump little hands. She wears a ratty cardigan sweater over her church dress, and still she shivers in the cool of the day's waning hours. It's almost dusk. The edges of the sky have turned indigo blue, and the low clouds are moving in, scudding the horizon with brooding gray monoliths. "Lord have mercy . . . what a world," she murmurs.

Miles shakes his head. "Suppose we do find these people, what the fuck you gonna tell them?"

She looks down. "I'm gonna tell them everything."

"What if these folks are as bug-fuck crazy as that preacher? Ever think of that? What if these people are just as fucking evil as Garlitz?"

Norma gazes back out the passenger-side window, the passing landscape tinted red now by the blood-filmed glass. "Then God help us all."

Darkness closes in around Lilly and Tommy as they creep silently down a farm road cutting between two scabrous tobacco fields. They move in a single-file line along a split-rail fence and communicate mostly with nods and gestures in order to avoid attracting the attention of lurkers.

For the last hour, they've noticed an increasing number of dead in the area, a few of which they have taken down with their bladed weapons. One came from inside a culvert, lunging at them with alarming velocity. Lilly managed to cleave its skull at the last moment with her rusty machete. Minutes later, another one surprised them as they passed a derelict grain elevator, the walker stumbling out of a musty storage room. The boy rose to that occasion by driving his crowbar through the thing's left ear.

Lilly now worries that they risk inadvertently stumbling upon a swarm. She has her silencer on her Ruger, but she wants to avoid using up her limited supply of ammo. She would like to be indoors—or at least under cover—by nightfall, and by the looks of the sky, that's not too far off. The roar of crickets has already risen like a tide around them, and the air has that clammy, pithy chill that it gets in the open country at sunset. The worst part, though, is the scent of death on the wind. Lilly can recognize the acrid, festering, sickly stench of a swarm a mile away. Only a mob of walkers can reek like that, and the odor is now sending a continuous wave of gooseflesh down Lilly's back.

They reach a lonely crossroads and pause. Lilly is about to whisper something to the boy when the tobacco leaves to their immediate left begin to rustle and quake. Lilly sees a massive figure moving toward them from behind the stalks, the breathy growling noise rising above the crickets. She pushes the boy aside and draws her Ruger.

From the tobacco plants bursts an enormous male in greasy dungarees, reaching and growling with monstrous hunger etched on its cadaverous face, its sharklike eyes practically luminous in the twilight. It wears a strange little hat that looks almost comical on its huge, livid head, and it smells of maggot-infested meat and scorched shit.

Lilly fires a single blast—the noise like a gunshot fired through a wet blanket, still loud but dampened—directly into the creature's cranium. The back of its head erupts in pink plumes of matter as the thing instantly folds.

For a moment, Lilly and the boy just stand there, staring at the fallen walker. For some reason, its attire gets Lilly's attention. She kneels and takes a closer look. The creature's hat has come askew in the fall, and Lilly picks it up. The pinstriped material, the silver, grime-flecked brim, the shape of it—all of it looks familiar. But at first

Lilly can't identify it. She looks at the gore-streaked dungarees, the gray fabric pinstriped, an empty tool belt still attached to the thing's midsection.

"He was an *engineer*." Tommy Dupree points excitedly at the creature's boots.

Lilly looks at the boy. "Yeah . . . exactly . . . a train engineer." She stands up and looks to the north. "Which means . . . I bet there's a station around here somewhere, or maybe a switchyard or something."

The boy stands up and excitedly looks toward the darkening horizon to the north. "You know what? It does look like there's something up there on the other side of that farm." He points. "See the water tower? I bet that's your train yard—c'mon!" He starts hustling northward, a spring in his step now.

"Who's 'Stupid'?" Bob breaks the silence, his voice echoing slightly in the long, straight mine shaft.

For almost an hour, he and Gloria have been trudging along the tributary tunnel—their boot steps crunching in the fine ashy dust— looking for the mining company outpost, exchanging small talk, discussing their inevitable bid to return to Woodbury. Bob believes the miners may have very well left a wealth of resources down here when they closed up shop years earlier.

"Say what?" Gloria walks along behind Bob with her lantern in one hand, the yellow pool of light shining down the endless channel of stone and the occasional dusty, cobweb-filmed support beam. About ten minutes ago, they had come upon a caved-in area that had evidently been worn away over the years by sewage runoff, leaving behind a narrow channel through which they could both, with some effort, squeeze. On the other side of the cave-in was an ancient mine shaft that smelled of fuel oil and dry rot.

"The hat," Bob says, shooting a thumb over his shoulder, indicating the visor Gloria is wearing, and always seems to be wearing, as though the thing is a good luck charm. "Says you're with Stupid, so I was just wondering—"

"If that was somebody in particular?" She smiles to herself.

"Yeah. Husband? Boyfriend?"

"Nope. Nobody in particular, Bob. I guess you could say it's every man I ever dated."

"Ouch. That bad?"

"Oh, you don't want to know."

"Sorry to hear that."

"Guess I ain't a very good judge of character, when you get right down to it."

"Well, I hope your luck changes someday."

"I appreciate that, Bob." She looks at the back of his head as they walk along single file in the narrow tunnel. "That's why it's good to meet somebody like yourself with some semblance of an intellect."

"Oh, I don't know about that." He chuckles. "I been accused of a lot of things."

"You remind me of my dad in a lot of ways."

"No kidding."

"Seriously, he was a self-taught intellectual, read all the time. Drove an eighteen-wheeler most of his life, listened to books on tape."

"Sounds like a good man."

"He *was*." Gloria keeps walking, but wipes her mouth at the thought of her old man. "He was kind, and he was kinda shy, but he knew a little bit about a lot of stuff."

They walk in silence for a few moments until Bob says, "Your dad . . . is he . . . ?"

"He passed before all this shit went down, thank God. I was an only child. My mom was in a nursing home in Savannah at the time of the outbreak. Her heart didn't hold out when it all went south. I buried her myself in a potter's field up to Hinesville." She swallows the unexpected wave of grief and sorrow as she walks. "Not the happiest moment of my life, I'll be honest with ya."

"Sorry to hear that, Glo."

She waves it off. "It's a miracle I made it to Woodbury. Told myself I was gonna go out west, go to the mountains, be a hermit." She laughs. "Hitchhiking ain't the best mode of travel these days, I can tell you that." A beat of silence passes, boot steps crunching, the rattle of her lamp. "How did you end up there, Bob?"

"I was traveling with—" He cocks his head, raises his Coleman, sees something in the darkness ahead of them. "Wait . . . hold on."

They come to a sudden halt. Bob gently puts a hand on Gloria's arm. She doesn't move. About fifty feet away from them, blocking their path, shimmering in the pool of light from the lantern, sits a small coal car. They cautiously approach. The little conveyance is about the size of a baby buggy, covered with mold and cobwebs, petrified, its wooden wheels almost fossilized with age. The closer they get, the more Gloria realizes the thing is covered in blood.

Bob pauses next to it and takes a closer look. Gloria leans in, holding her lamp high. "Is that blood?"

Bob wipes a fingertip across the surface of the carrier. "Sure is. Looks old."

"How old, d'ya think?"

"Hard to tell. Not ancient old. Not decades . . . but maybe a year or two."

He looks down. Gloria follows the pool of light as it sweeps across a pair of rails embedded like hardened arteries in the dirt floor of the tunnel.

"We're definitely in the neighborhood of that mining office," Bob ventures. "According to the map, should be right above us." He follows the rails. "Stay close."

Gloria does as he says, following along on his heels. Her hackles go up immediately. She feels that familiar tingling sensation at the base of her spine—she gets it every time something seems wrong—but she ignores it. She trusts Bob implicitly.

Shuffling along behind him, close enough to touch the fringe of thick dark hair hanging over his collar, she realizes that she actually yearns to do just that: touch his hair, run her fingers through those beautiful, gray-flecked black locks. Immediately she shoves the urge back down her throat, telling herself it's merely professional curiosity, an occupational hazard of being a lifelong employee of a beauty parlor.

For over twenty years, she had been the go-to colorist and cut-girl at the Curl Up and Dye Salon in the sprawling metropolis of Portersville, Georgia. She long ago lost count of how many heads she tinted, teased, and trimmed—but now that the world has hung up its going-out-of-business sign and the members of the post-plague society have let their hair go, she longs to get her hands on a pair of clippers.

On the other hand, Gloria realizes that she might as well face the fact that her interest in the texture of Bob Stookey's greasy mop-top is more than mere muscle memory. She has a thing for the man. But in this day and age, having a thing for somebody can lead to major problems—it can break your heart, or worse, it can get you killed.

"Okay . . . here we go," Bob murmurs from about a half step ahead of her, and the sound of his voice sends a cold current down Gloria's spine. She sees his hand shoot up, and then, in the light of their lanterns, she sees what he sees.

"Holy crap." She stops, and stares, and swallows hard as she registers the fact that the man slumped against the wall of the tunnel thirty feet away is missing the top of his head. He also seems to be missing his lower jaw. Dressed in the standard filthy dungarees and work shirt of a coal miner, with a blossom of inky-dark arterial spray visible across the tunnel wall above him, he still holds his suicide pistol in one cold, dead hand at his side.

As they move closer, the lantern light illuminates two more dead miners. One lies about twenty-five away from the suicide, the other is slumped against the opposite wall. Each of these men bears the grisly trauma of a point-blank head-shot wound. Bob crouches down next to the suicide victim with the quiet, world-weary authority of a seasoned homicide detective. "Looks like this one put the others outta their misery, then turned his own lights out."

Gloria pauses next to one of the other bodies and shines her light down at the gruesome remains. The maggots have long since had their fill of these poor gentlemen, and have left behind gray sunken shells inside the coal miner garb. Gloria shivers. "Looks like this happened a while back."

Bob looks around. He sees a set of iron steps embedded in the wall, and shines his light up at the top of the stairs, where a huge funnel of dirt slopes down through a manhole-style opening, blocking off entrance or exit. "Can't tell if they got trapped down here and then offed themselves when they realized it was a lost cause, or . . ."

He pauses, as though seeing the futility in the act of finishing the thought. Gloria looks up at the cave-in above the stairs. "Or they shut themselves off on purpose." She looks back at the pistol, frozen for eternity in the dead man's hand. "The outbreak happened about a year and a half ago . . . right? So this all coulda gone down right around that time." She sniffs, her allergies acting up. "You think the gun is still operational?"

Bob goes over and pries the .38 caliber police special from the dead hand. He sees old, faded, congealed candy wrappers on the floor around the man, a broken pencil, wads of paper smashed into the dirt. He checks the cylinder and finds three rounds remaining.

Gloria finds a shovel lying against the wall near the other two men. "This might come in handy," she says.

"Let me see that for a second."

Bob takes the shovel and walks over to the steps, prodding the wall of earth descending from the ceiling, extruding through the manhole. Granules of sandy dirt avalanche down, the cave-in shifting above him. "Stand back, Glo," he says with a grunt as he stabs at the earth. "Looks like the moisture has loosened it up."

A minute later, after Bob has grunted and groaned his way through several feet of earth, the cave-in gives, and he jumps out of the way as dirt starts flowing down the slope in one great heaving avalanche. The tunnel fills with dust, an acrid fog bank that drives Gloria back against the far wall. She coughs and coughs, and holds the collar of her pink Hello Kitty sweatshirt over her mouth and nostrils.

When the black dust finally clears, the steps become visible, leading up into the darkness on the other side of the manhole.

Bob looks at Gloria. "I would say 'Ladies first,' but I probably should take point."

"After you, Bob."

She motions at the steps, and Bob gives her a nod. He pulls his Glock, clips the lantern to his belt, and starts up the risers.

Gloria watches as Bob's upper body vanishes into the ceiling. Then she follows him up, neither of them yet comprehending the fact that the presence of the shovel indicates not only that the miners were able to get out, but that they *wanted* to be cut off . . .

. . . or wanted to cut off whatever it was that was in the room above them.

ELEVEN

Lilly and Tommy destroy three more walkers on their way across the switchyard, part of the same rail line that runs through Woodbury. Tommy runs in the lead position, clutching the crowbar, and Lilly brings up the rear, running backward, firing controlled blasts with her silencer on, first at the remains of a brakeman, then at a former yard worker, and finally at another dead engineer. They hustle past water towers, station buildings, warehouses, shipping containers, and flatbed train cars lined up along loading docks under tall, dark, powerless streetlights. Lilly deftly hops over track after track, each of which radiate across the weed-whiskered ground like the spokes of a giant wagon wheel.

Eighteen months of neglect has turned the switchyard into a swamp of standing water, bugs, and rust; and creeping kudzu and vines of ironweed slather every inch of the place. They close in on the small two-story frame building on the northeast corner of the property that faces the main track and parking lot (Lilly figures the abandoned passenger station is the best bet for harvesting supplies), and she begins to scan the place for a way in. The tall louvered windows are locked up tight and boarded, but there are numerous entryways, cloisters, and service doors. They reach the loading dock, leap onto the platform, hurry over to a closed garage door, and try unsuccessfully to open it. They move to an unmarked service door and find it equally stubborn, fossilized on rusty bolts and hinges.

Lilly's internal alarm starts going off—not because she senses danger inside the building, or even around the immediate vicinity, but because she gets a faint whiff of an odor on the wind that straightens her spine. The deep, black, oily nature of the odor speaks of swarms joining swarms joining swarms. And the last thing she wants to do is get pinned down in this godforsaken train yard. She points at one of the boarded windows. "Tommy, try jimmying one of those panels off."

The boy shuffles over to a boarded, arched window and slams the bar's teeth into a seam. The sound of cracking, wrenching wood issues forth as Tommy Dupree puts everything he has into his levering motions. The window gives with a creak, the bar forcing open a narrow gap. Tommy pushes the slat inward far enough to allow a human body to pass—barely. Tommy goes first, squeezing into the stationhouse. Lilly follows, cursing herself for having that second Pop-Tart that morning.

She lands on a cold parquet floor, scarred with decades of scuffling shoe leather and the wobbling wheels of Pullman dollies. She takes in the cavernous room, the graffiti-stained murals, and the high, skylighted ceiling, its fixtures hectic with bats, its gantries clogged with spiderwebs and bird nests. She scans the detritus and overturned carts and trunks, the ransacked offices behind broken glass doors, the cash registers rifled behind ticket booths, the cluttered box office counters strewn with coin wrappers and old canceled tickets. The place has been picked over. Lilly's heart sinks. In her dreams, she enters places such as this and finds cornucopias, treasure troves, steaming plates of roast beef and garlic mashed potatoes waiting for her on fine china.

She turns to the boy and has just started to say something to him when he cries out.

"Look!" He darts across the trash-strewn floor to the front corner of the station. "There's all kinds of stuff in there!"

"Oh my God." Lilly sees the object of his excitement and hurries up behind him. In her sudden delight, she doesn't smell the stench building outside the edifice, nor does she hear the telltale noise way,

way off in the distance like the rasping of high-voltage power lines. "I can't believe this is still intact—holy shit!"

They stand for a moment in awe of the vending machine. Either too much of a bother for previous looters, or perhaps missed in the race to grab all the cash in the place, the machine stands untouched, at least seven feet tall—an enormous convenience food dispenser with an unbroken glass front and coin-operated arm. Lilly sees Gatorade, soda, juice, bottled water, tortilla chips, popcorn, candy bars, gum, Life Savers, licorice, Fruit Roll-Ups, and even toenail clippers, disposable razors, toothbrushes, lint rollers, and travel pillows.

"It's beautiful," Tommy exclaims, sounding as though he's describing the Sistine Chapel.

"Look, there's even batteries." The awe in Lilly's voice is palpable— she might as well be talking about the Fountain of El Dorado.

"And Hostess fruit pies—I thought they stopped making those!"

"Let's look for something we can use to carry stuff. C'mon!"

They scour the disaster area of a station, looking behind closet doors, in vestibules, under ticket counters. In one of the offices they find a big gray duffel bag marked "BRINKS" crumpled in a corner, emptied long ago by God-only-knows-who. "Perfect!" Lilly grabs it, too excited to register the reeking odor of walkers building out in the neighboring woods. "Let's use that crowbar on the machine!"

They carry the duffel back to the vending machine and try forcing open the service door in the back of the thing, with no luck. The lock holds tight, the forked end of the crowbar merely gouging the steel. Finally, Tommy says, "Stand back for a second."

He swings the crowbar at the glass front as hard as he can.

Glass erupts with a harsh cracking noise, the shards falling into the guts of the machine, some of it spilling out across the floor, forcing Lilly to jump back.

They scramble to harvest all the goodies from the cubbies of the machine as quickly as possible, stuffing them into the huge duffel. Tommy wrenches some of the bigger items out with his crowbar. Soda cans roll across the floor and small bags of pretzels and Funyuns topple, Tommy kneeling down and scooping up every last one as though picking gold nuggets out of a stream. When they're done with the contents of the vending machine, they scramble to check out the rest of the rooms.

In an old musty administrative office, they find a treasure trove in a closet: nine-volt batteries, toner ink, paper, staplers, a magnifying glass, flashlights, paper clips, sealed cans of coffee, sweeteners, and powdered creamers. On the top shelf, Lilly finds the holy grail. "Bingo," she utters gleefully as she pulls down two ancient, shrink-wrapped, dust-filmed cartons of GE sixty-watt lightbulbs.

They carefully wrap the bulbs in layers of paper towels from the men's room before putting them in the duffel.

"That's getting a tad heavy," Lilly says, lifting the bag off the floor. She is far too distracted now to hear the chirring noises gathering outside, the buzzing sound of a hundred garbled growls closing in. "How the hell are we gonna carry this thing?"

"Use the strap," Tommy suggests.

"Yeah, but, the problem is—"

"Here, like this." Tommy snatches the strap out of her hands. He maneuvers himself under it and then lifts the bag with his shoulder. "See? Easy-peasy!" He starts to demonstrate how easy it is to walk with it when suddenly its massive weight buckles his knees and he collapses to the floor, landing hard on his ass.

"Yeah, I totally see what you mean," Lilly comments, deadpan.

Tommy looks down. "Fuck."

"Easy-peasy," Lilly says, and she's just started to laugh when she suddenly cocks her head at an angle as though hearing something important. "Wait a minute . . . fuck. Fuck, fuck, fuck."

"What?" Tommy looks at her. "What's wrong?"

"You smell that?"

"No . . . *What?*"

She rushes across the room, hurrying over to the window they'd breached in order to get inside. "Shit, shit, shit, shit," she murmurs as she peers through the crack in the boards. "God*damnit.*"

The figures appear in the distance, emerging from the trees and the road and the meadow, like a slow-motion flood tide rolling across the grounds of the switchyard. Dragging and bumping into each other, making those horrible raspy vocalizations that cause the hair on the back of Lilly's neck to stand up, the swarm practically encloses the property—bees drawn to the nectar of human activity, human smells, human noises.

"Okay, let's not panic." Lilly turns back to the room and chews a fingernail as she grasps for a way out. She looks around the room. No basement; surrounded on all four sides.

Tommy picks up her nervous tension as if he's a tuning fork. "Is it a swarm?" He peers out the window. "Holy fucking shit." He turns back to her. "Fuck."

"Okay, let's stay calm, and let's watch our language."

"Seriously?"

"Let me think, I'm not thinking straight." The odor intensifies as though the foundation is suddenly a rotting, festering morgue. The noise outside rises like a turbine that's growling, turning, revving higher and higher.

"Maybe we can stay inside this place." Tommy peers back through the window slat. "Maybe we can wait them out. Maybe they'll move on."

"That's a lot of maybes." Lilly paces, does a one-eighty, scans the walls, gazes into broken-down offices, thinking, panicking. "I don't think we can stay here."

"Why not?"

She looks at him, swallows. "Because I think they can smell us."

Tommy looks back out the window, sees something important, and points. "Wait!" He whispers now, afraid the front line of the horde closing in on the building might hear them. "Hold on!"

"What?"

He turns and gives her a grave look. "I think I know how we can escape."

For quite some time, Bob and Gloria gaze in silent awe at the strange interior of the Haddonfield Mining Company staging area, now illuminated in soft, green, ambient daylight. The place is apparently sunken into the side of a hill, and what was once a labyrinth of service bays, storage rooms, and work desks—the entirety of the space encompassing the breadth and width of an airplane hangar—has been reduced to a surreal nest of creeping vines, roots, and mossy decay. All the surfaces look as though they've been in a snowstorm of mold and dust. The high casement windows have all been breached, either by weather or walkers, the roots of ancient pines probing down through the gaps and spreading tentacle-like across the walls and the floor. A carpet of moss and snot green lichens covers everything—desktops, cabinets, coal cars, tools, gas tanks, shovels, and augers—and the smell of humus and earth chokes the air. A chill wind ripples through the place, tossing leaves across the floor.

"Looks like the inside of the Keebler elf tree," Gloria remarks, pulling her Glock and cautiously crossing the spongy floor.

"Watch those doorways." Bob has his .357 in his hand, and shuffles toward one of the exits. Many of the archways gape open, their doors dangling on ancient hinges. Bob doesn't like the odor coming from the far entryway, or the noise rising under the breeze swirling through the place. He approaches the open door.

From the depths of a mossy green vestibule, a shadow looms, the grinding noise of mortified vocal cords. Bob raises the revolver. A lone male walker appears around a corner, thirty-five feet away. It drags along on bony, emaciated legs, its face so skeletal and its mining garb so worn and rotted it lends the creature an air of mummification. The moldering atmosphere of the underground has taken its toll on the thing. Its eyes—or what's left of them—shimmer in deep, hollowed-out pits. Its teeth drip black ooze as it comes for Bob.

Bob aims the revolver and squeezes off a single shot—the bark as loud as a mortar blast inside the enclosed space, making Gloria jump—and the impact of the 125-grain metal-jacketed hollow point takes off the top of the creature's head. The soupy fluids of brain matter and blood spill out over the brim of the open skull as the thing collapses into its own spoor.

"Gloria," Bob mutters calmly, backing away from the archway, hearing more noises. "We gotta get the fuck outta here right now."

Across the floor, Gloria crouches down by a row of storage lockers. "I understand, I just think we should grab a few things first—this place is a gold mine."

"Coal mine," Bob corrects her, holstering his revolver, backing toward her, staring at the shadows looming just inside the far doorway, coming closer and closer, filling the air with the reek of stale feces and wormy meat. Apparently the entire mining company—the mechanics, the secretarial pool, most of the middle-management executives—turned and found themselves trapped in this nightmarish terrarium. Maybe they sought refuge here immediately after the outbreak . . . maybe they returned here once they died. Regardless, they're all coming down that baby-shit green hothouse corridor right now, and evidently they're famished. "Grab what you're going to grab, Glo, but let's get our asses in gear soon."

She breathes hard as she pulls a fuel canister sloshing with diesel out from under a cabinet. "Look at all this shit, Bob!"

"Goddamnit, Gloria—we don't have time!" Bob hears the chorus of watery growling noises from inside the vestibule. He runs over and slams the broken door against the jamb, the stench of walker practically choking him. He pulls a chair up to the rusted door and wedges it under the knob. "C'mon, just grab the stuff and let's go!"

Gloria stuffs sticks of dynamite, a first aid kit, axle grease, pickaxes and hacksaws, duct tape, an acetylene torch, miner's helmets with lamps, wrenches of all sizes, coils of rope, spools of safety fuses, and bottles of alcohol into her pack. She tosses aside canisters of oxygen, old boots, grappling hooks, and various pieces of miners' gear that she can't identify. Meanwhile, Bob is hurriedly shoving a stepladder across the leprous floor toward one of the high windows.

The door on the other side of the room rattles with the pressure of walkers trying to get in. Bob positions the ladder under the busted casement. "Glo, c'mon! I'm not kidding! NOW!"

Bob climbs the ladder as Gloria hauls the laden pack across the room. She starts up the ladder, Bob grasping her hand and pulling her, when the corner door busts open and a phalanx of reanimated dead floods into the room.

Two of the creatures are females, their faces desiccated leather, their eyes like milkweed pods. Some of the others still wear the short-sleeve dress shirts and clip-on ties of office drones—probably former Haddonfield employees—their shirts soggy with bile and old blood. They come clamoring and gnashing into the room, their doll's eyes seeking movement and human flesh.

"Shit—shit—SHIT!" Gloria claws her way up the ladder behind Bob, who is already punching out the remains of the broken windowpane above him. He reaches down to her and tries to pull her up when the closest walker—a former secretary with her reading glasses still dangling on chains around her mummified neck—reaches the bottom of the ladder and lunges at Gloria's legs.

"GLO! LOOK OUT!"

Halfway up the ladder, Gloria feels a weird pressure on her left boot and glances down right at the same moment the walker goes for her ankle, the female's slimy teeth snapping only centimeters away from Gloria's exposed flesh above the top of her boot. Gloria cries out a garbled yelp and kicks and kicks, and smashes her right boot into the sunken face of the dead secretary.

The delicate bones of the thing's brow ridge begin to crack, and Gloria keeps kicking until the creature lets go of her and blood bubbles from its nostrils, mouth, and ears. Then Gloria delivers one last tremendous kick to its forehead, its skull finally caves in, and the female slides down the bottom of the ladder and hits the floor with a watery smack.

"Hold on to my hand!" Bob pulls Gloria the rest of the way up as the other walkers reach the base of the ladder. He shimmies through the gaping window, and then yanks Gloria over the sill and out the jagged maw. Shards tear at her clothes and skin. Her overstuffed backpack nearly gets stuck, but she finally wriggles through and lands on a rocky spit of earth under the window.

The pine-scented breeze and overcast daylight calm Gloria down, allow her to breathe. She lies curled in a semi-fetal position in a clearing swimming with cottonwood snow. Her head spins from the excess adrenaline as she rolls onto her back. She feels as though she's been underground for a year. She looks up at the sky.

Bob kicks the ladder off the ledge and it falls down into the room, smashing on top of the ravenous walkers. Gloria stares at the treetops. She catches her breath. Bob kneels next to her. "You okay, kiddo? Talk to me."

"I'm good," she says, and gazes up through the canopy of massive, twisted, ancient live oaks. A thin, wispy layer of fog clings to the tops of the boughs and limbs, giving the forest a primordial cast.

"You sure?" Bob hovers, looking concerned.

"Absolutely." Though her head is still swimming, she manages to sit up. The weight of her pack drags on her shoulders. "That was a close fucking call, wasn't it?"

"A little too close," Bob says, touching her cheek. "You sure you're okay?"

She takes a deep breath. "Yep. All good. Let's get outta here."

He helps her up and takes a look around. The woods seem fairly quiet. There's a road visible through the trees, maybe a hundred yards away, up on a hill, a narrow blacktop ribbon cutting through the forest. Bob looks back at Gloria. "Can you walk?"

She nods. "You bet."

They've just started toward the edge of the clearing when pain stabs Gloria's hip. She stumbles, and Bob catches her. "Whoa, easy does it."

"I'm okay, I just need to rest a second." She shrugs off the pack, drops it, and lowers herself to the ground. Bob kneels in front of her, and she looks at him. "Sit down, Bob, you're making me nervous."

"Sorry." He sits next to her on a soft padding of old pine needles. "You're a trouper, Glo. Can't believe you got all that shit."

She smiles at him, takes off her visor, runs fingers through her hair. "I couldn't resist—you never know when you're gonna need a good stick of dynamite to liven up your next barbecue."

"You have a point there . . . sadly."

"Thanks for getting me outta there in one piece." She leans over and gives him a peck on the cheek. "Wouldn't have made it without you."

"Don't mention it." He smiles at her, and she can see something sparkling in his dark eyes, something thoughtful crossing his deeply lined face. "Gotta watch each other's backs nowadays."

"Hmmm . . . I thought I caught you watching my back the other day," she says with a smirk.

"You got me." Bob winks at her. "Guilty as charged." He pulls a canteen from his pack and offers it to her. "You want to wet your whistle?"

"Don't mind if I do." She takes a big pull off the bottle and hands it back. She watches him take a drink. "I understand that's about the only thing you're drinking nowadays."

He gives her a nod. "Yeah, well, this or maybe a bottle of Coke if I'm feeling festive."

"I'm proud of you, Bob."

"Hey, anybody can quit. . . . It's *staying* quit that separates the men from the drunks."

"I believe you're there, Bob. You made it."

They look into each other's eyes for a moment. Gloria gets very still. Bob reaches out and touches her hair, and she reaches up and touches his hand. He leans down, and she leans in, and they kiss.

The kiss goes on for a long moment, the passion kindling in both of them, the heat rising, so much so that neither hears the distant low burble of a high-powered engine, the squeak of brakes, or the sound of two car doors opening.

"I swear on my mama's grave I saw two people coming out of that shaggy-ass building down there."

Norma Sutters stands in front of a thicket of prairie grass and dense foliage, gazing down at the roof of the mining outpost. Her pinafore dress flaps in the wind, her abundant cleavage shiny with sweat. She squints to see better and cranes her neck, all to no avail. The rest of the forest is shrouded in shadow and the vaporous haze of cottonwood and dust motes, making it nearly impossible to discern any movement behind the trees. "I'm not imagining it, Miles, I'm telling you I saw them—a man and woman."

"You think it was them, the folks from the tunnel?" The young car thief stands behind her, fiddling with the lens dial on a pair of cheap binoculars. The Dodge idles behind him, both doors wide open.

"I just don't know."

Miles looks through the binoculars. "Wait . . . wait . . . I think I see somebody!"

"Give 'em here, sonny-boy." Norma snatches the binoculars away from the young man.

She looks through them, scanning the woods around the mining headquarters.

At last, she sees the shadow-bound couple on the ground in the darker shade of the pines. She adjusts the focus. She stares through the lenses and lets out a little cluck of her tongue. "Well, well . . . Them two don't seem too damn worried about getting attacked."

Bob gently lowers Gloria to the ground, his lips still locked on hers.

His senses fill with her smell—Wrigley's Spearmint, soap, sweat, and musk—and his mind goes blank. Sound fades, time stops. He doesn't think of Megan, his one post-plague crush, a relationship that crashed and burned in a charade of pity-fucks and death. He doesn't think of his impotence, which has plagued him ever since he was wounded by a mortar blast in Kuwait during the first Gulf War. He doesn't think of those vague wet-dream recollections of being a horny teenager in Slidell, Louisiana, frequenting the Bottoms Up Gentlemen's Club. He doesn't think of any neurotic obsession, fear, or insecurity. He thinks only of a calm sea, a great void in his mind—which is suddenly filled up with the essence of Gloria Pyne: her tender fingertips on his neck, her lips, her gray-green eyes, her breath on his face. The plague is gone, and the universe is now infinite in the cleft between Gloria Pyne's breasts.

Bob presses his face down into her bosom and breathes in her fragrance and feels as though he is floating. Gloria lets out a faint moan. She opens her legs and pushes up against him, and their faces return to each other.

Something stops them. Bob pulls back, cupping her face in his hands.

She looks up at him. "What is it? What's the matter? Did I do something—?"

Bob can tell something is wrong. He stares. "You feel hot."

"What?"

Bob puts the back of his hand on her forehead. "You're burning up."

She blinks, swallows hard, looks at him. "Yeah, I *thought* it was . . ."

"Oh no. No. No." Bob feels along the length of her arms, her hands, her fingers. He looks down her midriff, down her legs. He freezes when he sees her ankle. "Oh God no, no, *shit*!"

She sees it as well now: just above the top of her boot, where an inch-and-a-half-wide area of skin is exposed below the cuff of her Capri pants, a small nip the size of a kernel of corn, a bloody tooth mark—probably from the former secretary that had lunged at her on the ladder.

Bob hears a sound in the trees to the north, and instinctively draws his revolver, then levers himself to his feet. He aims at the noise.

Norma Sutters calls out to them: "Excuse me!—Hello!?!—Folks?!"

Her plump body wedged between two trees fifty feet above the mining company building, she musters up as much deference and humility as she can manage. "Sorry to interrupt y'all! Ain't got no gun or weapon!—We mean no harm!"

She waves her hands over her head in a gesture of amity, looking like a traffic controller on the tarmac of an airport, the flesh on the backs of her arms jiggling. "Got one question for ya! Is the lady named *Lilly* by any chance? We're looking for a gal by the name of *Lilly Caul*!"

TWELVE

The stationhouse window bursts open, two sections of loose board-
ing flinging off into space with the impact of Lilly's shoulder. Tommy
Dupree appears in the maw and leaps over the sill, vaulting through
the air and landing awkwardly on the hard-packed earth outside the
building, fifty pounds of vending machine products rattling on his
back. Lilly comes next, squeezing through the opening and jumping off the sill while gripping her Ruger with both hands, landing
hard, instantly assuming the Israeli commando posture that Bob
taught her, both feet planted firmly on the ground, maintaining her
equilibrium fairly well considering that she has the equivalent of a
small wardrobe locker roped to her back and a twenty-gallon container of fuel oil tied to her waist.

The air hangs heavy with putrid death-stench and vibrates with
the collective vocalizations of three or four hundred walkers. Tommy
doesn't hesitate, doesn't flinch, doesn't even break his stride as he
heads directly for the main branch of the railroad tracks, despite the
fact that the switchyard is virtually standing-room-only with walkers, scores of them blocking his path to the middle rails. Gripping
the crowbar with white-knuckle pressure, letting out a garbled war
cry, he puts his head down like a miniature fullback and barrels toward the tracks. He slams into a column of three, flinging two male
adults and a female teenager backward, stumbling willy-nilly on

their heels, emaciated arms pinwheeling stupidly, knocking others down.

The closest line of walkers—amounting to about twenty or thirty—turn their seemingly inebriated attention toward the commotion, locking their sharklike gazes on to Tommy. Swarms move with the hive behavior of bees—the outer rings of dead still oblivious to the humans in their midst, even while the inner rings begin to react chemically, turning, locking sights on their prey, slowly trundling heavy-footed toward the warm, breathing bodies.

If asked to describe the physical bearing of a walker, the first thing to pop into the average person's head might be a stroke victim—albeit an *angry, starving, ferocious, cannibalistic* stroke victim. But a swarm has a different feel. When walkers swarm—and sometimes grow to a number that would be considered a *herd*—they present dangers and wreak catastrophes that are almost biblical. They coalesce into a tsunami of menace that strums the deepest chords of primal, genetic terror in a person. They are an inexorable force of nature.

Lilly Caul feels this bone-deep fear start to work its cancer on her as she follows the boy toward the central track. Dizziness threatens to slow her down, make her stumble, steal her breath, and perhaps drag her down into a deadly blackout. She keeps her gaze locked on to Tommy Dupree.

The boy charges along in front of her, banging into walker after walker, screaming, kicking, flailing at them, pushing one onto another at the last possible instant to avoid getting snagged or bitten or slashed by the grinding of countless teeth. He buries the crowbar in the cranium of a ragged old woman with stringy, mossy white hair and pulls it out with a high-pitched howl that resembles the hysterical bark of a hyena. He slashes the crowbar wildly at another phalanx lunging at him from the left.

Lilly moves in tighter behind him, the Ruger gripped hard in her cupped hands. She squeezes off a few more blasts, scoring head shots on either side of the boy, sending body after body to the ground in wet, crumpled heaps. Her heart races, her vision blurring with each jarring stride as she pounds across the rocky earth.

Tommy reaches the turntable area, vaults across the outer rails, and scrambles up onto a lone flatcar in the center of the tracks. Lilly arrives at the turntable one instant behind the boy, and has to fire on three more walkers, each one of them old, gray, desiccated, and cadaverous—by the looks of them, former farm people in tattered work garb. Her blasts send chunks of aged skulls flying in mists of pink matter glistening in the sun, the dead collapsing to the ground, returning to the stillness that should have claimed them in the first place.

On the flatcar, Tommy has already shrugged off his pack and grabbed one of the giant tree limbs.

Behind him, Lilly climbs onto the rear of the conveyance and slips off her cargo, dropping the huge duffel and fuel canister onto the rotting planks. The flatcar rocks slightly as Tommy chooses one of the larger tree limbs, picks it up, and then steadies it on the ground next to the car. He glances over his shoulder.

"ON MY SIGNAL . . . PUSH!" Lilly yells from the rear. She, too, has grabbed one of the limbs, and now holds it as one would hold an oar on a boat.

By this point, the herd has shifted, drawn to the commotion on the flatcar. Many of them awkwardly cobble over corrugations of iron rails and weeds, approaching the central flatcar, their talonlike hands clawing at the air, their blackened lips as gelatinous as earthworms undulating around decaying teeth.

"Let's go already!" Tommy yells, jabbing his tree limb as one of the first walkers to reach the flatcar claws at his pant legs.

"TOGETHER NOW—PUSH!" Lilly pushes off with her tree limb as hard as she can, while Tommy does the same at the front end of the car.

At first, the flatcar barely budges. The wheels, mired in the undergrowth, slowly rip through tangles of weeds, squeaking noisily. Lilly puts everything she has into the limb, pushing as hard as she can. She feels the train car breaking free of the kudzu and wild ivy and ironweed, and the steel wheels beginning to turn on the rail.

More walkers arrive, clamoring to claw their way onto the car.

Tommy slams his boot down on a small female, staving in her skull as he pushes the car away from her. The diminutive body collapses and falls under the conveyance, the rear wheels slicing her legs in two. The flatcar picks up speed. Now Lilly finds herself pumping the limb as though rowing a boat, pushing and lifting, pushing and lifting, making the car roll faster and faster down the main branch. Near the front, Tommy also furiously prods his limb against the ground, until something unexpected happens.

"We're going downhill!" Lilly yells from the rear, the wind in her hair now, the car vibrating wildly as it picks up speed on the downward slope. She drops her limb. Tommy drops his bough and crouches down, holding on to an iron bolt to steady himself.

The track gently curves to the right. A few walkers along the edges of the rails stumble into the car's path, and get mowed down. The wheels thump over mortified flesh. Tommy screams as a severed arm tumbles across the car's deck, spewing a leech trail of blood.

The flatcar rolls faster and faster. The woods on either side start to blur past them. Lilly guesses they're already traveling thirty or forty miles an hour. The wheels drum on the rails, a syncopated beat, the tempo speeding up. Tommy starts to giggle, and then his giggle builds to outright manic laughter, and then his manic laughter builds to a triumphant wail: "TRY TO CATCH US NOW, YOU FUCKERS!— EAT SHIT!!—YOU PUS BAGS!!—YOU SLUGS!!"

Lilly glances over her shoulder and sees the herd receding in the distance. Just like that. They have slipped free of the plague of locusts.

She turns and sees the car careening down the gentle decline, and all at once she finds no humor in their situation. She finds nothing to celebrate.

They are on a runaway train car, with no way to stop.

"Hold still! Please, Glo! This is the only way!" Bob Stookey crouches in the claustrophobic rear bench-seat area of the Dodge Challenger as the car climbs past sixty in the northbound lanes of Highway 19. Bob has his pack open between his legs, his makeshift surgical instruments on an old newspaper spread out across the floor mat in front of him. Gloria lies on her back, her shoulders pushed up against the far door, her legs sprawled across Bob's lap.

"I don't know, Bob. . . . " She clutches his arm, writhing, drunk with terror. "I don't know—I don't know—I don't know about this!" She covers her face with her hands, her tears leaking through her fingers. It sounds as though she's giggling. Her visor has come loose and dropped to the floor, and her graying, dyed hair is matted with flop sweat. She hyperventilates. "I don't know I don't know I don't know I don't—"

"Okay, honey, look at me." Bob gently turns and cradles her face in his hands. "You have to try and breathe and stay as calm as possible. We only have a few minutes here . . . and there's no other option. It'll go down a lot easier if you just stay as calm as possible." He strokes her hair. "Look at me. Gloria. It's old Bob. You can trust me. You're gonna make it, and you're gonna outlive us all. Now, sweetie, I want to hear you say it."

"What?! You want me to what?!"

"I want to hear you say you're gonna outlive us all. C'mon, say it!" He finds a small plastic bottle between his legs, squirts liquid sanitizer onto his big, gnarled hands, and rubs it in. Lying on the newspaper between his feet are many of the items they found in the miners' office, including the acetylene torch, the rubbing alcohol, the first aid kit, the can of axle grease, and the hacksaw. He looks at her. "C'mon, Gloria, say it."

"Good try, Bob." She lets out a dry, mordant little giggle. She sounds intoxicated—woozy with fear. "Good fucking try."

"Hey!" He drops the bottle and grabs her by the shoulders, shakes her a little, and speaks crossly. "Who's the medic here? Three tours and an honorable discharge in Iraq!—I may not be able to make a soufflé rise, but when it comes to emergency field surgery I'm a goddamn Florence Nightingale! So do what I say and repeat after me, 'I'! Say it! 'I'!"

She swallows. She looks at him, her eyes groggy and disoriented. "I . . . "

" *'I am going to outlive all you guys!'* "

Her voice breaks, crumbles into a half sob. "I am going to . . . outlive you guys."

"That's exactly right! And when you're right, you're right. So now I'm gonna—"

A voice from the front interrupts: "Sir?" The young car thief pipes up from behind the wheel, calling out over the roar of 426 cubic inches. "Can I make a suggestion?"

"Make it quick!" Bob reaches down to his belt buckle, unclasps it, and quickly pulls it free from his pant loops. "Gonna need all hands on deck in a second."

"Sir, I'm not trying to tell y'all what to do." The young driver gazes nervously up into the rearview at the action in back. He does this while simultaneously weaving around standing wreckage, a maneuver that would send most drivers careening off the road and into a ditch. "But there's a rest stop coming up where we can pull off, and maybe you can do this on a picnic table or inside the shelter."

"No time for that!" Bob grabs Gloria's wriggling leg and holds it still, grasping it about two inches above the wound. The bite mark has already turned livid, a ringworm of red around the kernel-sized gouge. It has been Bob's experience—especially when dealing with gunshot trauma on the battlefield—that sepsis can spread within minutes. It can cause blood pressure to plummet, bring on shock, and make organs fail like the winking out of streetlights in a storm.

Unfortunately, he has no standard of reference by which to triangulate the relationship between his lifetime of experience with infections and trauma and the time it takes for a person who has been nipped to ultimately succumb. "Just keep heading north on 19 as fast as you can without rolling this thing," he orders the young driver. "Keep an eye peeled for Hannahs Mill, and that's where you'll turn west on Jeff Davis Road!"

"But what about—?"

"Just stay on course!" Bob's voice is as taut as a piano string. He palpates Gloria's leg, feeling along the tendons below her knee for the pulse of her peroneal artery. "I need to get her back to the infirmary we got set up in the tunnel as soon as possible—I can only do so much out here in the sticks!"

The woman in the passenger seat twists around and aims her calm, friendly eyes at Bob. "You want to give her the rest of that hooch? 'Bob,' was it?"

"Yes, ma'am, that's right. Sure. That would be good." Bob nods and starts winding the belt around Gloria's leg, making a field tourniquet as best he can. He guides the end through the buckle and yanks it back hard, cutting off the blood flow to the site, making Gloria moan softly, murmuring something that nobody hears. Five minutes ago, they had given her half the pint of Mad Dog that Norma Sutters stashes in her purse, along with a couple Seconal tablets that Miles Littleton keeps in his glove box. Now the narcotics and booze have begun to dampen Gloria's nerve endings.

"Here ya go." Norma leans forward and thumbs open the glove compartment. She fishes through the contents, pulls out a couple of small objects, turns, and proffers the pill bottle and the half-empty pint of Mad Dog as though they are peace offerings between two tribal elders. "She takes a couple more of them Seconals with the rest of that Mad Dog . . . oh Lordy, she ain't even gonna remember what year it is."

Another terse nod from Bob. "Okay, fine, good . . . Let's get them down her gullet quick."

They give the narcotics and booze to Gloria, who coughs and chokes, but eventually guzzles it all down. She burps and hiccups and heaves a couple of anguished sobs, and manages to say, "Never thought I would be partying with Bob Stookey quite like this." She laughs. Actually, it's more of a pained honk than a laugh, and it comes out on a breathless sigh, narcotic-fueled, feverish, and shot through with morbid irony. "Partaaaaay!" She giggles, and giggles, and her giggles deteriorate into garbled muttering that soon trails off.

Bob positions a towel under her foot. He picks up the hacksaw.

"Would you care to dance, Mister Stookey?" Gloria slurs her words

now. "Come here often?" More giggling. "Haven't I met you somewhere be—"

Bob saws into the meat of her ankle.

"GET READY TO JUMP!"

Lilly's voice, barely audible in the wind, reaches Tommy Dupree's
ears an instant before he sees the bend in the tracks a couple hundred yards away. He lies prone, on his belly, clutching an iron lever
mounted to the side of the flatcar, squinting against the gusts, as
the flatcar plunges toward the sharp curve, the drumroll noise of
the wheels rising, the undercarriage beginning to shudder and
quake. He can see Lilly Caul ten feet away, also on her belly, holding
on to the iron apparatus mounted to the front of the car.

Tommy realizes Lilly is absolutely right: They're going to fly off
the rails as soon as the car hits that turn—and they'd better bail, and
quickly. Tommy manages to lift himself up without losing his heavy
pack or getting swept off the edge of the car. He crouches with his
skinny legs pinioned under him, coiled and ready to spring. The
wind stings his face, makes him squint.

"ON THREE!"

At the front of the flatcar, Lilly also rises to a crouch and prepares
to vault off the hurtling conveyance. For one insane moment, crouching there in the wind, his brain crackling with panic, Tommy thinks
of Saturday morning cartoons. He remembers the Road Runner
occasionally going over a cliff, perhaps on a boulder or a log, and at
the very last possible instant (as the boulder is about to crash to earth)
executing a graceful little jeté and hopping off the rock at the perfect moment in order to land safely next to the enormous crater
formed by the impact. Is what they are about to attempt just as phys-
ically impossible? Is Lilly's crazy gambit here equally antithetical
to the basic laws of physics?

"ONE!"

The bend in the track looms closer and closer, a hundred yards
away now. Tommy lowers his center of gravity and prepares to make

his Road Runner–worthy leap. Reflector poles and tree trunks flicker past them as though they're approaching light speed.

"TWO!"

Tommy grips the iron lever beside him so tightly now that the vibrations travel up his tendons and strum his funny bone, sending jolts of electric current through him. He holds his breath and focuses on the blurry figure of Lilly, her back turned to him at the front of the flatcar. Tommy straightens, girds himself, tells himself he's ready to rock and roll. The sight of Lilly Caul—ten feet away, her shoulders tense and hunched over the front end, her legs cocked under her, her knees pointed outward like a baseball catcher's—fills Tommy Dupree with a sudden and unexpected injection of courage.

To paraphrase his late father, Tommy would follow this woman into the valley of the shadow of death.

"THREE!"

Lilly's piercing wail sends a bolt of fresh electricity through Tommy as he jumps.

Arms flailing, legs churning, Tommy soars through space, and for the briefest of moments, the entire length of the enormous conglomeration of wood, iron, and metal beneath him seems to plummet away from him, as though the earth has suddenly fallen away, or perhaps opened up to swallow the flatcar into its bottomless maw.

Tommy lands hard on his shoulder and rolls, his backpack tearing open and spilling its contents of tortilla chips, Life Savers, toenail clippers, disposable razors, toothbrushes, lint rollers, and travel pillows across a half-acre stretch of turf. The pain slams through him, a sledgehammer to the small of his back. He lands at an awkward angle against the trunk of a live oak. The impact knocks the breath out of his lungs and sends Roman candles across his line of vision. Gasping, trying to sit up, he sees Lilly landing next to him, the weight of her own huge knapsack slamming down on top of her, causing her to let out an agonizing grunt of pain. A tremendous thud rattles the ground, followed by a metallic shriek, and then silence.

Something blocks out the sun all of a sudden, something enormous in the sky, which rips Tommy's attention up to the heavens directly above the treetops. The entire sixty-foot-long flatcar has gone airborne. It rotates lazily in midair for a brief moment as it arcs out across an adjacent clearing—creating a surreal sight worthy of a Magritte painting, a locomotive in a fireplace—and then it crashes down in the grass beyond the bend.

The ground shakes.

Tommy lets out a sigh of air—half shock, half relief—as he watches the massive train car roll another hundred feet or so before shuddering to a stop, several of its axles and wheel assemblies broken loose, lying in the tall grass behind it. The air fills with a nebula of dust, which rises over the crash site and quickly dissipates in the breeze. Tommy lowers his head and lets out another breath of relief. Lilly has already managed to rise to her feet about ten yards away from him. "You okay, buddy?" she asks as she limps over to him.

"Yeah, I think so." Tommy levers himself up to a standing position. Dizziness makes him reel for a moment. "That was . . . yeah."

She inspects him for wounds. "Looks like you're fairly unscathed."

"Whaddaya talking about? I'm totally scathed. That was totally messed up."

She manages a tepid chuckle. "Yeah. Totally. But it was better than the alternative back there."

They hear a noise. Maybe a twig-snap somewhere behind the trees. Maybe shuffling footsteps.

Lilly looks over her shoulder and doesn't see anything . . . yet. "No time to pat ourselves on the back," she says, indicating the shadows of the woods. "All the noise of our little derailing incident is gonna draw the swarm. C'mon." Lilly starts picking up the goodies that fell from Tommy's pack. "Let's get this stuff squared away and get the fuck outta here."

Gloria's shriek erupts in the enclosed space of the Challenger's interior with the force of an air-raid siren. Blood backwashes all over Bob, and the car swerves. Bob bears down on the ankle, the handle of the hacksaw getting greasy from all the blood gushing up across his arms, down into his lap, and into the seams of the seats.

He knows he has to hurry. The slower he cuts, the more agonizing the pain.

Gloria screams louder—a raspy, keening howl, the sound of it almost metallic—as Bob feels the serrated blade of the hacksaw catch suddenly on the bone, the teeth seizing up, getting caught on the hard, brittle core of the ankle. He bears down harder. Gloria passes out, her body going limp. "Almost, almost, *almost,*" he utters between grunts as he tries to hack through her ankle, making her entire body jiggle with each nudge of the blade. "GodDAMNit!" Bob barks as he pulls the blade loose. "Gotta get better leverage!"

"Oh dear Jesus Lord, Lord, Lordy-Lord," Norma Sutters murmurs desperately into her lap, shaking her head, her shoulders slumped with sorrow.

Bob awkwardly pulls himself out from under the bloody mess of Gloria's legs, and he struggles to reverse his position, squeezing around between the seat-backs and Gloria to face her and then quickly finish the job. She moans. Partially conscious, delirious with pain, her head lolling, she manages to utter a name.

"I'm here, darlin'," Bob softly replies, and then says, "You gotta bite the bullet one more second and then it'll all be over."

Time seems to slow down, and suddenly stop, as Bob saws through the remaining few centimeters of Gloria's bone and finally wrenches the woman's right foot off, along with three inches of her leg above the ankle. It slips out of Bob's blood-slimy hand and splash into the puddle of blood that has formed on the floor mats. Blood floods the seats. Bob quickly grabs the torch and the lighter, and thumbs the acetylene on, and sparks the nozzle.

The faint thumping sound of the blue flame makes Norma Sutters jerk in the front seat, despite the fact that she's looking away, having averted her gaze for most of the procedure.

Bob cauterizes the ragged, oozing stump. The odor wafts, and it's terrible—a black, acrid fume—but the worst part isn't the smell. The worst part is the sound. The sizzling of burning flesh will live in the memories of each inhabitant of that Dodge Challenger from that day on. Bob feels something coming undone inside him, and lifts his finger off the torch's trigger, extinguishing the flame and leaving a black tarry cap on the stump.

Somehow, Miles has managed to keep the car at a steady fifty miles an hour throughout the entire procedure. Now he glances in the rearview at the aftermath in the rear seats. "Is it done?"

"Yeah, it's done," Bob says, looking down at the severed foot, wiping his blood-slick hands on a towel. "Get us home as soon as you can. . . . We ain't out of the woods yet." He regards the profuse amount of blood that has gathered on the floor mats, on the seats, and even across the inside of the windows. It looks like an animal was slaughtered. He drops his towel on top of the amputated foot and then tenderly puts a hand on Gloria's cheek.

She tries to speak, but all that comes out of her is a thin, wispy whistle of a sigh.

"You're gonna make it, kiddo," Bob tells her softly, stroking her feverish cheek.

She barely utters a labored response. "I'm sorry, Bob . . . but . . . I would . . . I'd . . . *rather not.*"

Bob looks at her. He tips his head to the side in confusion. He's not sure he just heard what he thinks he just heard. He leans down and puts his ear next to her quavering, blood-spattered lips. "Say again, sweetie?"

The words come out on a sigh, a dwindling volume to the voice. "I would . . . prefer to . . . just . . . you know . . . have this be . . . the end of the whole mess for me."

THIRTEEN

"Wait. . . . *What?*" Bob Stookey stares down at the face of a woman at peace, the eerie calm setting into her pug-nosed features. Bob panics. "No, no, no, no, no, no, no, no."

She gazes up at him through eyes filmed in opaque, milky suffering. "Let me go, Bob."

"Fuck, no!"

Her eyelids sink shut. "It was . . . a good run."

He shakes her. "Stay with us! There's no reason—"

"N-not like this . . . too much work."

"Gloria! Gloria!" He shakes her, he slaps her face. He's not even aware that he's crying. "There's no reason!—Glo!—DON'T DO THIS!"

Her eyes are closed now, her head lolling to the side, a soft death rattle wheezing out of her. The faintest words cross her lips, so soft that Bob has to press his ear against her quivering mouth. "Make sure I . . . don't . . ."

"GLORIA!"

". . . come back. . . . "

"GLORIA!"

On a long sigh: ". . . Please make sure. . . . "

"GLORIA!" He shakes her and shakes her. He can barely see through his tears. He tastes copper on his tongue—salt and tarnished metal—as the car swerves. Bob falls against the door, shaking Gloria, picking her up. He hardly notices the change in her tiny body. She has gone completely limp.

"GLORIA!—GLORIA!—GLORIA!" Bob holds her and cries and realizes the fingertips of his right hand are softly pressing the tender flesh above her carotid artery.

She has no pulse.

This fact reaches Bob's brain one nanosecond before he realizes what he has to do now.

He frowns, a tear breaking over the edge of his lower lid and tracking down his face. He pulls the .357 from where it was wedged between the back of his belt and his lower back. He collapses into the seat next to the flaccid, blood-soaked remains of Gloria Pyne.

Then Bob Stookey has a ferocious cry.

Inside the sealed windows of the muscle car, the blast pops dry and flat, like a balloon bursting, as the vehicle roars around the bend at the intersection of 74 and 18. The distinctive report of a .357 Magnum—when muffled by the glass and steel enclosure of an automobile, and further dampened by the hank of bunched fabric pressed down on Gloria Pyne's skull—emits a low thump that could easily be mistaken for a tire blowing or a chassis banging over a pothole, were it not for the unmistakable subsonic slap-back echo that now drifts over the treetops of the adjacent woods. To anyone within a five-mile radius, it might actually bring to mind the rattle of heat thunder on the horizon, or the low boil of a storm brewing in the far distance.

Lilly Caul pauses on the trail and looks up. She tilts her head and listens, waiting for more gunfire, but there is only that single muffled blast, now fading on the breeze. For a moment, she wonders if she imagined it. "Did you hear that?" she whispers to the young man coming up behind her.

Tommy lets out an exhausted sigh. "Hear what? No. What was it?—Walkers?"

"No . . . I thought I heard . . . Never mind." Lilly takes a deep breath and shrugs the straps of her knapsack a little higher on her shoulders. The straps have been digging into the nape of her neck for the last couple of miles, and now she hears the faint creak of her tendons as she stretches. Her pack weighs a ton, and feels like it's getting heavier by the moment. She tightens the bracing strap. "Let's go. . . . C'mon . . . we're almost there."

They continue down the stony, weed-riddled path as it snakes through the thickets.

Five minutes later, they see a glint of metal through a break in the foliage, and Lilly silently shoots a hand up, stopping Tommy cold in his tracks behind her. She hears voices. She motions for the boy to get down, be quiet, and hold on for a second. She crouches, wriggles off her pack, fishes in it, finds her binoculars, and peers through the lenses at the shimmer of purple metal-flake steel visible through the pine boughs and tall grass.

Lilly registers the sight as the front quarter panel of a car parked near the access hatch. It looks as though the car's doors are open, and that there are silhouettes of three or more figures sitting inside the vehicle.

A female voice says something like, "You gonna be okay?"

A gravelly male voice says, "Just gimme a second. . . . I'm fine. . . . Just a second."

Goose bumps crawl over Lilly's flesh. Several things register in her all at once, in equal measures of panic, confusion, and a weird kind of relief. She recognizes Bob Stookey's voice, but it sounds wrong—drained and trembly. And she does *not* recognize the other speaker.

Suddenly she hears the sound of shuffling footsteps behind her, in the middle distance, behind the trees, and the low buzz of growling.

Lilly twists around and makes eye contact with the exhausted boy. "Tommy," she whispers. "Listen to me. Get your crowbar out."

"Okay, but—"

"Sshhhh, just do it, and follow my lead." Lilly reaches down to her pack, puts back the binoculars, and zips it shut. Then she draws her Ruger from her belt, and whispers, "We got walkers coming up behind us, and I'm not totally sure what's going on up there with Bob and those folks, or who they are, or what they want. But I can tell something's wrong. I'd prefer to be safe rather than sorry."

The boy nods. "I get it—I'm ready."

"Let me do the talking."

Another nod.

Lilly rises, silently pushing her way through the foliage toward the clearing, and grips the Ruger with both hands—commando style—despite the fact that it's out of ammo. As she approaches the parked car, she sees that it's a vintage hot rod and it tics and diesels like a snoring beast as it sits at an angle across the clearing from the tunnel hatch. As she gets closer, she sees Bob kneeling down just outside the car's open rear door, as though praying, or supplicating, to someone sprawled across the rear seats. His shoulders are slumped miserably, as if his head weighs a million tons.

An enormous black woman in a threadbare floral dress and bouffant hairstyle stands outside the front passenger door, wringing her hands, waiting respectfully for Bob to finish whatever it is he's doing.

Lilly pauses just inside the netting of cattails and undergrowth that borders the clearing. She holds her gun on the portly woman. "Bob?!"

Bob's head rises with a start. "Lilly?" He looks around. "That you?"

Lilly steps out of the thicket and into the clearing, followed by the boy, who holds his crowbar as menacingly as possible. "What the fuck is going on?" Lilly demands as she trains the Ruger's muzzle on the woman. "Who are these people, Bob?"

"Take it easy, Lilly-girl." Bob speaks in halting wheezes, as though he can barely muster the energy to talk. "They're friendlies."

Lilly starts to say something else when the car's driver-side door squeaks open and a young African-American in a ragged hoodie and tight little braids emerges from the car with his hands up. "We're on your side, ma'am!"

"That's right." The portly woman has her hands up as well, and she gives Lilly a convivial little smile. "I'm Norma, and this here is Miles."

"Bob, what's wrong?" Lilly sees the lump of a figure lying prone across the backseat and sees the backwash of deep scarlet blood spattered everywhere inside the car, and it makes her stomach clench. She can hear the scuttling of walkers closing in from the woods. "Is that Gloria? What happened? Is she okay?"

Bob looks up at Lilly, and with a single, forlorn, anguished shake of his head, he tells Lilly practically everything she needs to know about what happened without uttering a single word. She lowers her gun, and she feels her chest go cold. She bows her head and lets out a heartbreaking sigh. "Oh God . . . Don't tell me she was . . . and you had to . . ."

"Lilly—?" Tommy's voice from behind her penetrates her shock. "We got four cold ones coming."

Lilly turns and shoves her gun in the back of her belt, then draws her rusty machete from its makeshift sheath on her hip. "Get back, Tommy."

"But what about—?"

"Just do what I say!" Lilly sees the foursome pushing through the foliage about thirty feet away, a female and three males in ragged work clothes. They have at least a couple of years of decay on them, their faces and exposed areas of flesh so corroded with decomposition that they appear to be made of stucco, with ghastly veneers of gray tissue vacu-formed around their sharp-angled skulls. Lilly starts to say, "Get back, everybody, and—"

She hears a commotion behind her and then hears Bob's voice barking suddenly, "GET OUTTA MY WAY!"

A blur of movement draws Lilly's attention over her shoulder. She sees Bob lurching away from the car, then stumbling toward her. Before Lilly can even react, Bob has grabbed the machete out of her hands.

"BOB, WAIT—!!"

He lunges toward the creatures, snorting with the mad pent-up rage of a wild bull. He lashes out at the first one, striking it between the pectoral and shoulder, making a divot so deep in its neck the entire cranium peels away and flops down across its back. Black blood oozes out of the crater the instant before the thing collapses, its head dangling upside down against its own back, the threads of arteries and tendons like the defunct wiring of some out-of-service automaton.

"Bob—?!"

Lilly stares as Bob Stookey grips the rusty, blood-stippled machete with both hands—Babe Ruth at bat, about to swing for the fences—and in front of his horror-stricken, wide-eyed fellow survivors, proceeds to lose himself in his labors.

Lilly Caul has seen walker massacres before. She witnessed the man known as the Governor rain the hellfire of an entire armada of .50 caliber machine guns and countless automatic assault rifles down upon a swarm of the things that had accumulated outside the fences of a medium-security prison in rural Georgia. The clouds of blood mist and physical matter that had filled the air from *that* particular mass annihilation would live for a long time in her memory. She had seen smaller, more intimate slaughters as well—like the time that band of men in Marietta had cornered a small group of biters in a loading dock area behind a Piggly Wiggly and systematically dismembered them and crushed their heads with the rear tires of massive stake trucks. But she has never—*ever*—witnessed anything quite like this.

Bob's cathartic rampage through that cluster of decrepit monsters continues with a wide, arcing, roundhouse blow of the machete to the skull of the next closest walker. The blade strikes the thing's cranium just above the earlobe, and slices the top two-thirds of the skull clean off as though Bob were popping a bottle cap. The ragged scalp and partial upper-fascia jettisons into the air on a meteor-tail of pink matter, falling end over end to the ground. What remains is a hollow, trembling mess of bloody mantislike mandibles and exposed teeth that shudder and chatter for a surreal instant before the rest of the body gives out and folds to the ground.

The surviving two creatures make futile attempts to close in on Bob, but the dark-haired man turns to them and makes primal grunting noises as he quickly, efficiently, rams the tip of the blade, one at a time, hard, at upward angles, through the roofs of each of their mouths, into their nasal cavities, through their parietal lobes, and out the tops of their skulls. One by one, the remaining walkers drop.

Bob takes in a deep breath and lets out an enormous howl of pure, unadulterated rage—shot through with the agony of loss—right before he slams a boot down as hard as he can on the head of one of the fallen. The wet crunch makes most of the spectators behind him turn away in disgust—all except Lilly. She puts her arm around Tommy Dupree and hugs his face against her midsection and softly whispers, "I really don't think you need to see this."

Meanwhile, Bob still has that machete gripped in both hands, and now he starts in on the motionless heaps. He slams the blade down on the moldering limbs and torsos as though beginning a vigorous session of firewood chopping. Lilly watches almost stoically, morbidly curious. The truth is, she loves this man, and she's proud of him—proud of him for kicking his drinking habit, proud of him for finding the tunnels, proud of him for saving the lives of his fellow survivors, for being the voice of reason, being loyal, and being a friend. For days now, Lilly has noticed little signs that Bob had grown sweet on Gloria, and now *this.* . . .

Lilly continues to look on without much emotion as Bob slashes and hacks and buries the blade in the gristle of mortified joints and stubborn bones, yanking it out with the help of his boot-sole. Blood spatters and blows back up at him, freckling his gaunt face, stinging his burning eyes. He looks like a demonic entity, and it begins to stir something deep inside Lilly Caul. *Whatever it takes,* she thinks.

Bob separates a leg from a hip with a single blow, a head from a neck, an upper body from a lower body, and the blood covers him now. Is he reenacting the amputation fiasco in the car? Is he exorcising something deeper, thornier? Lilly can't quite figure it out, but that's okay with her. Bob gets winded. The blade gets stuck for a moment and Bob lets out another feral yawp, almost simian in its guttural rage, but with pain in it.

That's when Lilly realizes that Bob is crying as he flails at the dead things. His tears fly off his face with each furious blow, his hitching sobs mingling with his hyperventilated gasps.

"Okay," Lilly says, taking a step toward him. "That's enough now."

She comes up behind him as he continues to lash away at the things on the ground. His energy has begun to flag. His head droops as he slashes wildly, fecklessly now. The sobbing has gotten the better of him. Lilly cautiously approaches. She puts a tender hand on his shoulder and he jumps, taken aback by her touch.

He turns and meets her gaze with his own feverish eyes, which now glitter with the madness. "What!—*WHAT!*"

Lilly doesn't say anything. She just nods her head, and keeps her hand on his shoulder, and keeps nodding and doesn't look away.

Bob lets the sobbing take him down into her arms, the grief loosening his grip on the blood-lacquered machete. The weapon falls to ground.

Then Bob loses it.

Lilly holds him and lets him cry it all out until there's nothing left.

They reconvene underground, in the private shadows of a side tunnel, in the deathly silence. They sit on folding chairs, and hold paper cups of instant coffee, and stare gravely at the floor as they listen to Norma Sutters' low, raspy voice give them the bad news.

Some of them had hoped the preacher was dead, figuring he must have perished in the chaos of the hordes that descended upon Woodbury last month. Now they sit very still and listen with morose expressions on their faces as Norma explains how the preacher stumbled upon her church with his two minions. She describes how he joined her in her search for Miles and the infamous caravan, and how the preacher had taken over the convoy when the priest had died, and how he had started acting strange and erratic almost immediately.

Then she pauses. The others wait. She licks her chapped lips as she looks into the eyes of each listener for a moment, gauging if and when and how she should tell them the gist of what she came here to say. At last, she clears her throat and says very softly, very casually, "He's building an army out of walkers."

Lilly asks her to repeat what she just said, and Norma does so, and Lilly has to hear it a third time just to register its meaning, and to take stock of it.

Her memories of the Governor's horror shows in the speedway arena with their gladiatorial walkers and grisly death matches are still fresh enough to make nightly appearances in her dreams, and she remembers all too well the defensive swarm of biters positioned outside the fences of that horrible prison at which she had killed Philip Blake. She also remembers Jeremiah attempting to wreak havoc in Woodbury by knocking down the barricades and summoning the herd. Over the two years since the plague broke out, many others have certainly tried to use walkers in various ways—as shields, as weapons, or as threats of one kind or another—but nobody else ever attempted it in such a delusional and grand manner as this.

"I'm afraid you're gonna have to explain just exactly what you're talking about," Lilly says finally to the plump black woman sitting across from her.

Dressed in a threadbare floral-print dress that strains at the seams with her girth, her décolletage brimming with massive bosoms, Norma Sutters has that warm, open, earthy face that Lilly has always associated with nurses, teachers, and den mothers. Against her better judgment, Lilly finds herself trusting this woman and her young juvenile delinquent of a companion.

Norma takes a sip of her tepid coffee and says, "Couple of nights ago, I couldn't for the life of me sleep one wink . . . tossing and turning all night to beat the band. I guess the old brain was just overloading with worry. So I got up and took a little walk."

In another part of the tunnels, a child's laughter rings out, making Lilly and the others jump. Barbara Stern has agreed to keep the kids occupied with games and lunch while Norma and Miles tell their story to the rest of the adults, but every few moments the children inadvertently make their presence known. Lilly looks down at her hands and sees that they're shaking ever so slightly, and this touches off some deep well of anger within her. She has barely come to terms with Gloria Pyne's death—they have to bury her sometime soon—and now *this*.

"I was about to go back to bed," Norma is saying. "I'd been walkin' for maybe a half an hour, circling the entire wagon train, when all of a sudden I see a light flickering in the woods. Thought I was seeing things at first. I get a little closer and I hear noises comin' from behind the trees, and that flickering light. I hear the most god-awful sounds coming from that light—human screams, walkers growling and such, I don't know what all."

Norma shudders, and Lilly feels a cold finger tracing down the back of her spine, eliciting a wave of gooseflesh along the back of her legs as she recalls Jeremiah's used-car-dealer face and huge pompadour of hair. David Stern sits on one side of Lilly and Harold Staubach on the other, and she can sense each man's hackles going up. Tommy Dupree sits behind her, and she can hear the boy's steady breathing, and it sounds rapt, transfixed. Bob is off somewhere dealing with his grief over Gloria. Lilly's worried about him. He's lost a lot in recent months.

"Curiosity killed the cat," Norma goes on, "and I get close enough to finally see what's going on in them woods without givin' myself away." She pauses again, and the others hang on her silence. "Now remember, this crazy preacher's been gathering these walkers for God knows what reason, and he's been torturing them biker fellas for days, and I have no earthly idea what he's up to, but I just know deep down in my bones it's all connected. So I hide behind a tree, and I see the strangest thing."

The momentary pause weighs down on Lilly like a massive yoke.

"The preacher's got about ten of them monsters, and I'll be damned if it don't look like he's *playing* with them."

David Stern knits his brow. "Whaddaya mean 'playing with them'?"

Norma looks down and takes another deep breath as though the very *telling* of this continues to take a physical toll. "Down in Florida, they used to have them dog races? Terrible things, those races, all that hard-earned money getting lost on liquor and shenanigans. Anyway, I don't know if y'all ever saw one of them things, but there's a little metal rabbit on a rail that pops up and then charges around that track so the dogs'll chase it real good?"

"I'm sorry, ma'am," David breaks in. "All due respect, what the hell does this have to do with the price of peas? If you'll pardon my impertinence."

She gives him a hard look. "I'm comin' to that part, if you'll just be patient with me; my mama always used to say that if words was nickels I'd be a rich girl. Anyway . . . you gotta understand, all the pieces to this puzzle was right in front of me—the torturing of them bikers, the collecting of walkers as though they was bobblehead dolls." She breathes deeply and shakes her head. "One of the RVs we found along the way—it had toys in it. Must have been a rich family and the children must have been spoiled and all, because there was remote control cars and planes and such, rechargeable batteries, cameras, electric guitars, and all kinds of gadgets you would never think you'd have any use for . . . but guess what?"

She glances around the dimly lit tunnel at all the dour faces soaking in her story, and she takes a deep breath. Here it comes.

"Here I am looking at this crazy-ass preacher leading this pack of walkers around like they was square dancers havin' a two-step. He's got this contraption rigged up, a battery-operated tape recorder, and a camera light flickering, and a little remote control car . . . and it's playing a recording of men dying. I swear. I ain't never heard anything like it—the screams of men being tortured to death, and a light blinking like that."

She makes a pulsing gesture with her plump little hand. She shakes her head, but before she can continue, Lilly Caul says what she's thinking in a soft whisper, almost under her breath. "Pavlov . . ."

All heads turn toward Lilly. She feels their hot, nervous gazes on her skin. She says, "*Pavlov* . . . as in Pavlov's dog . . . He's *training* them."

David Stern looks down and barely utters the words, "Can't be done."

"Well, now, see, that's kinda open for debate," Norma counters, "because I saw them walkers following that thing around like sheep following a sheepdog. That preacher's got a remote control—one of them little toggle switches—and he's leading them monsters around like . . . like the damn Wizard of Oz. And that ain't all." She swallows air for a moment. "Couple days later, he's got half the men in the place with him, off on some mission that he wouldn't tell the rest of us about. I was real curious by that point, so I got Miles to drive me out to the barrens, this flat meadow not far from our camp, where the preacher's got an old tow truck."

Miles Littleton, still an unknown quantity to Lilly, mumbles something from his seat behind the plump woman. Lilly can't quite make out what he's saying. He speaks softly, his face downturned, his voice garbled with nerves and self-consciousness.

"Go ahead, Miles," Norma Sutters urges. "You tell 'em what he was doing."

The young man takes a deep breath and looks up. "Okay, so, we been using this tow truck for hauling shit, right? Pulling wreckage off the roads and shit. But when I saw what they was doing with that motherfuckin' truck that night I could *not* believe what I was seeing. They had one them bikers strung up on the back, tied to the tow-arm like a carcass of some dead animal, bleeding and shit, and he was . . . he was still . . . he was making . . ."

The young man falters for a moment, at a loss for words, vexed by the very act of describing what he'd seen. Norma twists around, pats the man's knee, and says, "Take your time, Brother. It's okay."

Miles breathes as he remembers the terrible thing. "This dude was still alive . . . barely. He was screaming like a stuck pig . . . and they had one of them photo strobes blinking . . . and they were driving pretty slowly . . . and then I realized that the swarm was *following* them, the monsters were following that horrible noise of that dude dying . . . and then . . . then I realized what that preacher was doing."

Lilly stares at him. "What the hell was he doing?"

"He was *teaching* them things."

Lilly gapes. "I get that part, I get it, but why? What's the end game? What the *fuck* is he teaching these walkers to *do*?"

For a long while, Miles and Norma just look at each other. In fact, they take so long to get up the nerve to answer that the pause begins to make Lilly and the others in the tunnel that day feel very uncomfortable.

FOURTEEN

The preacher stands alone and unarmed in the purple glow of twilight on the soft, spongy ground of a secluded meadow. The air has grown still at day's end, the chill of night rolling in, the motes of cottonwood tufts drifting lazily through the dying rays of the setting sun. The drone of cicadas and crickets provides a white noise in his head, lulling him into a state of transcendent semiconsciousness, a state of meditative reminiscence.

CLICK-*FLASH!*

Jeremiah blinks, momentarily blinded by the ghostly corona of light lingering for a moment on his line of vision. He blinks again until his eyes adjust. Now he can plainly see that the walkers have surrounded him, some of them close enough to reach out and touch. The black odors and the low snoring of mortified vocal cords weigh down upon him with tremendous force. And yet . . . and *yet* . . . not a single one of the hundred or so reanimated corpses makes a move. It's as though they're idling, stationary, their mind-screens frozen, their calcified, desiccated brains processing some external stimuli for which they have no bandwidth. And this causes Jeremiah to feel ennobled, buoyant, all-powerful standing there, engulfed in the horde like this, surrounded by myriad silhouettes of the dead, the shimmer of a hundred pairs of eyes mesmerized now by something in the sky.

CLICK-*FLASH!*

Amidst the throng, the preacher recognizes a former mail carrier to his immediate left, the thing that was once a man now leaning to one side with its uniform torn and gouged and spilling entrails into the mail sack that still hangs habitually from its emaciated shoulder. It has been carrying its own entrails around like this for months, as if searching for an addressee. Many of the others have now aged and weathered and decomposed to the point of being unrecognizable as anything other than sacks of putrefied flesh that still manage to nominally walk. Someday soon, some of them will collapse and begin to disintegrate into the earth, never once pausing from their autonomic mission to feed. Will their teeth continue to gnash long after the soft tissues have turned to dust?

CLICK-*FLASH!*—CLICK-*FLASH!*—CLICK-*FLASH!!*

Jeremiah holds his ground, standing rock-steady, and he doesn't worry, doesn't panic. He hears his father's voice, the deep whiskey rasp that held him in such horrible awe in the darkness of his bedroom most nights: "*Yea, though I walk through the valley of the shadow of death, I shall fear no evil, for I am the meanest son of a bitch in the valley.*" Jeremiah remembers the time his father had sent away for the beehives—one of the old man's crackpot ideas for augmenting his military retirement pay and pension benefits—turning the backyard of their Jacksonville ranch home into a honeybee colony. Jeremiah had been in the throes of adolescence that summer, and had been acting out, rebelling—drinking and smoking and hanging out with the loose girls from that heathen institution known as Florida State University.

The old man had gotten drunk one night and dragged his only son out to the hives. And what he did to the boy on that hot August night still scars not only the flesh of the preacher's right arm, but the marrow of his soul. The echo of the old man's boozy baritone still reverberates in Jeremiah's dreams. "*Boy, it's high time you learned to inoculate yourself against the temptations of worldly women, the venom of the queen bee.*" Jeremiah remembers starting to scream like a stuck pig as his father gripped his arm and then thrust it down into the guts of the largest hive.

It had felt as though a million needles were penetrating Jeremiah's flesh that night, setting his arm on fire, spreading waves of horrible, hot electric agony up his tendons and nerves. He remembers passing out from the pain a minute later, the fading sound of the old man's voice, "*It's the only way, boy . . . the scourging of the flesh . . . the only way to become immune . . . the only way to withstand the poison of them fast women.*"

CLICK-*FLASH!*—CLICK-*FLASH!*—CLICK-*FLASH!*—CLICK-*FLASH!!*

The intermittent pop of silver light shakes Jeremiah out of his terrible reverie, drawing his attention over his shoulder.

He can see the small crane that rises off the back of the rusty, battered tow truck thirty yards away. He can see the photo-strobe that he'd found in that Chicago family's RV, now duct-taped to the apex of that block and tackle, a beacon flashing, implanting the horde with silent, behavioral triggers, the invisible strings of the puppeteer. The air trembles with the grating, grinding music of human suffering—the screams of the dying—now pouring out of ceramic loudspeakers. It soothes Jeremiah in the strangest of ways—he can feel the mob around him like schools of fish flocking around a living coral reef, ignoring him, brushing past him, spellbound by the noise and the light.

The preacher feels almost safe within this putrid sea of cadavers. He is finally *inside* the hive, and he is immune and he is all-powerful, a messenger from God, the last evangelist on the dying earth.

He remembers the early autumn chill that had swept through Jacksonville that summer, turning the honeybees into sluggish, intoxicated revenants of what they once were. He remembers waking up right after his scourging on the hard ground next to the hive and feeling nothing—a cold, numb, empty sensation spreading through him. He remembers seeing the flesh of his blood-pocked arm where all the stingers had embedded themselves in the skin like the barbs of long-stemmed roses. By that point, it had felt like his arm was asleep, prickling faintly. And yet he harbored no hatred for his father, who still stood over him like a redneck golem, like an angry

Old Testament god. The old man had been smiling. Surely, he was thinking of the life cycle of the honeybees.

When the honeybee stings a person, it can't pull its thorny stinger back out. It leaves behind not only the stinger but also a large part of its abdomen and digestive tract, plus a bundle of muscles and nerves and tissue. This enormous abdominal rupture kills the honeybee, but not before it flutters off into the ether, an engine dieseling long after it's been shut off.

My bees, Jeremiah Garlitz thinks, rather grandly surveying the outer boundaries of the horde that surrounds him. He breathes in the cloud of rubbery, rancid-meat odors, the stench of flesh deteriorated long past its crumbling point. He raises his sinewy arms to the heavens and rejoices: *My bees, my faithful bees . . .*

Late that night she finds him at the end of a side tunnel earmarked as a temporary infirmary.

The air smells of peat and musk, and the minimal light comes from a single battery-powered lantern sitting on a stool at the end of the tributary. At one time a channel for an underground spring, its walls of petrified roots long since worn smooth, its floor of hard-packed earth covered with tarp, the side tunnel now houses the meager sick bay. Makeshift gurneys of wooden planks on carpenters' sawhorses sit along each wall. A metal shelving unit with boxes of gauze, tubes of ointments, cotton tape, and bottles of homemade grain alcohol stands in the corner.

Bob Stookey sits on the floor next to the metal shelves, cross-legged, his head slumped, his back turned to the visitor who approaches cautiously. He hums softly, an old country tune that he's absently mangling. A body draped in a moth-eaten blanket lies on the sawhorse next to him, a pale hand dangling down. Bob clasps the tiny hand in his own, holding it as though comforting a small child rather than a full-grown woman who'd once worn the visor that now sits cradled in Bob's lap.

"Bob?"

Lilly's voice rises barely above a whisper. She can tell what's going on, and the sight of it presses in on her heart like a vise.

"Bob, I'm sorry but we have to talk."

He doesn't say anything. He just keeps humming a song that Lilly suddenly recognizes. Early on, Bob used to always play a George Jones cassette in his big old Dodge Ram pickup, and his favorite tune—one that he had practically worn out—had been "He Stopped Loving Her Today." Now he hums the soggy tearjerker with off-key indifference.

"Bob, we have a situation, and I need to—"

Lilly sees something that stops her in her tracks. Cold panic slithers down her midsection like an icy snake. In setting up the little medical bay, Bob and Lilly had procured several different kinds of antiseptics. One type—rubbing alcohol—they had found in profusion, in fact cases and cases of it, in the rear of the derelict drugstore. Another type Bob had retrieved from the burned, charred husk of the Dew Drop Inn, the Woodbury watering hole that he had frequented during his drinking days. He had remembered seeing bottles of Everclear and grain alcohol behind the bar that had been untouched by fire.

"There's always a situation, Lilly, haven't you noticed?" In Bob's other hand, the one that isn't clutching the hand of the deceased, is a fifth of grain alcohol. He takes another sip and winces at the burn. "We live in a goddamn constant situation."

Lilly's spirit deflates. Almost audibly, her hope and faith in Bob and in Bob's future, and in the future of all of them, drain out of her on a long, agonizing sigh. "Oh, Bob . . . don't do this. C'mon."

He looks down, ashamed. "Leave me be."

"You can't let this destroy you." She gently maneuvers her way past the gurney and sits down on the floor next to him. "There isn't a person here doesn't know what it's like to lose somebody."

He looks everywhere but at her. "I don't need a shrink, I just need to be left alone."

She looks at the floor. Out of the corner of her eye she can see the old cotton visor that Gloria used to wear—so old and worn, the balloon letters spelling out the phrase "I'M WITH STUPID" have faded to shadows—sitting on Bob's lap. Every few seconds he puts the bottle down and caresses the visor as though it's an infant sparrow needing to be nursed back to health. Lilly shakes her head. "She was a great lady."

Bob swallows another gulp. "That's for sure, Lilly-girl." He slurs her name as though it contains an extra "l," then adds, "That's for sure."

"She was a badass."

"Yep."

"We'll have a service."

"That's fine, Lilly-girl. You do that." His voice is flinty now, sharp with thinly veiled rage. "You have a service, I'll make sure to show up."

Lilly takes a deep breath and lets a few moments pass before saying, "I remember when Josh took that shot in the head by the Butcher, I thought I would never see the light of day again. I just figured it was over for me, and there was nothing I could do about it, and why even bother. But I didn't give up, I just figured . . . you know . . . one day at a time."

"Goody for you."

"Bob, c'mon. Don't do this to me."

He gives her a look. "I'm not doing *anything* to *you*. . . . It's not *about* you!" His bark makes her jump. "It's not always *about you*!"

She swallows back the urge to slap him. "That's not even remotely fair."

"Life ain't fair." His voice softens. "It never was . . . and it sure as hell ain't now."

Lilly shakes her head, gazes at the floor, and allows another long, anguished beat of silence to ensue while Bob quietly drinks and stews in his misery. Lilly tries to take deep breaths and figure out how to get him back. She needs him now, maybe more than ever. She starts to say something else but thinks better of it.

Who is she to give advice to this man? Who the fuck does she think she is—trying to be a role model, trying to force a particular mode of behavior on Bob Stookey? Lilly has her own foibles, her own fucking problems. Her nerves are as tightly wired as Bob's, maybe more so. And she's noticed that her temper is quicker, her shaking worse, her nightmares more intense since they've been driven underground.

Almost every time Lilly manages to get a wink of sleep—which is somewhat infrequent since they've been in the tunnels—she weathers a storm of claustrophobic, bloody, inchoate scenarios: bus doors closing on her dead father, her friend Megan dangling on the end of a rope, her former lover Josh lying decapitated in a trench of carnage, and every iteration imaginable of traps, cages, locked chambers, prison cells, and endless, featureless tunnels going nowhere. But the one that recurs the most, the one that truly haunts her, is an almost photo-realistic rendering of that day she killed the baby.

You know it's coming. It always starts the same way. You're ducking down behind a bullet-riddled truck while the air outside that Georgia state prison boils with gunfire. You always rise up the same way: your teeth gritted, your high-powered rifle clutched in sweaty hands, the taste of old pennies in your mouth, and the washed-out sunlight glaring in your eyes as you see the amorphous figure seventy-five yards away, trundling across the hot zone of the prison exercise yard. It always goes down the same rabbit hole. You feel the cold pressure of the scope on your eye, the blurry image behind the crosshairs (an anonymous man with the bomb cradled against his solar plexus). And that huge, greasy, sweat-glistening head with the eye patch yelling at you, *"TAKE THEM OUT, NOW!"*

Always the same. Always. Always the blast in time-lapse that echoes up in the sky, the distant blood mist enveloping two figures— one large, one small—a woman and a baby, their blood mingling in the ether like a sacrament. The anonymous man is a woman. The bomb is a *baby*. You just killed both. In cold blood.

On the whim of a madman.

Lilly closes her eyes and tries to drive the inexorable horrors from her thoughts. "You know what," she says, looking at Bob Stookey. "Gimme some of that."

He looks up at her, his eyes unfocused, bleary, vexed by this turn of events.

"What . . . this?"

"Hand it over." She grabs the bottle away from him. She takes a sip, and the liquid scrapes down her throat like barbed wire, then ignites a fireball in her gut. She flinches, and gulps down the rest. The fourth or fifth swallow turns her tonsils and uvula and soft palate numb.

Bob studies her, watches her shudder at the burning liquid agony. "That's one way to get me to quit," he says with zero humor in his voice.

"Crack another one," she says.

"Yes, ma'am." He turns and pulls another glass bottle from the middle shelf. He twists off the top, and takes a healthy pull. Then he hands it over.

She drinks, wipes her mouth, and looks him in the eye. "We don't have the luxury to grieve anymore. Are you listening to me? Do you understand what I'm saying? That was for the old times."

He nods. "Loud and clear."

Then Lilly tells him exactly what Norma and Miles told her about the preacher.

"I knew we should have finished off that sick fuck when we had the chance," Bob grumbles after processing the whole thing. The bad news seems to sober him slightly, turning him cranky, like a petulant child who's just been awakened prematurely from a nap. "Goddamned Holy Rollers are worse than the fucking biters."

"That's not all of it," Lilly informs him. "The worst part—the part she saved for the end—is what he's got planned for the unveiling of his little grand experiment."

Bob doesn't say anything, just takes another sip of the hooch and waits.

"He's planning an invasion." Lilly levels her gaze at Bob. The liquor has already started to work on her equilibrium, burnishing the edges of her vision with gauzy, soft-focus sunspots.

"An invasion of what?"

"Us."

Bob holds her gaze for a moment, wavering a little as though laboring to maintain his end of the stare-down. "How the hell does he think he's gonna . . . ?"

He stops. They share a glance, and Bob looks away. Lilly can see he's thinking it over, chewing on it; in his drunken state, the realization comes in waves, like a tide rolling in. Finally he looks at Lilly. "Maybe it's time for us to just pack it in, cut our losses."

She scowls at him. "The fuck are you talking about?" Now *she* has added a few consonants, the "f" coming out like "ffffh." She swallows bile. "You talking about surrender? You want to surrender to this maniac? Are you insane?"

"Did I say 'surrender'? I'm not talking about surrender. Cool your jets."

"Then what are you saying?"

Bob rubs his pouchy, bloodshot eyes. "I'm talking about cutting our losses and hightailing it out of here."

Lilly is silent for a moment.

Bob studies her. "I know what you're going to say; I know what you're thinking."

"What am I thinking?"

"You would never abandon your beloved Woodbury to some cracker redneck preacher with a chip on his shoulder. Am I close?"

Lilly looks down. "Something like that." She meets his gaze. "Bob, we can take this guy—we did it once before. We can shut him down, go preemptive on his ass."

"What, a hit squad?"

"Yeah, we could—"

"Now *you're* the one's insane."

"Bob—"

"Listen to me. This yay-hoo is a lot more than some backwoods Bible thumper. He's crazy, and he's the worst kind of crazy—he's *organized*. He can pull the wool over people's eyes. He can marshal large groups. You understand what I'm saying?"

Lilly sighs. The initial rush of intoxication has now transformed into a full-on wave of woozy nausea. She belches silently and feels her stomach acids churning. "Trust me, he can be stopped," she says finally.

"Lilly-girl, sometimes retreat is the best offensive strategy. Scorched earth. We don't leave him shit. And we make sure—"

"No! Stop!" Lilly takes quick breaths in a feeble attempt to stanch the warm knot of nausea tightening her gorge. She shakes her head. "I will not destroy my town for one evil asshole."

"It ain't your town, Lilly. It belongs to all of us."

"Well, right now it belongs to the walkers, and I'm not gonna turn tail and run. That's a chickenshit move, Bob, and you know it."

Bob throws the bottle against the wall. The glass shatters, the liquid exploding. It makes Lilly jump. Bob's voice gets low and taut. "That's right, I'm a chickenshit. I'm a coward. Why? Because I'm a natural born-survivor. It comes with the 'coward' part. Being a fuckin' hero gets you killed." He stares hard at her, pursing his lips bitterly. "Listen, you got a better idea, I'm all ears."

"Yeah, I got a better idea. I say we find this prick and put him down like a rabid dog."

"Lilly, blow the cobwebs outta your head. This guy's surrounded by his little army of followers, plus now it sounds like he's found a way to weaponize the goddamn stiffs. You want to traipse into that, you be my guest. I'm leaving! And I'm taking them kids with me. And whoever else has the common sense to come along, they're welcome to join me."

Lilly kicks the legs of the shelving unit and knocks over a row of bottles, which tumble to the floor, several of them shattering. "Fine! Whatever! Go! I'll deal with this guy myself!"

"Lilly—"

She springs to her feet, nearly knocking over the entire shelving unit. "Go! Take off! What the fuck are you waiting for?!"

"Hold your horses, calm down. . . . " Bob speaks softly now, standing, taking her by the shoulders. "I know you have big dreams for this place, and you see us getting it back one day, and that's great, I get that, but these people don't deserve to die just because one young lady's maybe got a bigger set of balls than everybody else."

"GO!" The volume of her voice makes her stagger, the dizziness and adrenaline and nausea coursing through her all at once, nearly knocking her over. She has to grab the shelf just to steady herself. "Go with God! I'll pack you a fucking lunch!"

Bob faces her with clenched fists, his face reddening with fury. "YOU CAN'T JUST DICTATE—!!"

He abruptly stops. The sound coming from behind them, from the tunnel's entryway, instantly stiffens his back and cuts off his rant. Lilly hears it, too, and it diffuses her rage like a bucket of cold water splashing in her face. She turns and sees Tommy Dupree standing in the opening, silhouetted by the lantern light behind him.

"I know how we can beat them bastards," he says softly, his voice coarse with gravity.

In his father's ratty cardigan sweater, his ruddy little face furrowed with grim determination, Tommy Dupree looks far older than his years. His fists clenched at his side as he stands in the arched opening, his slender form framed by worm-eaten beams and ancient earthen walls, he looks like a miniature sentry in some obscure Hummel diorama. Maybe his time spent in the wild with Lilly has changed him. He seems to have aged years over the course of the last horrible months.

Bob turns and looks at the boy. "I'm sorry, son, I didn't catch that."

Tommy takes a deep breath and repeats what he just said: "I know how we can send each and every one of them shit-bags back to the hell they come from."

Lilly looks at Bob, and then glances back at the boy, and then feels a hot, greasy belch coming as she falls to her knees and roars vomit across the tarp-covered tunnel floor.

PART 3

The Great
Steel Oblivion

"Behold I am sending you out as sheep in the midst of wolves,
so be wise as serpents."

—Matthew 10:16

FIFTEEN

In the carbon black darkness of the clearing, as crickets drone and engines tick in the background, a voice seems to come from thin air, deep and modulated like the voice of a god, disembodied at first as the eyes adjust. "We pretty near lost half our people tonight. . . . Just slipped away under the cover of darkness."

The voice pauses, and the listeners—five men, each in their third decade of life, former laborers and tradesmen, all spooked now as never before—look down at the ground and remain silent.

"I understand the latest ones to leave were the Thorndykes," the voice says, and pauses again, a single orange speck of light from a cigarette glowing brighter as the speaker takes a vigorous drag off a hand-rolled smoke. "The Kentons, too." Another pause. "I understand people are troubled by my . . . *methods* . . . the events of the last few days . . . my *experiments* on them bikers. People don't appreciate my . . . *using* walkers in such a manner."

"Can I say something?" James Frazier speaks up. The young man with the sandy hair scratches the side of his grizzled cheek as he measures his words. He runs fingers through his hair. "It's just . . . some of the folks with kids . . . they get a little nervous with this kinda stuff going on."

"I understand that," Jeremiah Garlitz says with a paternal nod. In the darkness behind the glow of the cigarette, his deeply lined face and prominent jaw give off the feeling of a jack-o'-lantern. "They have every right to abandon the cause, and I wish them all well. Every last one of 'em."

"Look, I'm not saying we don't—"

James abruptly falls silent, his thoughts, the big speech he wanted to make, all of it tumbling down like a house of cards when he hears another surge of atonal screams and growls—hundreds of feral vocalizations—swelling on the night breezes from the east. He glances over his shoulder and takes another reluctant look at the area beyond the circle of trucks and RVs, down a wooded slope and across a vast tobacco field.

In the darkness, it's impossible to make out the details of the throng—except at regular intervals when the strobe flashes. Each time the light flickers, a swath of the super-herd is momentarily illuminated, from this distance looking like a vast leper colony stuck in mid-shamble, a necropolis of the damned, all of them hunched and mesmerized by the noise and light, some of them reaching futilely for the source of this magical pied piper of screams, the sea of mottled, putrid faces a monolithic audience waiting for a play.

After only a couple flashes, James Frazier has to look away, back at his spiritual guide.

"They don't understand what we're up against," the preacher says as he tosses the butt and pushes himself off his perch on the stump. "They don't understand the savagery of these tunnel dwellers."

The preacher ambles over to the edge of the clearing and gazes out at the meadow of the dead, the arrhythmic pulsing and flickering stamping their afterimages on the darkness. His coattails flap in the wind. His big hair tosses. His voice comes out deep and cold. "These people took us in, me and my congregation, what was left of us. Offered us refuge at first. But they had no intention of giving us solace and succor."

He turns and gazes at James and the four other men. Chester Gleason looks up from the ground, his eyes gleaming with nervous tension. "What'd they do?"

"They began to kill us, one by one," the preacher utters in a low tone, the lies flowing off his tongue. "The idea was to feed us to the swarm outside the walls of their town. Use our bodies as fodder, as bait, as a way to keep the herd at bay. They were going to slaughter all of us." He looks at each man now, and the way he fixes each of them in his smoldering gaze makes James Frazier look away at the dark horizon. "They did it before, and they'll do again . . . do it to some poor unassuming family that hobbles into their web." The preacher pauses and lets out a sigh. He kicks the dirt. "I understand if y'all don't want to be a part of this mission that I have been charged with by God."

"We didn't say that," Chester murmurs mildly as he stares at the ground.

The preacher takes a step closer to the men. "In the book of Revelation it says, 'He that leadeth into captivity shall go into captivity; he that kills with the sword must be killed with the sword.'"

Chester keeps looking at the ground, but he's starting to nod.

"I'm going to bring the medicine for these people in the form of the dead, an army of the damned—*an eye for an eye.*" Another big dramatic pause. "Gonna make damn sure these people never victimize another survivor again. Gonna take that town back in the name of the Lord, and whoever wants to be along for the ride is welcome to stay with me. Whoever wants to leave has my blessing."

Now Jeremiah turns his back on them, and appears to be pondering the flickering horde in the distance. But what he's really doing is waiting.

He doesn't have to wait long.

The next afternoon, the caravan sets out on its grandiose mission in earnest. The ten remaining vehicles cut a swath of dust and carbon monoxide up the Interstate 75 basin, avoiding the petrified wreckage blocking much of the four-lane by traveling single file along the arid ditches running parallel to the shoulder. The three heavy-duty trucks lead the convoy, setting the glacial pace at about three miles an hour. The five RVs rumble along behind them, some of their roofs occupied by gunmen armed with sniper rifles.

Jeremiah's command center—the rust-spotted, eggshell-colored Winnebago formerly owned by Father Patrick Murphy—rolls along near the end of the procession, fishtailing over intermittent patches of decomposing remains, throwing a wake of dust and rotting organic matter off its massive rear wheels. Behind the Winnebago rattles the big tow truck, with its enormous rear crane, its gigantic twin rear tires crunching through the detritus. They pass a mile marker, its battered green facing faded and bullet-riddled.

They are exactly thirty-five miles from the town of Woodbury, Georgia. At this pace, their estimated time of arrival would be dawn the next day.

Very few of the drivers or passengers in the caravan keep close watch on the sea of shadows behind the tow truck. Every so often, on the shifting winds, they hear the watery, creaking chorus of growls, and the fading screams of the prisoner. If they chose to do so, they could catch a glimpse in their peripheral vision of the long shadows of countless shambling bodies. The mob is growing. With each passing hour, more and more of the dead come out from behind dilapidated, derelict barns and groves of sickly oak trees and piles of overturned cars. Most of the convoy's members are somewhat disturbed by this spectacle, but these are the repressed, the sheep, the stalwart. They now have their own flashing strobe light, in the form of Reverend Jeremiah Garlitz.

At this moment, in fact, this volatile guiding force sits on a bunk in the rear of his RV, while his minions, Reese and Stephen, take turns at the wheel.

Jeremiah sits barefoot, in shirtsleeves and trousers, gazing into a small rectangular mirror that he has canted against the headboard. Using a disposable razor and skin lotion, he carefully shaves the last nubs of hair from his head, leaving behind a pale dome of mottled skin, as smooth as a peach. He believes now, like the monastic clergy of yore, that he must shed all his pride and vanity and worldly possessions before he leads his flock into battle. He ponders his blotchy, reddened face. Aside from the psoriasis, he looks very presentable.

He finishes, wipes his scalp with a towel, and then moves to the window embedded in the rear door—a slat of grimy glass no wider than a necktie—and peers out. In the ashen sunlight, he can see the throngs of his new congregation.

They are hundreds strong, their styles of clothing, their facial features, even their genders, worn away by the rot and ruin of maggots and weather and time. They move almost as one, brushing against each other languidly, twitching in the pale sun, bumping shoulders and snarling in excruciating, oblivious hunger, the hundreds of sets of teeth visible even at this distance, like tiny kernels of white corn in the rotten husks of their faces.

Silver light blinks across their rank and file, apparent in even the bright daylight, flashing with metronomic regularity—the strings of the puppeteer—and accompanied by the echoes of human suffering.

The onyx-colored tow truck spews a swirling fog bank of smoke from the homemade biodiesel, the miasma rising out of its vertical stack, curling around, and engulfing the rear of the truck, where the human bait writhes in agony on its sacrificial gantry. The subject is the last of the surviving bikers—a big, pear-shaped, bearded Viking with teardrop tattoos and enormous sagging pectorals—now reduced to a sobbing mess in his shit-stained underwear and bloody, lacerated skin. A loop of barbed wire is wound around his expansive belly, gathered behind him, and connected to a winch. Each time his shrieking fades and deteriorates to garbled sobbing, the tow truck driver thumbs the winch button and the barbed wire tightens slightly, eliciting more agony.

The previous subject had not been as boisterous, and had died prematurely, the shrieking going silent shortly after the winch had literally cut the man in half. But the preacher had learned from the fiasco, and now the pressure is being applied with great moderation, calibrated for optimum pain rather than catastrophic injury. Plus, the Viking's girth should provide hours and hours of racket, the slow bleed-out unlikely to kill the man for at least a day or two. The preacher had found that the beasts responded better to live sound than recorded.

He turns away from the window and wipes the last spot of lotion from his gleaming, shaved head. He tosses the towel, looks around the RV's cabin, and decides to rest. Tomorrow will be a big day. He sees his Bible on a shelf above the sleeping berth to his left, tented open to Revelations, the chapters and verse he had been studying the previous night. He picks up the worn black book and lies down and continues reading about dragons and horsemen and slaughtered lambs and angels clothed in clouds and the number 666.

At length, he falls into a deep and profound sleep and dreams he's sitting on a stone bench on the edge of a precipice overlooking a valley of scorched, burned, blackened woods. He wears a tunic, as though from another time. The wind tosses his hair.

"Are you my son?"

The voice comes from behind him, a soothing, oily voice . . . the kind of voice one would expect a snake or a lizard to have if snakes or lizards could talk.

Jeremiah turns and sees a tall, dark man in a long black robe. The man's face is gaunt, sunken, cadaverous, his long coal black hair loose. His yellow eyes seem to absorb not only the light but all the energy around them. A pair of knoblike polyps extrude off the top of his skull like horns. His smile makes Jeremiah's flesh crawl.

"I've never even met you," Jeremiah finally replies in a breathless, nervous whisper. Then he says, "I have a church—I'm tax-exempt."

The tall man glides over to the bench, takes a seat next to Jeremiah. "I bid you greetings at long last."

"Are you . . . ?"

The tall man nods. At this close proximity, his flesh looks iridescent, like the scales of a fish. He smells of smoke and embers. "I am indeed," he purrs. "You once thought of me as your adversary."

"You're the Enemy . . . ?"

The man raises a tapered index finger, its nail sharpened to the point of a claw. "Ironically, no. I am no longer the enemy. I am merely a cog in the machine of prophecy."

"Prophecy?"

The man nods. "You are the son, the follower of fate, and this is the Rapture, and it is your destiny to turn the entire human race."

Jeremiah doesn't understand. "Turn them to Jesus?"

The laughter that tumbles out of the tall man recalls a million barking hyenas. "Oh, dear, no . . . That's adorable. Your destiny is no longer to proselytize Christianity. That ship has sailed." More oily laughter. "On the contrary, your destiny is to turn every human being into the walking dead, each and every last soul."

"This is my destiny," Jeremiah repeats as though learning a lesson in school.

The tall man puts his arm around Jeremiah, the touch of the man's hand like a cold compress. "It is written, you shall be the last of the human race, the last true human on earth. You shall rule the hordes as a king. You shall become a god in human form."

In the dream, Jeremiah jerks back with a start when he realizes the tall man has his father's bulbous, ulcerated nose, his father's droopy, bloodshot eyes, his father's crow's-feet and cleft chin and five o'clock shadow, and Jeremiah opens his mouth to say something but nothing comes out.

His father smiles.

Barbara Stern hurriedly gathers the six children at the end of the main tunnel near the west exit. She catches her breath, adjusts the straps of her pack, then pulls her unruly gray curls back into a ponytail and quickly snaps a rubber band around the hank of hair. Clad in her anachronistic floral-print muumuu with the gun belt around her midsection, Barbara surveys her young charges. "All right, here's the deal." She speaks to the kids in her patented tone, a mixture of two parts den mother and one part drill instructor, and she fiddles with her gun belt as she talks, securing the cumbersome pistol with its long suppressor into the holster. "We're going to go up top on a little adventure."

"Like a field trip?" Tiff Slocum asks with wide-eyed wonder. One of two identical twins, the cherubic little eight-year-old girl wears the same soiled jumper as her sister, Mercy Slocum. The two girls have been compulsively wearing the things since the group went underground. Weeks ago, Barbara had discovered a forgotten box of hand-me-downs in the courthouse basement earmarked for Goodwill, and had brought different outfits into the tunnels, but the twins insisted on dressing in the same threadbare jumpers every day of their lives from that point on, forever and ever, amen. They claim the blue gingham jumpers are good luck, and had informed Barbara of this just this morning.

"*Exactly* like a field trip," Barbara replies, cupping her hand around Tiff's little cheek and giving the girl an encouraging smile.

"What are we studying?" little Lucas Dupree asks, his blond bangs, badly in need of a trim, dangling down across his big doe eyes. He clutches at his sister's dress, as he's been doing all day. In fact, Lucas and Bethany Dupree have been clinging to each other, practically without a break, from the moment they were brought into the tunnels. Still shell-shocked from the loss of both of their parents, they are indispensable to each other, and that's fine with Barbara. She needs all the comfort and succor for these children she can get, and she'll get it wherever she can find it.

"We're studying how to survive an attack," Barbara says, choosing not to mince words. "Now, I want everybody to follow me in a single file. Do you all remember what that means? 'Single file'?"

In the back, Jenny Coogan shoots her little hand up as though sitting in the fourth grade back at Marietta Park Elementary. The little girl wears thick eyeglasses, one of the lenses cracked. "It means, like, walking in like a single line?"

"Everybody knows what 'single file' means!" Tyler Coogan snaps at his sister, making an exaggerated, dramatic gesture of complete exasperation with his sibling's colossal ignorance. The ten-year-old wears OshKosh jeans and a Braves baseball cap and looks like the Campbell's Soup Kid. He shakes a lot, which breaks Barbara's heart. It's one thing to see an adult trembling like this, whether it's illness, terror, the cold, or withdrawal . . . but it's quite another to see a child this age with a chronic case of the shakes. Somehow, it puts something that Barbara can't quite come to terms with in perfect perspective—whatever that perspective might imply. She's not sure. But she knows it's not good.

"Okay, enough with the squabbling." Barbara claps her hands and then points at her eyes. "Look at me. Everybody, look at me. I'm going to climb up and make sure the coast is clear, and then I want you all to follow me quickly, quietly, in an orderly fashion, and try not to talk unless it's absolutely necessary. Okay? Everybody clear on that? We good?"

Most of the children give her earnest nods or shrugs, except Tyler, who has his hands on his little hips, his petulant expression suddenly puzzled. "There's no coast in the middle of Georgia. What coast are you talking about?"

Barbara gives the boy a look. "I'm lost. What are you referring to?"

"You said—"

"Oh, right, right. Very astute. That's correct—there's no coast up there." She pats the boy on the shoulder. "But there's walkers, so I want you to follow me quickly and quietly, okay?"

"Sure, whatever." The boy shrugs, trying to keep himself from shaking by thrusting his hands in his pockets. "You already said that."

"Okay, so right now I'm going to climb up there, and I want you all to make a line and keep your eyes on me and wait for the signal." She looks around at all the little faces. The fear is so thick it seems to pollute the air. Barbara manages a smile. "Here goes."

She turns and maneuvers her feet into the steps embedded in the petrified hardpack of the wall.

She climbs. The manhole cover is locked in place by vise clamps that Bob procured from the ruins of Woodbury Paint and Wallpaper. The moisture tends to rust and congeal everything in the tunnels within days, and Barbara has to struggle a bit with the clamps in order to loosen them. She grunts and finally loosens the lid, then feels the half dozen pairs of young eyes on her as she pushes it up and partially open.

The fecund odors of the forest and the acrid stench of the dead greet her, wafting on the afternoon breeze. It's almost six o'clock and the daylight has faded to an indigo glow behind the trees.

"Okay, listen up, people," Barbara whispers over her shoulder to the kids. "When I say go, everybody follow Bethany up the ladder."

She glances back outside at the immediate area—a narrow clearing in the woods bordered by thickets of creeping vines and foliage—and it appears to be walker-free at the moment. About a hundred yards away, through a break in the trees, Barbara can see her destination: *the main building of the derelict train station.*

"All right . . . ready, set, go!"

She pushes the manhole the rest of the way open, and the iron lid flops to the dirt. She climbs out and pauses on the edge of the opening. She pulls the .45 tactical pistol with its four-inch suppressor (originally taken off the remains of one of the Governor's men) out of its holster, thumbs the safety off, and sets it to single action. Now *she's* shaking. She can hear the distant dead getting agitated. Twigs snapping nearby. Her post-outbreak gun skills—if not the accuracy of her aim—have improved dramatically, but she wants to avoid having to shoot in front of the kids if at all possible.

Bethany Lucas is the first child to emerge, peering nervously over the lip of the hole. Barbara helps the little girl wriggle the rest of the way up, and then assists her little brother, who comes out still clutching the tail of Bethany's Hello Kitty sweatshirt. Barbara motions for Bethany to stay put and whispers, "Stay right there, honey, until I get everybody else out."

Bethany crouches down, her little brother beside her, furiously sucking his thumb.

Barbara gives her a reassuring nod and whispers, "It's okay, just stay there until we get everybody out." She turns back to the hole. The others come out one by one. The Slocum twins emerge, wide-eyed, scanning the woods in fits and jerks. Tiff Slocum looks as though she's already hyperventilating. Barbara strokes the girl's shoulder and points to a spot on the mossy ground behind Bethany and Lucas. "Girls, just stay right over there for a second."

Jenny Coogan comes out next. She has a tragic look on her face, her lips pressed together tightly, chin jutting, fists clenched, eyes glassy with fear. Barbara can tell the poor little thing is fighting a losing battle with her fears, but God bless her, she's trying. That's all Barbara can ask of anyone. Just try to be fucking brave and get the fucking job of survival *done.*

"Okay, everybody, look at me now, and remember what I told you earlier," Barbara addresses the gaggle of children in a low whisper after the last of them, Tyler Coogan, has emerged and shoved the manhole cover back across the top of the aperture, then quickly brushed dirt across the lid to camouflage it as best he can. Barbara whispers, "We're going to hurry—but not too fast—across that train track to the building on the other side."

A shadow looms behind little Tyler, something slithering out of the foliage.

Things start happening quickly. Barbara can't get off a shot quick enough to neutralize the sudden attack, and the biter lunges at Tyler. It's a gangly middle-aged male in farmer's overalls with a sunken skull, milky white eyes, and flesh weathered to the consistency of parchment. It snaps its jaws at the empty space that Tyler's foot occupied a moment ago before being yanked out of harm's way.

One of the girls lets out a piercing little wail, as shrill as a teakettle whistling, and a switch goes off inside Barbara: *That's it—cover blown—now it's a race.* There are more screams as Tyler kicks at the monster. Barbara fires at the thing—the blast of her Charter Arms .44 Bulldog making a thin, muffled pop, like a wet firecracker—and the tree behind the creature erupts. *C'mon, Annie Oakley,* she thinks frantically. Tyler scoots away as fast as his little butt and legs can carry him. The walker claws at the boy, snagging a piece of his Osh-Kosh jeans. Barbara fires again. The blast chews a chunk out of the thing's shoulder, barely fazing it, hardly slowing it down. But her third shot hits the bull's-eye, creating a trough through the crown of the thing's skull and punching through half its rotting frontal lobe.

Pink soupy fluid gushes out the back of its head as it deflates and collapses.

Tyler scurries into Barbara's arms. She catches him and hugs him to her breast, and lets him silently sob for a moment, but only a moment. The shift in the tide of shadows behind the trees all around them can be felt more than seen, can barely be heard under the rustle of the wind through the pine boughs. "That was a badass move on your part," Barbara soothes the little boy in her arms. "But now, the thing is, we have to move even faster."

He looks up at her through tears. "What are we waiting for?!"

In Olympic track and field, a gold medalist can traverse a hundred yards in a little under ten seconds. A high school track star can do it in maybe eleven seconds flat, perhaps a little less. But on *this* day, as the dusk begins to close in on the outskirts of Woodbury, and the horde—drawn to the noise of terrified squealing—surrounds the children, Barbara's gaggle charges across that weed-whiskered lot toward the train station with a purpose far more intense than that of those competing in a track meet. There is no official record-keeping for preschoolers running the hundred-yard dash, but if there were, one would have a difficult time dissuading Barbara Stern that each and every one of her kids now deserves a medal.

They reach the side door of the ancient wood-sided edifice at the same moment the horde crosses the adjacent tracks and starts toward the fresh young meat in their midst. Tiff and Mercy Slocum begin jumping up and down in panic, and Lucas goes deeper into himself and the folds of his sister's sweatshirt. Barbara refrains from looking over her shoulder—she's too busy fishing for a key in her dress pocket, while recalling that the last time she visited this building, the Governor was in charge of things around here, and they were using the station warehouse for the safekeeping of valuables and confiscated items. Barbara finds the key, thrusts it into the lock, turns the tumblers, and throws open the door.

They pour into the building one at a time, some of them tripping over discarded packing straps and trash on the floor. A few of them tumble and fall. Barbara brings up the rear and slams the door shut behind her.

She lets out a heavy sigh of relief as the thudding noises of walkers bumping into the door and brushing up against the boarded windows start reverberating. Barbara pulls the shade down on the barred door-window and leans back against the wall, another sigh issuing out of her. The kids help one another up, some of the younger ones still whimpering. Barbara asks if everybody's okay, and she gets nods all around from the little troupers.

Catching her breath, Barbara drops her pack—heavy with her extra ammo, batteries, a walkie-talkie, and provisions—and then regards the dusty room.

The high ceiling has long fluorescent fixtures that haven't seen power in over a year. The tall windows on the west side of the room are boarded on the outside, painted over with black Rust-Oleum on the inside, the air permeated with sour-smelling must. Boxes and crates rise to the rafters on all sides, some of the stacks forming aisles down the center of room, where more crates and pallets brim with forgotten riches such as oil paintings, cash drawers from store registers, home safes, wardrobes draped with furs, and all sorts of expensive knickknacks, ivory, fine china, and heirlooms.

Barbara shakes her head as she takes a closer look at the center aisle. She remembers the Governor scouring the abandoned homes along Bartee and Narnina Streets, trolling for valuables that might be of use if the apocalypse ever slouched to an end. Barbara remembers thinking it was sick, and thinking of Hitler harvesting gold teeth from the dead.

She reaches down and opens a velvet-lined jewelry box. Inside the compartments lie the tarnished and gleaming worldly treasures of some long-forgotten Southern dowager. Barbara picks up a tiny diamond-encrusted broach in the shape of a uniformed black attendant, a racist symbol reminiscent of little black lawn jockeys— "Pickaninny Pins," they used to call them—and it brings on a wave of unexpected emotion. She shakes her head some more as she throws the ridiculous lavaliere back in the ridiculous jewelry box.

"Listen up, everybody!" She doesn't take her eyes off the jewelry box. "I want everybody to move to the other side of the room where there are no windows. Do it now, please. . . . No talking, just move!"

The kids drift to the far side of the room, each of them wide-eyed, nervous, jittery. Bethany Dupree takes charge and motions for Lucas and the younger kids to hurry up. They all crowd together under a huge Regulator clock that stopped at midnight many months earlier and will probably never tell the correct time again.

Barbara pulls the .44, double-checks the safety, and calls out, "I want everybody to go ahead and cover your ears!" The four-inch suppressor apparatus—contrary to what the movies say—does not completely silence a pistol; it only suppresses the blast, taking it down a few decibels from its normal harsh, sibilant boom.

She fires a single shot into the jewelry box, sending shards of wood, velvet, stainless steel, and precious gemstones up into the air.

The echo finally dies down, and then an avalanche of silence presses down on the warehouse. The kids freeze—gaping, terrified. Barbara sighs. She holsters her gun, then turns and walks over to the side door.

She pushes the shade aside a couple centimeters and peers outside at the grounds, the far outskirts of Woodbury, the wall off to the right, and the rooftops of the town buildings beyond the barricade. "I know you are all too smart, too grown-up, and too brave to be treated like babies." She says this loud enough for the kids to hear her, but she doesn't take her eyes off the horde of walking corpses outside in the setting sun, crowding the train yard and milling about the town's welcome sign. "Am I right?"

A few of them—Bethany Dupree, the Coogans—mumble affirmatively.

"Then I'll give it to you straight. There's a war coming. Not a play war, not a pretend war—a real one. It's not a game." She turns and looks at them. "We have a job to do. We need to be very, very quiet— above all other things—no matter what happens. Do you understand?"

They tell her they understand.

She nods. "Good." She looks back out the gap between the barred window and the shade. "Good." She thinks about it. "No talking unless it's absolutely necessary. No laughing, no fighting."

She hears one of the kids approaching her, the footsteps cautious, hesitant. Bethany Dupree stands beside her. "Mrs. Stern?"

"Call me Barb."

"Okay . . . Barb? Can I ask you a question?"

Barbara looks at the child, looks into those soft, guileless blue eyes. "Of course, honey."

"Who are we fighting? The walkers?"

Barbara nods. "Yeah . . . sort of."

The girl licks her lips. "We're gonna have a war with the walkers?"

"Yes."

The girl thinks for a moment. "But . . . haven't we already been doing that?"

Barbara ponders the question, then looks back out at the multitude of ragged figures shambling aimlessly about the outskirts in the dusky light. When she speaks again, it is in a lower register, her voice shot through with grave foreboding. "Not like this, sweetie . . . not like this."

SIXTEEN

"FUCK!" Miles Littleton kicks the brake pedal and skids the Challenger across a weathered macadam in the middle of Thomaston Woods. He comes to a screeching halt on a hairpin that sits at the top of Mullins Hill. His headlights throw two beams of silver through the foggy, dense wall of birches in front of him. His heart races. His mouth is dry. He stares as he registers what he's seeing.

He slams the shift lever into park, leaves the engine running, and gets out. He pads across the shoulder, down a gravel slope, and through about fifteen feet of oily-dark forest, batting away the gnats and vines and slender pine boughs that claw him in the face. He comes to a gap in the undergrowth, and peers out through the opening.

In the distance, down in a vast patchwork of fallow brown tobacco fields, in the pale moonlight, he sees the shadows of the slow-moving motorcade. From this distance, illuminated by the pinpricks of light from torches and headlamps, the convoy vehicles look as tiny as figures in an ant farm, and harmless—almost festive—as they churn westward, traveling in a narrow, single-file formation in the center median of Highway 74 like a radiant yellow string of fireflies.

It takes a moment for the shapes behind the last of the vehicles to register in Miles's brain.

At first, it just looks like the wind is blowing up gouts of black earth into the atmosphere behind the caravan, or that perhaps he's looking at a vast bank of fog rolling in, or that maybe it's just his eyes playing tricks. He curses himself for not bringing the binoculars. What the fuck was he thinking? Things are moving very fast, and shit is slipping through the cracks. But there's nothing he can do about it now.

He squints. Swallows hard. *Is that . . . ? No . . . it can't be. No fucking way.* But the more he stares at that enormous carpet of moving shadows behind the convoy's rear end, the more he comes to terms with it. "Holy fucking shit," he murmurs, and turns away from the scene.

Cobbling up the slope, his heart hammering in his chest, he rushes back to his ride. He throws open the driver's door and rifles through the contents of the passenger seat, grabbing the RadioShack walkie-talkie.

He presses the Send button. "Yo! Sister-girl? You there?" He lifts up the button and hears nothing, not even static. He presses it again. "Yo! YO! Norma! Lilly! Anybody! Y'all hear me?!"

Nothing. Not a single crackle of static or hiss of white noise.

He looks at the back of the device, opens the tray, and dumps out the single nine-volt battery. He looks at it. The terminals are corroded. It looks ancient. "Goddamn motherfucking batteries!"

He tosses the worthless two-way radio into the backseat, and he revs the engine. He grips the shift knob, slams the level down into drive, and nudges the foot-feed. The transmission engages, and the car lurches, pressing him into the seat.

Heading back down the hill, swerving around abandoned wrecks, Miles listens to the ticking clock in his brain and does the math. Woodbury lies seventeen miles to the west. At the rate the convoy is going, they'll reach the town in eight to ten hours.

The attack will come at first light the next morning.

Bob Stookey has the shakes. He does his best to deal with them as he power-walks as fast as his arthritic legs will carry him through the narrow, leprous channel of ancient Georgia clay, his flashlight bouncing off the rusty earthen darkness that plunges ahead of him into the void. He's in a hurry, ignoring the tremors.

He has a job to do.

The tunnel wends its way east toward Elkins Creek, and with each passing support beam it gets shaggier and shaggier with stalactites of roots and calcium deposits hanging down like chandeliers. The passageway—once a zinc mine—feels as though it closes in on a person the farther west he goes, like it's a giant gullet swallowing all who dare to traverse its depths.

Currently Bob can't tell if this phenomenon is imaginary or real, but he currently *can* detect a quickening of his pulse and a feeling that his pack is getting heavier and heavier the deeper he penetrates the mine shaft. His boots squeak rhythmically on the stony floor, and his breath wheezes out of him with the syncopated huff of a lame horse. Because his hands are greasy with cold sweat he can barely hold on to the flashlight, but that's okay. Lives depend upon his getting to the cave-in, and he won't let his relapse get in the way of his mission.

They say your first reaction is the truest. They say your original thought, your initial gut feeling, is *always* the correct course of action. But when Bob heard the boy laying out his plan—a deceptively simple way of not only fighting back, but fighting back hard and decisively—he experienced a wave of emotion. The Dupree boy reminds Bob of some of the young Marines he patched up over in the Middle East so many years ago—not in specific ways but in the intangibles: the way young men will go inside themselves when threatened, the way a street fighter will get that cobra calm before striking out with feral intensity. The boy had looked almost dreamy as he'd proposed the insane stages of his strategy.

The more Bob thinks about it, the more it makes sense. Choose your favorite cliché: You fight fire with fire. Take the battle to the enemy. A strong defense is a strong offense. Remember the fucking Alamo.

He stops for a moment, ears ringing, guts burning with nausea. He digs in his pocket and finds his medicine—the battered metal flask a remnant of his hard drinking days after the death of Megan Lafferty—and he thumbs off the cap. He takes a quick swig. Not too much. Just enough to keep the trembling under control. Like methadone. It's funny. Bob used to joke with the Governor that he needed his medicine to get through the day. Now the alcohol is serving as just that: *medicine*. For the last twenty-four hours, Bob had secretly been treating his condition with measured doses of hooch. There's no pleasure in it, no high, no buzz . . . just a constant leveling of his nerves, like outboard directional jets on a spacecraft.

Bob knows this is the only way. Otherwise he would either drink himself into oblivion or go through the horrible symptoms of withdrawal again—the delirium tremens—resulting in seizures and dry heaves. Either way, he would be no good to anybody right now. So he calibrates and administers these sips at regular intervals, and he focuses on the task at hand. He replaces the cap and continues on.

He makes a turn and starts to see the telltale signs of a stream carving its way above him through the earth—in the beam of his flashlight, the icicles of sandstone and calcium dangle down, growing longer and longer, the roots glistening with moisture and the barnacles of mold clinging to the formations. He notices the air getting more and more fetid and musty, like the inside of a rotten gourd. He shines his light on an object looming straight ahead.

In the murk of the flashlight beam, the overturned coal car looks like a fossilized baby carriage lying upside down—the landmark Bob remembers from the last time he came here, ironically to rescue that bug-fuck crazy preacher and his flock of followers. Bob knows the creek is above him. He picks up his pace.

As he trundles along, he pulls the walkie-talkie from his belt. Thumbing the Send button, he says, "Hey Lilly-girl, you got your ears on?"

Nothing but static.

He thumbs the button. "Can you hear me? Lilly? It's Bob. Over?"

Through the sizzle of bad reception, he hears a ghostly wisp of a voice: *". . . Go ahead, Bob. . . . "*

"I'm coming up on the cave-in."

". . . Good, Bob, set it up as quickly as possible. . . . "

"Copy that."

He puts the walkie back on his belt, and stops suddenly. His heart pounds. He hears a noise. He clicks off the flashlight. The tunnel plunges into darkness. Radiant fireflies swim in his field of vision, a faint blur of purple methane glowing as his eyes adjust. He pulls his .357 Magnum and carefully flicks the safety off. Then presses the flashlight against the barrel and clicks it back on. The beam reveals a slight curve in the tunnel fifty feet ahead of him. He remembers the turn from the last time he visited this area, and the cave-in that lies just beyond it.

He can hear the watery vocalizations of a biter, faint but unmistakable, coming from somewhere in the darkness just around the bend. He carefully moves forward, holding the flashlight against the revolver. The noise rises. He shuffles cautiously around the corner and suddenly comes to a halt.

The cave-in that occurred only a couple of months ago lies thirty feet away from Bob in the oval pool of the flashlight beam. The forty-five-degree slope of loose earth blocking the tunnel is the color of mildew, and a single reanimated corpse protrudes from its center as though it's a prisoner yoked and bound by stocks. Only its hairless, mottled head and part of its shoulders stick out of the dirt, and the confinement somehow seems to be eternally agitating it.

Bob approaches it with a sigh. "Look what we have here," he says under his breath.

Snarling noisily, its iridescent eyes widening at the glare of a flashlight in its face, it bites at the space in front of Bob.

"Something I want you to know," Bob says. He presses the barrel against the creature's forehead. At this close proximity, with Bob standing only inches away from the thing, the smell is overwhelming, its flesh the consistency of spackling compound, as pallid as bread dough. It's not often Bob gets a chance to address one of these things in such an intimate fashion—just the two of them, close quarters, smelling each other. "Her name was Gloria Pyne," Bob informs the creature, then squeezes off a single blast that blows a divot through the top of its skull.

Magnified by the enclosed space, the roar deafens Bob for a moment.

He jumps back, trying to avoid the flood of black cerebro-spinal fluid gushing down into the dirt as the thing's ruined head and shoulders instantly sag and hang lifeless in the merciless beam of light. Bob spits. He scowls at the ventilated scalp, the decaying mass of brain matter now visible and glistening inside the gaping hole in the bone and dermal layers.

In his life, Bob Stookey has never felt such hatred deep in his marrow.

The muffled sound of other cadavers milling about behind the wall of loose earth shakes Bob out of his daze. He swallows the grief welling up in him—just his mere mention of Gloria's name, spoken aloud in this lonely, godforsaken tunnel, has put the squeeze on his heart—and he spits again, shaking it off, taking a deep breath. "Don't worry, folks, I haven't forgotten you."

Time to get down to business. He carefully shrugs off his pack and sets it gently on the ground. He unzips it, fishes around, and gingerly pulls out the wooden cigar box with the words "DYNO NOBEL" stenciled on the sides. He crouches, shines the flashlight on it, and opens the lid. The sticks are nestled in sawdust.

"Got a message from Gloria for ya," Bob murmurs under his breath as he pulls the first stick of dynamite from the box he and Gloria found in the mining office. He rises up and carefully inserts the dull end of the stick into the cave-in wall near the ceiling.

He inserts three more sticks into the cave-in at key junctures along the ceiling, then winds the ancient safety fuse from blasting cap to blasting cap. There's no telling if the fuse is viable; God only knows how long the stuff was down there in that mining office. Bob's not even sure if it'll ignite the explosives. Nor is he certain the caravan will pass this way en route to Woodbury. It's all guesswork at this point, but what else can they do?

He inserts a half dozen more sticks into the dirt ceiling. Then he unwinds the fuse-coil along the tunnel about fifty feet or so and finds a bucket on which to sit. He sits down, and he pulls his walkie-talkie. "Okay, it's all set. Over."

A moment later, Lilly's faint voice crackles through the static: "*. . . Okay, stand by. . . .*"

Bob says, "Will do," then releases the button and puts the walkie back on his belt.

Then he waits.

And waits.

Miles Littleton yanks the wheel and careens off River Cove Road, then rushes headlong down a narrow dirt path that winds through the dark woods, his headlamps sweeping across dense walls of foliage, the vibrations rattling his bones and making the rear end of the Challenger fishtail in the dirt. The muscle car throws a tidal wave of dust behind it as it roars toward the grove of trees outside the tunnel entrance.

Normally—as instructed by Lilly—Miles would park about a mile away, where the fleet of vehicles used by the tunnel dwellers lies hidden under the cover of thick live oaks. But time is of the essence now, and he can't spare the fifteen-minute walk from the fleet to the tunnel entrance.

He slams on the brakes just as the car rounds the final curve.

The inertia sucks him forward, throwing debris, as the Challenger goes into a sideways skid. He jerks the wheel into the skid, expertly preventing the massive, low-slung sedan from going into a spin. The car scrapes to a noisy stop a thousand feet south of the tunnel entrance near a dry riverbed.

Miles lets out a tense breath, throws the door open, and leaps out.

He charges through the shadows until he comes to the ragged red bandanna on the stick, barely visible in the darkness. He sees the string sticking out of the ground, tied to a stump, and he grabs and pulls. "Hey! Lilly! Norma! It's me!"

He waits.

"Yo! YO! Folks! Let me in! It's Miles!" He tries to pry open the manhole cover, but they have the clamps in place, the tunnels on high alert. He knocks. "Yo!—People!—LET ME IN!"

The ground around the manhole vibrates slightly as somebody pulls off the clamps and pushes it open. All at once, Lilly Caul's sweaty face appears in the darkness below, and her arm shoots up, and she clutches the collar of Miles Littleton's worn hoodie. "Jesus Christ, Miles, you're going to draw the whole fucking swarm!"

He climbs down the embedded steps behind her and hops down onto the hardpack floor of the tunnel. The impact sends stars across his field of vision, and he's momentarily blind in the gloomy atmosphere of the underground. He hears Norma's voice.

"What in the love of Christ is going on? Wasn't you supposed to radio in?"

"Goddamn batteries," Miles says between heaving breaths, blinking as his eyes adjust.

Lilly's voice is closer. "Didn't we check them?"

"I don't think so." Miles leans down with his hands on his knees as he catches his breath. He can see Lilly Caul standing over him with an ammo magazine in one hand, a walkie-talkie in the other. Miles looks at her. "Them damn things were shot, leaking shit all over the insides of the radio. Walkie was dead as fuck."

"Damnit, I told Bob we should've—" Lilly starts to say when Miles speaks up.

"They're closer than we thought. *Dude.* I think they're gonna be here by sunup."

Lilly looks at him. "What?" She licks her lips, looks around the narrow chamber of petrified earth and ancient pilings. By this point, Tommy Dupree, David Stern, and Harold Staubach have each heard the commotion and have come over to stand behind Lilly with tense expressions. Speaking almost to herself, Lilly says, "That's like, what . . . like an *hour* from now?"

Miles shrugs and meets her gaze, but he doesn't say anything.

David Stern compulsively wrings his hands. He wears a black windbreaker with the Falcons logo almost completely worn off its breast pocket, the underarm areas already damp with stress sweat. "Are you absolutely sure?" He gapes incredulously at the young car thief. "We need to be sure."

Miles nods. "I saw 'em on the west side of Thomaston Woods, heading up 74, about five miles away from the crossroads."

"From Highway 18, you're talking about?"

Miles nods. "And the worst part, they got like twice as many walkers as we thought—it's like a fucking army following along behind them—like a hundred motherfucking *marching bands*—just following along as happy as ya please!"

Lilly looks down, chews her lip, thinks, and then looks up at Miles. "How long ago was it you saw them at Thomaston Woods?"

Miles shrugs. "Like half an hour ago?"

"Fuck!—FUCK!" Lilly raises the walkie-talkie to her lips and thumbs the button. "Bob? Can you hear me?"

Sitting in the darkness of the Elkins Creek tunnel, directly under the town of Carlinville, Georgia, Bob jumps at the sound of Lilly's voice crackling out of his two-way, echoing in the desolate passageway. "*. . . Bob!—BOB!—BOB!!—GODDAMNIT, TALK TO ME! . . .*"

Bob hits the button: "I'm still here, girlie-girl, you don't have to yell."

"*. . . Light it up, Bob, do it now—NOW!*"

He stares at the two-way. "Now?"

"*. . . YES, DO IT NOW!—WE WERE WRONG ABOUT THEIR ETA—DO IT RIGHT NOW!!*"

He drops the radio and fumbles with his lighter and finds himself praying that the antique fuses will work.

Bob Stookey is no atheist. He has his own conception of who God is, and how busy the man must be. But right now, as Bob touches the Bic flame to the end of the safety fuse, and the jute sparks to life, he asks if God might perhaps have a moment to do him this one favor.

The preacher hears the first explosion coming from behind him as he's standing on the RV's running board—a surreal version of Washington crossing the Delaware—his red-stained face, black mourning suit, Wellington boots, and cue-ball head shining dully in the predawn murk. The night sky flickers above him like a photographer's strobe, and the aftershock thumps against the back of the camper.

At first he ducks instinctively, as though he's being shot at, and then, momentarily vexed, he twists around to gaze back at the walker horde.

He sees the second and third explosions burst the ground open along the outskirts of Carlinville, in the gloomy light appearing as oil gushers sending particles of black earth heavenward in brilliant orange plumes. The vast black spouts blossom into the pale gray sky, kicking up the tail half of the walker herd like a carpet being rolled up.

Jeremiah once saw a real honest-to-goodness twister while doing a tent revival meeting in Arkansas, and it looked a lot like this—trailer parks, whole communities, entire neighborhoods, seen from a distance, appearing to dissolve and get sucked up into the fury of the tornado. Tiny particles that first appear to be unidentifiable trash or debris turn out to be swing sets, chimneys, entire cars, entire homes. The sight of it makes a person's soul contract inward with primordial unease—Mother Nature throwing one of her nastiest tantrums. And now *this*—this abomination—is bringing it all back in one great booming rush.

The preacher ducks again as the first projectile lands on the roof of the trailer, a dark, glistening object that bounces off the bonnet and tumbles across the front quarter panel, landing on the running board a few inches from Jeremiah's boots. It gets lodged behind the fender long enough for the preacher to identify it as a severed human hand. Other objects begin raining down on the RV—arms, feet, half a torso, a few ruined, decapitated heads—sending particle bombs of blood and tissue down across the windshield so profusely that Reese Lee Hawthorne, who is behind the wheel and struggling to hold the vehicle steady in the storm of carnage, flips on the windshield wipers.

"STAY ON COURSE!" Jeremiah howls at his driver. "KEEP ON GOING!"

The preacher then fishes his walkie-talkie out of his suit pocket and throws a quick glance over his shoulder to assess the damage. In the haze of the blasts, he can see the massive tow truck weaving to and fro, the flickering light and the sounds of human agony still pulsing, and beyond that, he can see that a huge portion of the population of biters has been vanquished, the rear half of the swarm either disintegrated by the explosions or scattered across the seared brown earth in lifeless, smoking lumps of flesh. Jeremiah squeezes the walkie-talkie's Send button and screams into the mouthpiece: "Brother Stephen, don't you dare stop that tow truck! Don't you dare slow down! We still got hundreds of them things marching with us! These people can*not* turn back the tide of fate! DON'T YOU EVEN THINK ABOUT STOPPING!"

Jeremiah hears a noise from the front of the caravan and whips around.

His eyes narrow with fury.

Cowards!

Bob Stookey peers over the top of the overturned coal car, and sees something horrible developing in the distant dark reaches of the tunnel.

He had been crouching behind the wrecked conveyance for the last five minutes, first watching the fuse sparkle and spit and wend its way along the ground to the dynamite, and then ducking down behind the car with each thunderous roar as the sodium carbonate and nitroglycerine did their jobs. But now the aftershocks have started creaking through the tendons of the ancient mine shaft.

Bob turns on his flashlight, shines it down the length of the tunnel from which he has just come, and springs to his feet when he sees the ceiling joists beginning to sift dust down through the darkness a hundred yards away. He starts backing away when he sees the sides of the shaft starting to bow inward like warped, surreal, Salvador Dalí sculptures melting in time-lapse. And he turns and breaks into a trot when the tunnel begins caving in.

Miners call it a bounce. When a shaft bounces, the entire topography of the earth changes. Streams alter their course, boulders crack, and entire tectonic plates shift slightly. Bob hustles along for about a minute—heading back toward the Elkins Creek main branch and the Woodbury sewers—but when he hears the thunderous low rumbling rising, he glances back over his shoulder, aiming the flashlight beam at the depths behind him.

The leading edge of the cave-in has closed the distance to about a hundred feet, and it's gaining. The entire mine system is collapsing behind Bob, and within seconds will reach him and devour him and bury him in the cold black eternal void and that'll be all she wrote. This gets Bob moving in a dead run, which isn't easy in such a narrow, confined space. He bangs and scrapes against the fossilized surfaces of the wall as he charges westward. The cave-in gains on him, practically nipping at his heels.

He reaches the underside of the creek just as the tributaries on either side of him fold. The noise is immense—like a series of depth charges at the bottom of the ocean—and it makes Bob quicken his pace. Now he's hurtling as fast as his poor old legs will carry him, sucking dusty air into his lungs, the tidal wave of blackness pushing up behind him, swallowing everything in its path. He gasps and flails and sprints down the main conduit while the flashlight beam bounces chaotically across the ceiling and walls, and the weight of the encroaching collapse—now right behind him—presses in on him. The noise deafens him and threatens to drag him down. He drops the flashlight. He charges through absolute darkness for another eternal moment of agonizing terror before his knees buckle.

He trips and falls, sprawling face-first, sliding for a few yards in the cinders.

He bangs against the corner of two intersection tunnels and then lies still, waiting for the cold, dark, final curtain to draw down over him.

SEVENTEEN

"C'mon, baby, it's now or never! DO IT!"

The sound of Molly Frazier's voice from the Winnebago's passenger seat girds the driver, and he shoots a feverish glance over at his wife, nods, and then yanks the wheel. The RV sends up a shriek as it skids into a sharp turn, then roars down the narrow dirt road that disappears into the forest.

James Frazier has had enough. He's not going to fight some insane war against people he doesn't even know, using walkers as weapons, alongside some preacher who seems to have lost his mind.

Hands welded to the steering wheel, James can see in the mirror the foliage and limbs scraping the sides of the camper. He can also see the rest of the convoy behind him in disarray, some of the other vehicles pulling away and making a break for it in the opposite direction. Thank the Lord, he's not the only one.

The young, sandy-haired man with the kind eyes and scraggly beard has been debating with his wife for over twenty-four hours now about whether they should stay with the preacher or slip away as so many others have already done. James and Molly Frazier both come from Pentecostal church backgrounds, with extremely conservative, strict parents and overbearing fathers. They never truly clicked with Father Murphy—too liberal, too Catholic, too ethnic, too *something*—but it was better than struggling on their own. They needed the familiar security of church people—no matter the de-nomination.

But when Jeremiah Garlitz came along, the Fraziers—and many others, for that matter—saw a kindred spirit, a man from their world, a leader who spoke their language. This is the saddest part of this whole mess to James Frazier—what they *could* have had if Reverend Garlitz had kept his wits about him. They could have had the peace and satisfaction of not just surviving the plague, but truly living in the Holy Spirit.

Now, as the pale predawn light starts to bruise the shadows of the forest along Elkins Creek, and James steers the camper toward the farmland to the north, both he and his wife sit in the desolate silence of the RV's cab, unsure of what sins they're committing by fleeing the caravan . . . or what fate has in store for them up north.

Bob Stookey opens his eyes.

He lies in darkness, a cold weight pressing down on his legs, but he realizes with some measure of pleasant surprise that he's still breathing. A faint glint of light is visible out of the corner of his eye, and he has to twist around into an awkward position in order to see that his flashlight has fallen and rolled about thirty feet away, and now lies on the tunnel floor, shining off an adjacent wall.

Bob takes deep breaths and rises to a kneeling position, his joints screaming with pain and stiffness. His greasy black hair hangs in his face. He wipes it back and shakes off the dizziness and looks around the dark, crisscrossing tunnels, the ancient joists above him dripping with condensation and whiskers of roots. He quickly pieces together what just happened. The cave-in must have run its course to the point that the wave bumped up against the reinforcing beams and stonework of the intersecting tunnels.

He looks down and sees the shards of plastic and electrical guts of his two-way radio. He must have fallen on the device in all the excitement and smashed the thing to pieces. His pulse races, a cold rivulet of panic traveling down the pathways of his spine.

"Shit, shit, shit, shit, shit, shit," he mumbles as he struggles to his feet, his ribs stitched with pain where he smashed into the wall.

Time continues ticking away—he's not sure how long he's been lying incapacitated here—and now there's no way of keeping in touch with Lilly. He has a feeling the dynamite blasts were too little too late—something about the urgency in Lilly's voice, the rumbling overhead. Now that bat-shit crazy preacher could already be attacking. Bob goes over and snatches up the flashlight, and then starts trotting down the central conduit, heading back toward town as fast as his battered old bones will allow.

His side starts aching immediately, but he ignores it. He picks up his speed. The flashlight beam bounces ahead of him. He has no way of gauging how far away he is, or how long it will take him to get back home. The long main branch that connects Woodbury with Elkins Creek goes on for almost three miles, and has a sameness to it, a regularity of ceiling slats and congealed hardpack walls and intermittent dead cage lights hanging down on antique cables.

He looks for a milestone as he lopes along, huffing and puffing laboriously, his .357 banging on his hip. He looks for a sign he's closing in on the home tunnels, but the gray rotting walls and calcium deposits and random discarded tools pass in a blur. He picks up his pace. His heart hammers against his chest. He knows he's already put a mile or two between him and Elkins Creek, but how long will it take to cover the remaining mile or so?

The dry silver oval of light dances across the darkness ahead of him, illuminating more and more of the depths of the mine shaft. He feels like a rat in a maze. He thinks of Lilly and David Stern and Harold and that poor hapless gal Norma and that kid Miles trying to hold off the preacher's army of sycophants. He thinks of those children locked up in the stationhouse with Barbara. He runs faster.

It takes him a while to realize that his chest has started to pang and that his huffing and puffing has deteriorated into painful wheezing. Again, he ignores it. He keeps charging along as swiftly as possible, leaping over wrecked coal cars and errant detritus from generations of runaway slaves, miners, and undocumented fugitives.

The tunnel seems to stretch away from him, a telescope turned backward, a dream in which he can't get anywhere no matter how hard he runs. His chest throbs with pain, the pressure squeezing in on it now. His neck gets stiff. His left arm twinges with knifing jolts, his joints seize up. He slows down slightly, and then he gets mad and runs harder. The light beam bounces. The walls blur. He gasps for breath. He's getting dizzy. His ears—deafened by the blasts—can now hear only the syncopated drumbeat of his huffing breaths. His jaw begins to ache. Pain shoots down his arms.

He slows to a hobble, holding the flashlight with one sweaty hand, the other hand now on his belly. Nausea churns in his gut. It feels as though a metal band is tightening around his chest. The back of his throat burns, flaring molten hot with each breath. He moves his free hand up to his sternum, where it feels like an elephant is standing on his chest between his pectorals.

His hobbling slows to an awkward trundle as he hunches in pain. The vomit comes up without warning, retching out of him on a watery, garbled yawn, spattering the front of his filthy chambray shirt and his clodhoppers. There's not much in his stomach so the puke isn't very productive, but it's noisy and slows him down to a stagger.

He finally stops and leans down and puts his hands on his knees. He's soaked in perspiration, and his sweat has gone icy cold and clammy. He drops the flashlight. The pressure on his chest is immense now, a thousand-ton headstone weighing down on his heart.

His heart.

His *goddamn heart*.

He falls to his knees. Holds his chest. His situation registers in stages. First, he can think only of Lilly and the others, and how he has to simply work through this momentary delay because he knows better than most that a boatload of other causes can bring on symptoms that merely *resemble* a heart attack.

That's when the vertigo and breathlessness pour over him and drag him down. He collapses, still holding himself, heaving and gasping ragged breaths off the tunnel floor, the puffs blowing up little clouds of black dust.

The second stage of his realization comes to him then on a tide of white-hot anger: *You idiot, you fool, you're supposed to be a man of medicine, and now look at you. Look at you. At the worst possible moment! All the careless living finally catches up to you!*

All the booze and late nights and cigarettes and red-eye gravy and grits dripping with butter and bacon grease and fried chicken and banana cream pie—all the punishments he doled out to his heart over the years—were coming home to roost.

Flopping onto his back in a sudden paroxysm of agony, the sharp pain slicing a chasm down through the center of his chest, he hugs himself and gasps for air. He stares at the ceiling through tears. His lungs heave for air that comes only stubbornly. His flesh crawls. The third and final revelation comes then, on a wave of despair.

This is the big one—the heart attack his doctor back in Augusta had been warning him about for decades—and it couldn't have come at a worse time.

A tear breaks out of the corner of one eye and tracks down the left side of his face. He stares at the wormy, tangled convolutions of the tunnel ceiling in the dim, angular beam of the fallen flashlight, and feels the fist close around his heart and the concrete filling his lungs and halting his blood flow, and everything going all fuzzy and soft focus on him. He knows what comes next, and he thinks about not being able to ever see Lilly again, not being able to fight alongside her, not being able to see her glittering hazel eyes taking in the strange circus the world has become.

All this passes through his mind in a millisecond that feels like an eternity.

He thinks of the kids. He thinks of holding the little Dupree boy, Lucas, on his knee a couple of days ago, playing This is the Way the Gentlemen Ride and getting a magnificent giggle out of the child, and for some reason feeling an enormous and unexpected sense of accomplishment; just to get that giggle in these dark times is a salve on the soul. Bob never married, never knew what it was like to have children, but he loved kids, and he adored these little ragamuffins that Lilly and he had taken in after Woodbury's fall. He loved the

Slocum twins, their elfin faces reminding him of two little marzipan dolls, the way their eyes twinkled when Bob showed them a four-leaf clover he found on a supply run last week.

These children represent the hope to someday restore the world to the way it was, and they mean everything to Bob, and now, lying in the throes of cardiac arrest, he thinks of the preacher and his bug-fuck crazies getting their hands on these kids. He thinks of these children in the line of fire. He thinks of them being in grave danger this very instant.

Bob starts to crawl, his left arm completely numb, his legs worthless, his lungs on fire. He makes it a few inches before collapsing. He breathes through his nose, puffing little blooms of cinder dust.

He starts again, dragging his failing body along with agonizing slowness, a few centimeters at a time. It feels as though his chest is about to rupture. He breathes in steel wool, but refuses to give in to the pain.

He keeps crawling, and keeps his hot gaze locked on the unforgiving darkness ahead of him.

The eastern horizon goes from a deep cobalt blue to a washed-out gray, the first light of day pushing back the shadows in the woods around Woodbury.

The air snaps with the chill of early morning and the whir of the aviary as a dark figure emerges from a hole in the ground, hastens across a clearing, and climbs the nearest live oak.

The butcher-birds in the high branches screech their blood-thirsty shrieks as a greeting, or maybe a warning, as the figure finds a vantage point and digs in a pocket for a pair of binoculars. Dressed in his threadbare hoodie, his delicate braids flagging in the breeze, Miles Littleton hooks an arm around the tree's center trunk to steady himself as he scans the barrens out beyond the tobacco fields.

Through the lenses he can see a narrow panorama of derelict

farmhouses, wreckage-strewn two-lanes, and dry riverbeds dissecting the Georgia hinterlands like the desiccated veins of a vast corpse. He sees the tinsel shimmer of the Flint River snaking southward in the new light.

He blinks. About two and a half miles away, a low thunderhead of dust rises off Cove Road. He blinks again. He adjusts the focus and gapes at the massive inkblot of vehicles and the myriad shadows fanning out in their wake, coming this way, moving with the slow certainty of a black glacier.

"Fuck me," Miles mutters, and lets the binoculars dangle and bounce around his neck as he climbs back down in a hurry. He hits the ground and charges back across the clearing to the manhole cover. He lifts it, then lowers himself down through the breach.

Footsteps converge on him as soon as he drops to the tunnel floor.

"Well?" Lilly's voice crackles with tension, her fists clenching involuntarily as she stands before him in her camo jacket, her hair pulled back taut in a ponytail. She has a bandolier belt slung across her chest, the row of fully jacketed bullets nestled between her small breasts.

Miles gives her a grave look. "They've already crossed the Flint."

"Fuck!" Lilly swallows dryly and looks around the room at the others gathering behind her. Harold Staubach holds a 12-gauge against his hip, his russet brown face shiny with sweat. David Stern stands behind him in the shadows, his AR-15 slung over the shoulder of his silk roadie jacket. Norma Sutters comes trundling up behind David, her plump features coalescing into a frown.

"Gonna be blowing in here in like maybe a half an hour? Something like that?"

"Okay, okay . . . all right." Lilly swallows hard again, focusing with laser intensity on the task at hand, looking down the length of the main tunnel. Less than a hundred feet away from her, the passageway plunges into darkness. They've been trying to conserve power and lightbulbs by burning only the absolute minimum number of cage lights. Now Lilly walks over to the wall and flips the switches

Bob installed as a safety measure a few days ago. "Here's what I need: I need everybody to listen closely, because I only got time to go through this once."

The others get very still as the cage lights flare on, one after another, down the length of the main conduit, past the makeshift nursery with its fleet of cribs and cots, past the side tunnels, past the temporary infirmary and the storage room, and out beyond the far chain-link barriers.

"Norma, I'm going to need you to go get the dummies. Bring them back in here on the double, as many as we have—it'll have to be enough. Miles, you help her."

Norma and Miles hustle down the center-aisle tunnel toward the storage room.

"David and Harold, I'm going to need you guys to go ahead and set that safe zone up as quickly as you can, then take your places and get into character."

David Stern looks pained, panicky. "Lilly, we're going to need more than two guys."

"You'll have Miles and Norma, too, as soon as we're ready down here. And Bob when he gets back." She remembers that Bob is late, which a bad sign, but she pushes the dread from her mind. "If all goes well, Tommy and I will be able to join you soon enough."

"How the hell is anybody gonna find us?"

"Look, we got three working walkie-talkies, right? You take one, I'll have one, and I'll give one to Norma. Three teams: Harold and you, Norma and Miles, me and Tommy."

"But what about Babs?"

"What about her?"

David wipes his mouth. "That stationhouse is really exposed out there—I don't know—seems like we could have found a safer place."

"There's nothing we can do about it now. C'mon. Let's get to work—WHILE WE'RE YOUNG!"

Lilly claps her hands briskly, and the group scatters. Lilly rushes across the lounge area and starts rearranging chairs. David and Harold head toward the sewer entrance fifty feet away. They vanish around the corner and their footsteps recede into the dripping silence.

By this point, Norma and Miles have returned with the first pair of dummies. Norma speaks quickly, tersely, almost under her breath: "Had enough clothes from the Salvation Army drop to make five of these things but we're gonna have to go back there for more if we want to make all of *us* up all raggedy-ass." She drags an effigy across the floor and drops it on a chair. "They're pretty rough. But from a distance? I don't know. Like my mama used to say, 'On a galloping horse, you don't look half bad, babygirl.'"

Garbed in rags and hand-me-downs, the dummies are filled with old newspaper and trash, the faces hewn from pairs of nude-colored panty hose stuffed with more paper. They look like the kind of objects a group of protesters might burn during a demonstration.

"Them walkers are pretty fucking stupid," Miles ventures, setting a dummy on a chair. "But I wonder if they're stupid enough to buy *this*."

"They'll buy it," Lilly says. "Trust me. C'mon. Let's get the others in here."

A minute later they have five of the effigies sitting in formation around the lounge. It's a surreal sight, even for this place, and Lilly stares at the things for a moment before she looks at Norma and Miles. "Okay, one last thing before I cut you guys loose."

Norma looks at her. "What's that, child?"

Lilly has already unbuckled her belt and unsnapped her jeans. "Pee on them with me."

For a moment, Norma looks at Miles, who looks back at Norma, then looks aghast at Lilly.

"C'mon!" Lilly pulls her pants down, shoves off her panties, and hovers over the lap of the first dummy. "Pee on them."

David Stern and Harold Staubach find the Dromedary Street manhole only minutes after they turn the corner beneath the intersection of Dromedary and Date Lane. The air hangs thick with a fog of methane and ammonia-stench, and they have to wade through six inches of brackish mire in order to reach the exit point.

They can see thin beams of the day's first glimmer of sunlight slicing down through the seams of the ancient manhole, celestial rays of light piercing the motes and demarcating the sewer's egress. Neither man says a word as they reach the bottom of the embedded stone steps. Working quickly and silently, David helps Harold up the steps first, then follows with his assault rifle dangling and twisting on its strap.

The older man struggles for a moment with the rusty cover, but eventually manages to force it open a few inches, wide enough to let in an enormous rush of acrid, reeking walker-stench. Harold pulls a small mirror from behind his belt and sticks it up into the daylight. Bob Stookey procured a dozen of these small makeup mirrors earlier in the month from the ruins of the town drugstore, and they have been invaluable to the tunnel dwellers.

Now Harold Staubach probes the mirror far enough to see a reflection of the street corner.

In the small oval of glass, scores of walkers are visible milling about the central intersection. To the left, a row of boarded storefronts overlooks a sidewalk riddled with the dead. Some of them continually brush against each other, while others idle in slumped, stationary positions in front of jagged broken windows, drooling black bile from their liver-colored lips as though waiting for their reflection to deliver some imminent message.

Harold rotates the mirror forty-five degrees to the left until he can see their destination.

Beyond the walker-infested street corner, a half a block north, two enormous semitrucks sit facing each other across the massive town entrance. Harold's heart rate kicks up a few notches. He can see the vacant lot adjacent to the gate, a square acre of wild, overgrown prairie grass littered here and there with overturned oil drums, discarded tires, and human remains all but picked clean by birds and weather and the ravenous dead. Some of the skeletons are so sun-bleached they look almost white, but other than these macabre reminders of the plague, the lot is fairly clear of walkers.

"You ready for this, my friend?" Harold asks somewhat rhetorically.

No response from David.

"We've been as quiet as mice for like a million hours now—when do we get to talk?"

The voice—as soft as the coo of a little bird, but also full of righteous indignation—penetrates Barbara Stern's racing thoughts and makes her whirl away from the window with a start.

In the dim light of dawn, which seeps through the cracks of the boarded windows, Barbara sees little Mercy Slocum standing directly behind her, hands on her hips in an elfin impression of long-suffering annoyance. The girl's frowning, cherubic face has chocolate stains on it; Barbara broke out the last of the stale candy bars twenty minutes ago, and they were gone in seconds. The walkie-talkie was then turned off to prevent the frenzied voices of David and the others from making the kids more nervous than they already were. Now Barbara is resorting to games in order to keep the group as quiet as possible.

"Get away from the window, sweetheart," Barbara says, gently, shooing the girl back toward the others. "You're gonna lose the game."

The other children huddle together at the opposite end of the room, standing around a couple of makeshift cots, watching this exchange with keen interest. Their toys and books are strewn across the floor around them. Bethany Dupree—the de facto spokesman for the children—also has her hands on her hips in a melodramatic display of exasperation. "These games are just a trick," she announces.

Mercy Slocum shuffles over to her twin sister, and the two of them stand there, facing Barbara in their matching threadbare pinafores, arms crossed sullenly across their little chests as though waiting for an apology. To Barbara they look like a Diane Arbus photograph, more wraithlike than childlike, as though torn from an album of Dust Bowl American poverty. "You're treating us like babies," Tiffany Slocum weighs in. "We want to know the truth."

"Ssshhhhhhhh!" Barbara comes up and kneels before them, speaking very softly and yet forcefully. "The time to be the most quiet is now!"

"Stop saying that," Lucas Dupree commands, his tiny chin jutting indignantly.

"You told us this was a field trip," Bethany says. "That was a lie. And then you told us there's a war coming but you won't say with who!"

"Sssshhhhh!" Barbara puts her finger to her lips. "I'll answer your questions only if you promise to whisper."

"What's going on?" Bethany demands in a petulant whisper that comes out more like a grunt. "And don't lie because we can tell when you're lying—kids can always tell. That's something adults will never, ever, ever understand. Kids know. Trust me on that, Mrs. Stern."

"Call me Barb."

"What's going on? Is it like a walker attack or what?"

Barbara lets out a sigh. "Some bad people are coming here to kill us."

The children all go very still—even Lucas Dupree, the youngest of them, only a year or two out of diapers, stares gravely back at Barbara—which pinches Barbara's heart. To see the face of a child looking so sullen, so weary, so grim—maybe in some ways this is the worst part of the plague, worse than getting devoured by the dead. To see a child devoured by *life*. At last, Bethany summons up a response. "Is it because they want our stuff?"

Barbara shrugs. "I swear to you, sweetheart, I don't know what they want. Revenge? The town itself?" She pauses and looks into the faces of these miniature old souls, as spectral and haunted as ghosts. "They believe God is on their side, which makes them even more dangerous—especially the preacher, Jeremiah."

Bethany cocks her head. "You mean that big guy in the black suit?"

Nodding glumly, Barbara can't lie anymore. "That's right, sweetie."

"That's stupid!" Bethany tries to wrap her brain around this. "He's not a bad man. He showed me a magic trick once, gave me licorice. He's a good man."

Barbara slowly shakes her head. "Not so much, honey . . . not so much."

The little girl starts to say something else when the strangest sound echoes on the wind outside, the sheer incongruity of it silencing her and stiffening each child's spine.

Barbara shushes the children one last time. "I want everybody to stay together, stay very still, and stay as quiet as possible until I tell you it's okay." She looks at them as the noise outside rises. Under the rumble of machines, the keening, knife-edged sounds of human screaming drift across the outskirts of town. "I'm going to go back to the window now, but nobody move."

Her binoculars bounce on her chest as Barbara hurries across the room.

She stands with her back against the jamb and carefully pushes aside the makeshift shade until a thin wisp of light shines in. She peers through the binoculars, scanning the southeast corner of town.

In the long shadows of dawn, about a quarter of a mile away, where Gates Road splits off from Highway 74 and the milky rays of sunlight cant down through the adjacent woods, she can see a thundercloud of dust and exhaust approaching.

With one hand, Barbara slowly, instinctively reaches down to where her revolver is tucked into its holster on the side of her muumuu, her hand caressing the waffled surface of her .44 caliber Bulldog's grip.

EIGHTEEN

At precisely 6:53 a.m. Eastern Standard Time that morning, in the gelid air and pale blue light of the forest south of Woodbury, without warning or precedent, an outsider with very specific orders enters the town limits on foot from Reeves Road, then creeps under the trees, a heavy pack jangling on his back. He consults a hand-drawn map as he moves silently through the undergrowth, his heavy lumberjack boots snapping twigs and crunching over ancient humus.

He finds the red bandanna fluttering in the breeze, tied to the tip of a stick thrust into the ground. He turns west and walks about ten paces, past a pair of softly humming generators camouflaged under skeins of leaves and twigs. A moment later, he locates the manhole cover embedded in the dirt, a relic from earlier in the century when a new sewage system was introduced to the area. He kneels, shrugs off his pack, and takes out his tools.

C-clamps go down on the edges of the lid, securing it to the paving stones around the outer ring. He tightens the clamps with channel locks. Then, just to be sure, he moves a small boulder from its mossy home under a nearby tree and sets it down on the manhole cover.

A few more stones go on top of the cover, and then, satisfied with his work, he goes searching for the other manhole entrance.

Twenty minutes later, at exactly 7:13 a.m., 250 yards southeast of the Woodbury train yard, the remaining members of the preacher's convoy boom across the Woodbury town limits in a cyclone of noise and dust and the rising stench of the dead. The tow truck driven by Stephen Pembry has lagged behind a mile or two, awaiting orders, keeping the throngs occupied in an adjacent tobacco field with the mesmerizing intervals of flickering light.

Meanwhile, the caravan follows the access road that winds along the edge of the forest, traveling single file, until they come to a dry riverbed where a yellow bandanna flaps and flags at the apex of yet another stick thrust into the ground. The flag stands near the mouth of a culvert, the gaping maw of which is crisscrossed by rusty, barnacled iron bars. Reese Lee Hawthorne and Stephen Pembry discovered this culvert on one of their reconnaissance trips, and now it will serve the mission well as a back door into the tunnels.

Jeremiah's RV skids to a stop, the other trucks slamming on their brakes behind him.

In the aftermath of the mass exodus that followed James and Molly Frazier's surprise flight from the fold, only a half dozen vehicles remain, and now these six small-duty pickups and flatbed trucks raise a fog bank of fumes—the homemade biodiesel burning dirty—as they scuttle to a halt behind the preacher.

By this point, the morning sun has crested the palisades of black oaks along Elkins Creek, and the woods south of town appear almost Paleolithic, with celestial sunbeams cutting down through the motes of fluff and insects that teem in the chill air. God has bestowed a beautiful day for a reckoning. And adding to all of the preacher's euphoria and good fortune is the fact that the immediate area is far enough away from the tunnel entrance for him and his followers to remain unheard and undetected by the heathens underground.

The RV's cab doors squeal open, and the preacher hops out one side, Reese Lee Hawthorne out the other. The preacher's gleaming bald pate shimmers in the shafts of light filtering through the trees, his black coattails flapping in the wind as he pulls his walkie-talkie out and presses the switch. "Brother Gleason! Talk to me!"

Through a crackle of static, Chester Gleason's voice squawks out of the device. *"It's done! It's done, Brother! All of them rabbit holes are locked up tight—and I can hear them down there!"*

"Well done, Brother!" Jeremiah releases the button, his hands shaking in the cold sunlight. His skull feels too big for his scalp. His flesh crawls with adrenaline as he ticks off the to-do list in his head. "All right, next!" He turns to the men gathered around him, his disciples, his holy warriors, his wolves. "Louis, use the winch to pull them bars."

One of the men hurries back to his truck, hops in, and throws it in reverse. He backs up to the riverbank, twelve feet away from the culvert opening. Reese Lee Hawthorne circles around the back of the pickup and disengages the winch hook, pulling the cable across the dry ditch and then hooking the end around the ancient grill-work of bars covering the culvert opening. He gives a signal.

The engine revs. Black exhaust spumes from the vertical pipe. The truck lurches, pulling the cable taut. Rear wheels dig into the muck, spinning for a second. The bars creak and groan. Off to the side, the bald preacher watches with voices in his head and the fire of madness in his eyes.

The bars finally snap, slamming down on the ground and sliding across the riverbed.

Lilly Caul finishes up making her last-minute adjustments to the tunnel, stuffing bloody bandages from the infirmary into the torsos of the makeshift mannequins, when she feels a slight tremor in the bones of the sewer—a faint temblor that is *sensed* more than *felt*—resonating up through the soles of her boots.

She stands very still for a moment, cocking her head, listening. The silence seems laden with potential, a tuning fork still vibrating slightly but not revealing anything specific.

She grabs her walkie-talkie off the spool table and squeezes the button. "Miles? Can you hear me?"

Nothing but static from the other end.

Nobody hears the gibberish tumbling out of Jeremiah's mouth as he stands back in the warmth of the morning sun, surveying the cool shadows of the woods around the gaping culvert opening. His voice has a low, musical, and breathless tone as the nonsensical syllables pour out of him, sounding like an approximation of an actual language but not a real one, more like the patois of a babbling infant possessed by the spirit, preverbal, preliteral.

In the Pentecostal church, it is believed the Holy Spirit enters a person at critical times, and the result is this fluid vocalizing of speechlike syllables, which lack any connotative meaning or any comprehensible pattern, but are considered by true believers to be sacred speech. Scientists refer to this phenomenon as "glossolalia" (or the putative speaking of natural languages previously unknown to the speaker). But in Jeremiah's case, it is clear that the tongues being gibbered are those of his father. The garbled scat issuing out of him comes directly from the old man's repertoire—all-pervasive, all-encompassing, all-powerful.

"Pardon?" The voice next to him snaps him out of his reverie. "What was that?"

"Huh?" Jeremiah turns and looks into the gaunt, gray, deeply lined face of Louis Packard, his winch operator, as the man puzzles over the sound of the tongues. Jeremiah smiles. "Oh . . . yes . . . I was just . . . humming an old hymn . . . a favorite of mine. 'The Old Rugged Cross.' "

"Brother Stephen's truck is coming up the hill with the walkers."

"That's excellent, Louis."

The gaunt man chews nervously on his cheek. "Brother, you know I'm with ya one hundred and ten percent."

"What is it, Louis?"

"These people gotta go, and I'm with ya, till the bitter end."

"What's wrong?"

The gaunt man lets out a tense sigh and speaks in a low whisper. "We're never gonna get them things to go inside them tunnels, never in a million *years*."

The preacher just smiles. He can smell the rising tide of death on the breeze as if it were a storm front rolling in. He hears the rumble of Stephen's tow truck, the human screams silent now, the prisoner long ago succumbing to blood loss and exposure. He senses the weight of the throngs coming up through the woods behind the truck, the unholy choir of watery snarling and growling noises rising on the wind.

He glances over his shoulder and sees the tow truck materializing around the corner of the forest road, the sea of shadows rolling in behind it in the flickering strobe light. He turns to the others. "Everybody in your vehicles, lock the doors!"

Then Jeremiah goes over to his RV, snaps the latch on the side door, leans inside, and pulls out a box marked "COX REMOTE CONTROL DUNE BUGGY."

At last, a voice crackles through the static spewing out of Lilly Caul's walkie-talkie: *". . . Yo! Yo, Lilly! We're here, we was just dodging a few biters, but I can read you loud and clear now, go ahead!"*

Lilly feels the walls of the tunnel contracting around her like the innards of a living thing reacting to poison in its system, and it makes her stomach clench as she thumbs the switch and says into the mike: "Have you made it to the church yet? Over?"

". . . Yes, ma'am, got the clothes, now on our way to the safe zone. . . ."

"Good, awesome . . . I gotta get the fuck out of here, I'm getting the willies down here all by myself."

". . . Copy that, see you in a few."

"Right."

Lilly whirls and hurries down the length of the main conduit toward the manhole. But even now, as she trots along, she feels the cold fingers of claustrophobia tightening around her neck, stealing her breath, sending cold currents of panic down her spine.

Ahead of her, the tunnel seems to blur out of focus, slipping into a double image like motion picture film jumping out of registration. She has dealt with excruciating claustrophobia for most of her life, ever since she accidentally locked herself in a coat closet at her cousins' house in Macon when she was nine years old.

Now she feels the old prickly panic returning like cold fingers wrapping around her spine.

The tunnel spins. She nearly trips. She slows down and braces herself against the wall. She realizes that she hasn't been in the tunnels alone in a while, maybe ever; it's hard to be sure right now. She blinks, rubs her eyes, tries to ignore the dizziness that's washing over her and to fix her gaze on the steps embedded in the wall at the end of the main conduit.

In her bleary line of sight, about fifteen feet away, the faint indentations in the crumbling stone wall are apparent, and she edges toward them as fast as she can without falling flat on her face. The vertigo courses over her, threatening to knock her off her feet. She holds on to a brace. It feels as though her head is about to loll off her shoulders, and her gorge rises, but she wills herself not to throw up and to keep inching forward.

She reaches the steps at the precise same moment she first hears the sound.

The faint, far-off noise is so strange and incongruous at this moment—in this dark, moldering place—that she freezes, her brain like an engine seizing up. She doesn't even look over her shoulder at first. She simply stands there, one hand on the middle rung of the steps, her entire body gripped in glacial, dreamlike paralysis.

Something moves at the dark end of the tunnel, glimpsed only peripherally, at first registering as a small animal darting around the corner.

She whirls around and sees a small remote control toy rolling toward her. *What the fuck*, she thinks. *Is this part of that*—?

The closer the toy gets, the more clearly it comes into view: a metal-flake orange dune buggy with fat little tires, a tiny whip antenna, and a couple of outboard devices duct-taped to its hood. It sends up a flash of silver strobe light at odd intervals as it rattles closer and closer, but the strangest and by far worst part is the recording being played back through a miniature speaker affixed to the toy car's rear bulwark.

When she was in college, Lilly Caul once accidentally stumbled upon a website called Comeuppance-dot-com on which Islamic fundamentalist terrorists posted old clips of people being beheaded and other various and sundry horrors. Before she had the good judgment to quickly navigate away from the visual trash heap, she got a good look at a grainy video of a British journalist being tortured before the shaky lens of a consumer camera. But oddly, it wasn't the sudden and tawdry terror of seeing a human being reduced to a naked bloody mass of agony—the man hanging upside down from a meat hook as he's whipped and scourged with barbed wire—that disturbed Lilly the most. It was the *sound*—the terrible, indelible screaming noises that were coming off the little YouTube clip.

You can't fake the sound of human suffering—especially at this intensity. No actor in any horror film can approximate the true texture of a tortured shriek. The quality of the sound is so specific, so harsh and shrill, as to be almost *feral* in its timbre. The clamor has an unmistakable electric-shock effect on the human ear.

Lilly hears this very sound coming out of a miniature speaker on board that toy, accompanied by the rising odors of dead flesh wafting through the tunnel. But it's the noise that holds her rapt as the contraption wheels toward her. She stares and stares as the little thing seems to aim itself directly at her feet.

The dune buggy bumps into the toe of her boot and bounces back slightly.

Lilly stares, transfixed, as the thing bumps her again and again, thumping against the steel toe of her work boot, as though trying to plow *through* her. At this close proximity, Lilly can see the tiny pencil-thin camera taped to the buggy's hood, the radio signals causing the thing to back up, jack its wheels, and make an attempt to go around her.

She snaps out of her fear-spell then, and gives the thing a hard kick, sending it into a sideways roll.

The toy car smashes against the tunnel wall and breaks apart into shards of plastic and rubber—the camera strobe hanging by a thread, *but continuing to blink.*

That's when Lilly sees the shadows at the opposite end of the tunnel, formed by a single yellow cage light dangling down somewhere in the side tunnel, the shapes creeping across the earthen floor like puddles of black ink slowly but inexorably spreading.

She sucks in a tense breath when she sees the first biter coming around the corner. For a terrible moment, Lilly remains motionless, horror-stricken, almost morbidly fascinated by this catastrophic breach of the area that was only minutes ago living space.

The lead corpse appears to be a former businessman, maybe a salesman—perhaps middle-aged at the time of death—now clad in a tattered seersucker suit so worn and stained with bile it looks like butcher paper. Its bloodless face puckers with hunger as it comes down the tunnel toward Lilly, at a fairly rapid pace for a walker, the others following on its heels, shuffling along with troubling velocity. There's a female in sun-bleached gingham—maybe at one time a farmer's wife—and a couple of teenage children in gore-encrusted overalls, most likely farm kids.

Within seconds, there are too many to process at a single glance: twenty, a hundred; Lilly quickly loses count. The tunnel fills with the guttural, watery clatter of putrid vocal cords. The lead creature closes the distance between him and Lilly to fifty feet, the others brushing and scraping against the walls behind him, the stench so thick now Lilly feels as though she might throw up after all, except that she has no time for such frivolities as vomiting.

She scuttles up the embedded steps to the underside of the manhole cover and tries to push the lid open.

The thing won't budge. The monsters are closing in. She shoves harder against the bottom of the cover, the clamps on the lid holding tight. The former salesman is now thirty feet away and closing.

Some of the other creatures have meandered toward the lounge area, where the urine-soaked effigies sit in a macabre tableau around the spool table. But the half dozen or so creatures in the lead have locked on to Lilly's scent, and come toward her in a blur of clenching teeth and palpitating jaws and arms stiff with rigor mortis reaching blindly for her tender flesh.

She frantically pushes against the stubborn manhole cover until her fingers throb with pain and her arms twinge—all to no avail.

The salesman reaches the bottom of the steps, coming to within three feet of Lilly's boot soles, and now she's forced to make some instantaneous choices and calculations: She has one extra ten-round ammo magazine wedged behind her belt, and one .22 caliber Ruger on her hip, sheathed in leather and with ten rounds in the grip. She also has a twelve-inch Buck knife on her other hip for close-quarter confrontations.

In one awkward motion, she holds fast to the top rung with her free hand and quickly draws the Ruger with the other. She squeezes off a single blast into the top of the salesman's skull. The pop sets off the tinnitus in her ears, and the backsplash of oily matter makes her flinch, as a rosette of bone and tissue in the top of the creature's head shuts off his reanimated nervous system.

More of the creatures clamor toward her. She aims the gun at the manhole cover, shields her face, and blindly fires point blank at the outer edges of the iron. The blast makes her jump. The ricochet sings past her face, hot spit on her cheek, ears deadened further.

No good. Waste of bullets. Now what? Think, think, *think*.

Her mind goes as blank as a television screen at the end of the programming day.

White noise.

The plague has had a strange and somewhat unexpected winnowing effect on people. Traits that were once considered flaws, even personality disorders, now help a person survive. Paranoia, narcissism, impulsiveness, greed, sociopathy, even cruelty now become assets. Indeed, the one cross that Lilly Caul had always borne in the old world has proven to be a rarity among the survivor class, and perhaps has enabled her to emerge as a leader. Call it pathological persistence.

Even now, with the discovery of the locked manhole, followed by her mind going blank, Lilly refuses to allow a scintilla of doubt to enter her mindscape. She hears the dissonant chorus of phlegm-clogged snarling and the clacking of teeth, and she doesn't even have to look. Out of the corner of her eye, she can see dead things pressing in on her, dozens of them—males in bile-stained dungarees, females dragging useless mangled limbs, grotesque former children chewing at the air, and assorted senior citizens now reduced to emaciated bags of brittle bones and weathered flesh stretched taut like Visqueen. The gruesome party has Lilly on its radar now, and the partygoers want their hors d'oeuvres.

Hopping to the floor of tunnel, she bangs into a gangly male before the thing can bite and knocks it back on its heels into three others, all of whom go down like bowling pins. More move in, and Lilly kicks at them as they lunge at her, one at a time, doubling them over, sending them to the floor. She shoots a younger female in the head, turning its face to pulp as it lurches at her.

Blood spatters Lilly's face as she backs deeper into the tunnel, counting bullets. Three down, seven to go in the gun, ten behind her belt. She's going to need all the ammo she can conserve.

More and more biters pour into the tunnel, a slow-motion stampede coming around the far corner, in all shapes and sizes, flowing toward Lilly with the certainty of a rising tide as she coughs and gags and flinches at the terrible odor. The stench is incredible, so powerful and thick that she can feel it on her skin as she continues to back into the darkness. She reaches down and draws the Buck knife from its hip sheath. She brings it up just in time.

A younger male with parchment brown skin shrink-wrapped around its skeletal face suddenly pounces at her, mouth gaping, black gums filled with slimy teeth. She thrusts the knife at it. The roof of its mouth impales itself on the point of the curved blade.

Lilly swings the male into two females, and the former young women stagger and fall backward over their clumsy feet. Lilly shoves the male—its mouth still engaged with the knife like a fish on a hook—back in the other direction, slamming it into two other males lumbering toward her.

The impaled creature shudders backward, knocking the others over.

But then things go from bad to worse, as the knife finally slices up through the thing's putrefied nasal cavity and the skull opens up. The knife pops out the top, and the creature's head cracks apart—coconut-like—into halves, each fragment tumbling to the floor. A geyser of tarry fluids gush out of the thing for a moment, the lack of blood pressure causing the blood to ooze more than spray, as the headless creature remains upright for a single horrible moment.

"DIE ALREADY!!"

Lilly slashes at the air in front of the headless thing as it finally sags to the floor. Others instantly move in to take its place. Lilly keeps slashing and screaming and slowly backing deeper into the labyrinth.

David Stern had been in the process of naming these side tunnels, and the one Lilly is backing toward now is called Tributary B—a narrow channel of hard-packed earth that connects the deeper maze of zinc mines to the town sewer. Lilly realizes if she can make it to the chain-link barrier drawn across its opening, and maybe get the thing open quickly enough, she can escape.

More biters move in—a cross section of ages and genders, most of them slimy with mold and sun-bleached—too many for hand-to-hand combat. Lilly fires off six more shots in quick succession. Brain matter spumes and splatters the tunnel walls all around her, bodies collapsing to the floor, one by one, making watery splats.

Lilly has spent almost a year practicing her aim, ever since Josh

Hamilton had taught her how to quick-draw and hit moving targets, and she has gotten pretty good at it, better than most, but now she sees the far end of the tunnel—the makeshift infirmary and the lounge with its pee-soaked effigies and the dining area with all its broken crockery and the storage nooks—completely overrun with monsters. They squeeze elbow to elbow into every square foot of space, pressing up against the walls, faces mashing against one another in a macabre, twisted corruption of a subway at rush hour.

The horrible sight of it weighs down on Lilly so heavily that she doesn't notice the next wave of assailants lunging at her until it's too late. A former obese woman—now with flaccid drapes of flesh hanging off her like excess dress fabric—manages with her hooked claw of a hand to snag a piece of Lilly's sweatshirt. Lilly rears back and fires. The bullet misses the top of the fat lady's head by a mile and goes into the ceiling. More biters close in. Lilly fires again. The gun clicks empty.

"FUCK!—FUCK!—FUCK!—FUCK!—FUCK!—FUCK!—FUCK!—FUCK!—FUCK!!"

Fumbling awkwardly with the gun, ejecting the clip, fishing for the fresh magazine, trying to get it into the hilt, hands oily with fear-sweat, more creatures coming at her, slamming the magazine home, cold-dead fingers reaching for her, cocking the slide, teeth chattering inches away from the exposed flesh of her hands and arms . . . she makes a tactical error. It's an honest mistake. Anybody could have made it.

She shoots a quick glance over her shoulder to see how close she is to the tributary.

The change in the center of balance is just enough to throw off her equilibrium, and she stumbles over her feet. She feels herself falling. Again, she compensates too severely by clawing at the wall for a handhold, a brace or a board or *something* to stop her fall, and in the process, the gun slips from her grip.

She collapses onto the small of her back, the Ruger skittering off across the floor.

NINETEEN

All at once everything slows down, and the ringing in Lilly's ears drowns out every other sound, and the pain bolts up her spine and seizes her arms and legs. She tries to scoot away from the onslaught, but now an enormous male moves in on her. A former farmhand in blood-soaked work pants, its shirt torn in half, revealing sagging pectorals the color of earthworms, it pounces on her legs.

Lilly wriggles under its dead weight, trying to get to her knife, but the thing has her pinned to the floor, and the creature's mottled face is folding open like a clamshell, exposing rows of greasy, moldering incisors, which gnash and clack noisily as they close in on her throat. Lilly manages to get her hands around its head.

For a moment she prevents it from devouring her, holding it at arm's length.

Over the course of that terrible instant, holding that snapping turtle of a head, engulfed in the odor of its hellish spoor—a mixture of rotting meat and that inimitable lower note of oily, black death-stench—Lilly looks into the thing's eyes. Just for a split second, she registers something glinting behind the dead sharklike cataracts. Cruelty? Madness? Rage? Agony? Maybe all of these things shimmer for a moment behind the creature's gaze as it regards its human food. But then, something breaks the spell.

Lilly feels a breathy puff of noxious wind on the *side* of her face, clammy and fetid, and she realizes she's lying right next to the chain-link barrier stretched across the tributary tunnel.

The thing on top of her snarls and drools as it looms closer and closer to her neck. Her strength dwindling, Lilly takes one last, heart-breaking glance at the narrow tunnel behind that chain-like barrier. She can see the passageway stretching back into the dark void, a single pool of yellow light from a solitary cage lamp hanging down, and she realizes it might as well be a million miles away. She realizes she has no more options. She has no more tricks up her sleeve. She feels her strength draining away.

For the first time in her life, she realizes it's time to give up.

More creatures close in. At least a dozen of them—mostly males, a few ravenous shells of older women, one gruesome child with half of its face torn open and leaking gristle and teeth—come at her from all sides. She feels the shuddering, drooling, wriggling head in her hands begin to slip out of her grip.

Einstein said time is relative, and anyone who has been unlucky enough to be engulfed by these hellish creatures knows the tenuous connection between the passage of time and the human mind under great stress. People in car wrecks see every detail in the split second before impact. Soldiers on the battlefield have reported witnessing the very bullets that put them in wheelchairs hanging in the air like moths before striking them. Lilly experiences something similar in the suspended beat of time before the first set of teeth sink into the soft flesh of her neck.

She closes her eyes, and she half expects her entire life to flicker across her mind-screen in some extravagant Cecil B. DeMille montage of her childhood, maybe a series of gauzy images beginning with her nursery in that airless little knotty-pine room in the rear of the Alton Street house. From there, we go to her first grade class picture in Hastings Park down by the river, her boyfriends, her milestone moments, and maybe even her high school graduation with her father, Everett, proudly carrying around her mortarboard hat and her little mimeographed diploma as though they were the Nobel Prize.

Part of her longs for this kind of storybook closure, but of course none of it appears to her, and now she sees only the minuscule red cinders down in the center of a monster's eyes burning into her retinas, floating across the dark field of her vision, as the air fills with the infernal noise of garbled snarling and she feels the cold breath of her assailant as its head finally slips through her sweaty fingers. She holds her breath, waiting for the teeth to plunge into her, when suddenly she hears a loud bang.

Her eyes pop open at precisely the same moment that the head above her explodes.

To the trained ear, the blast of a .357 magnum, especially in the confines of a narrow subterranean tunnel, makes an unmistakable roar. Deeper and more thunderous than the sound produced by smaller handguns, loud enough to puncture eardrums, the sonic boom rings out as if a giant wrecking ball had slammed through the biter on top of Lilly. In accompaniment with the echo of the gunshot, fluids and brain matter erupt in all directions. Lilly flinches as a wet spattering of blood splashes into her face, while the rest of the skull and rancid brain matter are blown sideways across the tunnel, hitting the opposite wall with a splat.

The body stiffens for a moment before collapsing on top of Lilly, the lifeless weight pressing down on her so hard it knocks the wind from her lungs. She frantically looks around, trying to grasp the import of what just happened, but the blood of the headless lump is now flowing out all over her, and she can't breathe, and she sees something out of the corner of her eye.

A series of three more flashes—like sparks of magnesium flaring in the dark, touched off by a firing pin—flicker in the shadows of the tributary.

Three more biters go down around Lilly while she tries to wriggle out from under the weight of the massive corpse pressing upon her—three more heads blown apart by large-caliber bullets, spraying brain mist against the opposite wall and sending body after body deflating onto the floor. In some far-flung compartment in Lilly's traumatized brain, she registers the fact that only hollow-point bullets could do this kind of damage, the projectiles expanding on impact, sending battering rams through mortified brains.

And in a deeper compartment, Lilly realizes there's only one person around here that she knows of who uses these soft-point dumdums.

Suddenly, she sees two things in her peripheral vision that get her up and moving: the shadow of a human being to her left, behind the chain-link barrier, crawling toward her, and her pistol, the .22 caliber Ruger, with its fresh magazine of ten rounds, lying ten feet away on the tunnel floor. She moves quickly, before the next wave of biters can swarm her, and lunges across the tunnel. She grabs the pistol and jacks the slide and spins and squeezes off four quick blasts into the heads of approaching biters.

Pink mist flashes in the darkness—more tissue spraying the adjacent wall—and three of the closest walkers collapse in flaccid heaps on the floor.

By this point, the single shadowy figure in the tributary has managed to crawl the remaining fifteen feet or so to the Cyclone fence barrier, and now this unidentified man begins to fumble with the cable ties on its outside edges that secure the screen to the tunnel opening. The man seems to be injured or otherwise incapacitated, his hands clumsy on the knotted cables.

"Bob?"

Lilly lunges toward the barrier as it shivers and quakes in Bob Stookey's oily hands. The cable finally breaks loose, and the chain-link section collapses outward onto Bob.

"BOB!"

The impact knocks the him backward. He trips and falls onto his spine, the rusty chain link pressing down on him. He lies there in a supine position, trying to breathe, trying to speak, his eyes bugging in agony. His flesh is pasty white, his eyes rimmed in livid purple, his lips gray and bloodless. His lungs heave, expanding and contracting under his filthy, blood-soaked chambray shirt with the urgency of a bellows fanning a dying fire.

Lilly slips through the opening and pulls the barrier off the older man.

A swarm of about twelve new walkers converges on the gaping maw behind Lilly as she frantically lifts the barrier up and hurriedly slams it back in place, securing it with the cables. A few of the creatures try to force their way out, pushing on the chain link before the barrier is secured. Grunting and groaning with effort, Lilly lets out a howl of rage as she struggles with the cables, her hands greasy with sweat, the creatures pushing up against her, their dead fingers trying to worm their way through the open links. She finally gets the cables wound tight.

The pressure of the swarm strains the fencing, bowing the chain link inward, but the cables hold.

Lilly flops down beside Bob. She pulls him into a furious embrace, smelling his trademark scent: Marlboros, sweat, Juicy Fruit, and Old Spice. She cradles his head to her collarbone and strokes his hair and softly murmurs, "Thank you, thank you, thank you. . . . We cut that one real close . . . too close. . . . I thought you were a goner, you old geezer. . . . God, it's good to see . . . Thank you, thank—"

He hasn't said a word. She can feel his chest palpating. His skin is cold and clammy. His shirt is soaked through with sweat.

Lilly backs off an inch or two and takes a closer look at Bob's face, which is draped in shadows from the meager cone of light above them—and that's when she starts panicking. She can see by the color of his skin, the way his eyes have gone pink and glassy, the way his nostrils flare and his lungs heave as he tries to speak but is able to make only strangled grunting noises, that he's having some kind of seizure or attack.

The word "heart" bubbles up from the deeper pools of Lilly's unconscious.

She saw her uncle Mike have one years ago, before her very eyes at the kitchen table at Grandpa Buck's place in Valdosta. The heavyset house painter was Everett's older brother, and had spent a lifetime of catting around and drinking heavily and sampling every form of fatty food and fast women that life had to offer. Divorced three times, a parolee from the U.S. Penitentiary in Atlanta for wire fraud, Uncle Mike surprised no one when he bowed his head that night at the dining table like he was either praying or about to take a header into his collard greens.

The strangest part—especially to a seventeen-year-old girl—was the casual way he looked up and said, 'Oops . . . here comes.' Like he was expecting a package or a court summons. And everybody around the table knew what he was talking about, and everybody knew what it entailed. Nobody panicked, nobody rushed to the telephone. In fact, they immediately got into an argument regarding what vehicle they should deploy to take him to the hospital.

Lilly remembers waiting for the man to clutch his chest dramatically and flop onto his back in seizures of agony like in the movies, but that never happened. Uncle Mike might as well have had a gas bubble that night that he needed to simply belch out—in fact, Lilly had learned later that this was exactly what a heart attack felt like . . . *at first*. That night, before they took Mike Caul away, Lilly saw her dad's brother writhing in pain on the couch out in the living room, complaining that it felt like an iron vise was tightening around his chest. Lilly remembers his skin color going so pallid and gray it looked as though the man was made of marble.

Bob Stookey has this same coloration right this moment in the dim light of the tunnel, as though he's been in agony for quite a long while now, his face so drawn and lifeless it looks like someone has sucked the air out of it. The fleshy bags under his eyes are so wrinkled they remind Lilly of the skin of a balloon that has been deflated. Lilly's heart begins to race. She rises to a kneeling position, cradles his head, and says, "Bob, can you hear me? Can you understand?"

He manages a nod, and then a sort of crooked grin. Very softly, very breathlessly, he says, "Don't have to . . . *yell*. . . . I'm old . . . but I ain't deaf."

Lilly recognizes in his halting, wheezing words the sound of an oxygen-starved, late-stage heart attack. A tremendous stab of emotion slices through her as she realizes he probably crawled all this way from the Elkins Creek junction in unimaginable pain. She takes him by the shoulders, gently lifting him so they are eye to eye. "Bob, is it a heart attack, ya think?"

He manages a nod.

"Can you breathe?"

With great effort: "Not . . . great . . . no."

"What do I do? Tell me what to do. You're the fucking medic."

He swallows with difficulty and looks like he's about to fall asleep. He manages a shake of his head, probably indicating there isn't shit she can do. His eyelids flutter for a moment.

"Stay with me!" She shakes him. "Breathe!" She straddles him. "I'm going to try CPR!" She barely remembers it from her lifeguard days, but what the hell else is she going to do? "Here we go!" She crosses her hands on his upper sternum and gives him three sharp nudges. She has no idea what she's doing. "Breathe, Bob! Breathe!" She bends down and pinches his nose and breathes into his mouth, three sharp breaths. "Breathe!—Breathe!—*BREATHE!*"

Bob's eyes have rolled back in his head, and his body has gone limp.

"No!—No!—Goddamnit no!!—No fucking way!!" She clenches her fists and pounds his chest as hard as she can. "You fucking asshole!—You don't do this to me *now*!" She hunches down and blows into his mouth as though trying to inflate the balloon back to where it was. "Bob!—Stay with me!—Please!—Bob, please!!"

Behind her, the swarm reacts to the commotion, the chain link rattling as they press inward, harder and harder, the watery growls rising into a hellish dissonant commentary. Lilly looks over her shoulder at them. "SHUT THE FUCK UP!!"

She feels something tugging at her sweatshirt and looks down and sees Bob's huge, coarse hand clutching the fabric of her shirttail as though holding on for dear life. He looks as though he's trying to say something. His liver-colored lips tremble, his mouth working desperately to get words out.

Lilly climbs off him, kneels next to him, leans down, and tries to hear.

Bob's voice is drowned out by the clamor of the swarm, the husky baritone growls bouncing off the walls and the inside of Lilly's skull.

She turns and shrieks at the biters at the top of her lungs. "YOU FUCKING SACKS OF SHIT!!—SHUT YOUR FUCKING ROTTEN MOUTHS!!!"

Bob tries desperately to speak. He clutches her shirt with the last soupçon of energy left in him. She kneels down and pushes her ear to his lips. She concentrates on the breathy whisper coming out of him. The word "love" and the word "you" are the only things she can make out at first. Then she hears the words *"Lilly-girl"* very clearly, and she registers the complete sentence: "Love you, Lilly-girl."

"Bob?"

His grip on her shirt has loosened. His hand falls to the tunnel floor. His body relaxes and goes still. She shakes him gently.

"BOB!"

His face has changed. The furrows of wrinkles corrugating his brow have smoothed out, and so have the crow's-feet around his hound-dog eyes. The pain has left his face. An expression that Lilly can only think of as *tranquil* has passed over his features.

"Oh Jesus . . ."

She embraces the lifeless shell in her arms. She hugs him tighter than she has ever hugged another human being, and she keeps hugging him for a long time in that gloomy tunnel with the atonal chorus of snarls echoing off the walls, reverberating down the arteries of the labyrinth.

Lilly tenderly lays the body back down on the tunnel floor, and she closes its eyes. She leans down and plants a soft kiss on the forehead. Her tears fall onto the chest, soaking into the tattered denim shirt. She wipes her eyes. She feels something cutting into her leg, something sharp, and looks down.

Bob's left hand—frozen in death—clutches a bundle of dynamite. Lilly stares at the ten-inch paper sticks wound with duct tape.

She stares at them for a long time, thinking, listening to the horrible grinding noise of the dead.

TWENTY

The preacher rides on the RV's sideboard the whole way around the north outskirts of the village. The morning has turned raw and overcast, a thin layer of haze filtering the pale sun, and Reese Lee Hawthorne drives the camper with caution, the other vehicles chugging along single file behind him, a flash of fully automatic gunfire from an AR-15 or a machine pistol sparking out the windows now and again when the edge of the horde gets too close or one of the stray drones happens to shuffle out into their path.

The town is ringed in hundreds and hundreds of walking dead, all of them showing the patina of two-plus years outdoors on the endless treadmill of super-hunger. With skin like old wax paper that's been wadded and smoothed back out, eyes buried in sacs of pus, articles of clothing so sodden with bile they have the consistency of greasepaint, these pathetic creatures have turned the atmosphere hanging over town into a rancid cesspool of decay. The thousand or so walkers swarming Woodbury have stalled for some reason, stuck in a loop of lumbering circles around the derelict parks and boarded storefronts—the slow dance of a phonograph needle skipping over and over again on the same groove.

Reverend Jeremiah Garlitz squints into the ashy, diffuse sky as the light glints off a sign on the empty bullet-riddled water tower east of town—"WOODBURY: A PEACH OF A PLACE"—and he smiles. His bald dome crawling with gooseflesh, his eyes stinging from the acrid tang of death on the wind, he wishes his father could see him now. The preacher has become the spiritual guide of the unwashed masses, the ruler of the End Days. He will take this town back from the dead in the name of Master Sergeant Daniel Herbert Garlitz and all that the old man stood for—discipline, rigor, purity, faith, and a bone-deep fear of God: the foundation of a new society.

"Okay, let's get to work!" The preacher gazes over his shoulder at the other vehicles coming up on each flank, and he gives a signal—a circular motion with one index finger—and the four pickups, two flatbed trucks, and one tow truck rasp to a stop one at a time on the bare ground of a vacant lot about fifty yards east of the main gate.

The incriminating tracks go unnoticed by the preacher and his men, the markings already fading to ghostly traces among the myriad furrows and ruts crisscrossing the sandy earth of the lot. Over the last couple of years, countless footprints and tire marks have left their imprints on the square acre of weeds and bare ground, only to blow asunder in a matter of days. The most recent set of tracks—a series of mysterious, inexplicable, parallel grooves spanning a width of almost forty feet—are nearly gone.

This is the nature of Woodbury's topography. When the town was originally established in the nineteenth century, it bore the name Sandtown for the proliferation of white sand that covers the ground here. And even today, the powdery stuff gets into everything, from gas tanks to laundry hanging on clotheslines. Some claim to feel the grit in their teeth whenever they eat. Tire tracks—even those of a huge unidentified conveyance the size of a battleship—don't last long here.

Now, all around the lot, vehicle doors creak open. Men climb out of cabs. Guns sit on hips and rest on shoulders and remain in holsters. Not a single man bothers to take cover. Careful reconnaissance has convinced everyone that the town is currently populated only by the dead. No reason to hurry. A spirit of inevitability pervades. Manifest destiny. They will make this their home, their base of operations, their seat of power amidst the ruins of the plague—just as Brother Jeremiah has promised them.

The preacher hops off the running board, his 9mm Glock in his right hand, the safety off, cocked and ready. "On my signal!" he calls to his men. "And make every bullet count, boys!"

He pauses and stands calmly before the swarm, as if impervious to the dangers coalescing near the hole in the barricade less than a hundred feet away. Several of the biters have reacted to the noise of the convoy and the sound of the preacher's rich baritone voice calling out over the wind. The monsters turn, one by one, and lock their sharklike gazes on the man in black and his associates fanning out on either side of the lot.

Jeremiah calmly surveys the southeast corner of Woodbury and the throngs gathered inside the gap in the wall, and he's about to give the order to fire . . . when he frowns. He clearly remembers two massive semitrucks parked grille to grille across the huge gaping opening in the barricade—the makeshift castle gate. Where the hell are they? And something else is bothering him: The configuration of the wall seems to have changed.

More of the walkers have started to shamble toward him, sniffing him and his men, locking on to them like ravenous dogs on the hunt, drooling and snarling wetly, closing the distance to fifty feet or so. Jeremiah stares at the street corner just inside the break in the barricade, and he notices that somebody has moved the wall, perhaps recently, and most definitely hurriedly. He can see the marks on the pavement, and the new boards shored up against the weathered planks of the original wall. It doesn't occur to him that there could be a safe area behind this hastily repositioned section of barricade spanning a square block between Dogwood Lane and Jones Mill Road. It doesn't register immediately because he smells the encroaching wave of dead and sees the walkers coming toward him—now only thirty feet away.

He decides it's time to clear this town for good, clear it in the name of the Lord.

Crouching down in the rancid darkness of the tributary, the air buzzing with the moaning of the dead, Lilly Caul feels her soul sinking into the primordial sediment beneath her, draining out of her as she holds the limp form to her chest, stroking the dead man's hair, cradling the back of his skull as though he were a sick child.

She can still detect the faintest whiff of Juicy Fruit gum radiating off the body—that sickeningly sweet, powdery candy smell—just beneath the pervasive stench of mortified flesh, and this breaks Lilly's heart. It's as though Bob Stookey's life force stubbornly refuses to relinquish this realm. In the form of a stale piece of Wrigley's chewing gum still lodged somewhere in the man's mouth, Bob's essence holds on long past his death. Lilly's tears trace the edges of her cheeks. As hot and bitter as scalding vinegar, they soak the edges of Bob's filthy chambray shirt.

Lilly's right hand slowly moves down to her right thigh. "I'm so, so, so, so, so, so, so sorry, Bob. . . . We could have made this town work."

She feels the tiny, nubby beavertail grip of her bowie knife. She closes her eyes and wills her hand to wrap around the knife's hilt. The webbing between her thumb and forefinger presses against the handle as she slowly, reluctantly draws it out of its sheath. Her other hand remains on the back of Bob's head, gently cradling his skull. She discreetly lifts the blade.

"I love you, Old Hoss," she whispers into his ear, tenderly kissing a hairy earlobe. Her voice is drowned out by the churning, rasping chorus of growls rising up behind the barrier of chain link twenty feet away.

With one hard, sharp thrust, she drives the tip of the blade into the back of the man's skull between the cords of his neck, never once breaking her embrace, never once pulling away from his ear.

The blade sinks at least six inches into his brain.

Jeremiah gazes up at the darkening sky, takes a deep, girding breath, turns, and starts to give the order to clear the walkers when he hears a strange sound.

A voice coming from *behind* him, emanating from the heart of the swarm, belonging to a living person, piercing the din: *"NOW!—FIRE!"*

Jeremiah whirls around just in time to see the four walkers leading the pack suddenly throw off their tattered overcoats and bile-spattered rags.

The preacher stares, paralyzed with shock, his gun still gripped at his side as he utters under his breath, "What has Satan wrought . . . ?"

The four lead walkers reveal themselves to be living humans camouflaged in the garb of the dead, covered with gruesome muck, their scents drowned by layers of death-stench harvested from a corpse. Each of them is holding an assault-style rifle. Jeremiah manages to raise his Glock and get off a single shot before diving for cover under the RV.

The preacher's round goes high and to the left, pinging off a high-tension wire.

Then things begin to transpire very quickly, over the course of a single minute and a half, all of it practically happening at once, beginning with Harold Staubach's answering the blast with a quick controlled burst from his Bushmaster, lighting up the air between him and the other men, strafing the side of the RV with a necklace of sparks as the preacher rolls under the camper's massive chassis. Some of the other caravan members immediately lunge behind open truck doors and fenders, instinctively taking cover, while others try to get off shots before leaping behind vehicles. Within seconds, the four faux monsters unleash hellfire. David Stern empties a Tec-9 machine pistol on full auto directly at Chester Gleason. The grizzled laborer tries to return fire with his HK416, but the weapon jams, and the volley of armor-piercing rounds perforates his chest and his left shoulder and his neck, sending him staggering backward in an envelope of blood mist. He's dead before he hits the ground. At the same time, Norma Sutters stands on David's right flank, firing her AR-15 wildly, not really presenting much of a threat, but howling a spontaneous war cry supercharged by her skills as a gospel choir director. Fifty yards away, Stephen Pembry leaps out of his tow truck with an old M16, and tries to fire, but before he can squeeze off a single shot, one of Norma's stray rounds strikes him full-on between the eyes—the definition of a lucky shot—and sends him staggering backward, his skull snapping back in a fog of pink spray, the impact knocking him to the ground, where he will lie and expire over the remaining seconds of the skirmish. Miles Littleton fares a little better in the aiming department, as he brooms the area with a fusillade of .308 caliber bullets from his AK-47, some of the rounds finding the two gunmen crouched behind pickups thirty yards due west. The armor-piercing bullets penetrate the flimsy layers of Detroit steel, fiberglass, and upholstery, hitting each gunman dead center, perforating lungs and carotid arteries and sending the men flinging backward, arms pinwheeling into the oblivion of weeds and organ failure. By this point, the preacher has attempted to return fire from under the enormous Winnebago, but his 9mm pistol is woefully outmatched, its fire rate far too low to make a dent in the attack. The three avengers are now simply spraying the general vicinity with un-controlled volleys—spitting centipedes of dust and debris off the ground, strafing the sides of vehicles, leaving chains of divots and tufts in the metal, pinging and ringing off grillwork and fenders, bursting door glass, vaporizing windshields into sheets of sparkling particles that implode across dashboards and seats. Three more ac-olytes go down. Earl Jerico, a pear-shaped man in denim and a Braves cap, gets it in the neck and shoulder, spinning in a bloody pirouette before slamming into the side of his pickup and sliding to the ground. A skinny, tattooed former biker-for-Jesus named Thurston Breen manages to dodge the spray of high-caliber slugs as he races for cover, but absorbs a series of gut shots while trying to crawl under the chassis of his flatbed stake truck. He rolls out from under the vehicle and curls into a fetal ball and dies more slowly than the rest. Many of the stray ricochets and errant blasts go into the oncoming surge of walkers, but it doesn't take long for the mass of reanimated corpses to overrun the vacant lot—despite the crossfire turning the air into a cloudbank of blue smoke—most of the dead flowing in from the adjacent streets and meadows. The four disguised guardians of Woodbury now slam new magazines into their weapons and begin to back away slowly—according to plan—as the oncoming horde engulfs the lot. Chester Gleason's body attracts a large number of the early arrivals, at least a dozen or more of the creatures descending upon his remains, their hunched forms rooting down into him for the truffles of his still-warm organs. The feeding frenzy intensifies as more of the things flood the battle-ground and find the other victims of the gunfight: the wounded, the fallen. David Stern orders his fellow counterassailants back into the safe zone behind the wall at Dogwood Street—his voice hollering above the din: "HURRY!—HURRY!—HURRY!" They all turn and trot after him. Harold Staubach doesn't see the glint of gunmetal fifty yards behind him, sticking out from under the Winnebago, as Jeremiah takes aim. Nobody sees the preacher fire off a single shot until it's too late. Harold is approaching the safe zone when the solitary round rips through his shoulder, throwing him off his feet and sprawling him across the asphalt road. Almost instantly, with-out a word, two things happen in response: Miles Littleton opens up on the camper, firing three controlled bursts from his AK, driving the preacher back under the RV, and David and Norma simulta-neously grab hold of Harold by the shoulders and start to drag him toward the fence at Dogwood Street. But they're too late.

The street before them crawls with walkers, drawn to the com-motion of the firefight, so many that David freezes practically in mid-stride, surveying the ragged mob of the dead weaving toward him, drunk with hunger and kill-lust, arms reaching, and yells at the top of this lungs: "PLAN B!—PLAN B!"

For a long while, in the noisy darkness of the tributary, Lilly remains in a desperate embrace with Bob's remains, the knife still buried to the hilt in his skull. Her eyes have welled up again as the warmth of his cerebro-spinal fluids continues to gush around the knife's hilt and run down her arm and under her sleeve. She's soaked with it. She hears a slight release of something that sounds like a faint puff of air, but Lilly can't tell if it's coming from the wound or from Bob's lungs. His body remains limp and lifeless in her arms.

The noise of the dead rumbles and chugs nearby, drowning out the faint and distant crackle of gunfire. It feels to Lilly as though a storm is gathering inside her as she gently lays the body back down on the tunnel floor. She positions the head so it's facing straight up. The puddle of blood beneath it has spread like black motor oil across the cracked hardpack floor. She carefully rests Bob's hands on his midsection.

Ancient Egyptians buried their dead with family pets, tools, scrolls, food, even coins for the afterlife, as though the deceased were simply embarking on a trip. Lilly digs in her pocket.

She puts her lucky coin—an old Buffalo nickel that her father, Everett, had given her—on Bob's eyelid. She leans down and softly kisses the bridge of his nose. She touches his cheek one last time, feeling the storm front moving in from deep within her core. Black clouds of rage start to migrate up through her, pulling a dark shade down across her field of vision.

Rising to her feet, she gazes back down the tributary and sees the swarm—now at least a hundred or more squeezed into the main conduit—pressing against the waffle of metal links. Their wormy gray faces puckering with hunger, their milky eyes wide with bloodlust, they drool and sputter and moan and try to squeeze their blackened fingers through the two-inch-square triangles. The Cyclone fencing barely holds, creaking with the pressure of their collective weight. It looks as though the barrier is about to snap.

Lilly reaches down to Bob's holster and pulls his .357. She snaps open the center and sees only two rounds remaining in the cylinder. She feels along the underside of his belt and finds the tiny leather pouch with the speed loader. She pulls it free and sticks it in her pocket. She digs some more and finds his lighter and a roll of safety fuse. She removes his watch and pockets it. The anger fuels her now, courses through her veins, galvanizes her, gets her up and moving. She rises to her feet, and walks across the tunnel to the chain-link barrier, and she stands there for a moment.

Her close proximity stirs the creatures into frenzies. The growls rise into gravelly ululations, like the howls of hyenas, the cold eyes widening, teeth gnashing frantically to get a piece of her. Some of them push harder, warping the chain-link fencing inward to its absolute limit. The odor is incredibly horrible.

Lilly stares impassively at them. She comes to within inches of their moldering mouths. She stares into their empty eyes. The rage-storm inside Lilly has begun to unleash torrents of adrenaline, lightning and thunder rumbling, squalls of emotion erupting in her veins.

The bundle of dynamite sits on the floor near the chain-link barrier.

Lilly pulls the detonator cord and the roll of safety fuse from her pocket, never once taking her eyes off the creatures trying to squeeze through the screen of fencing and get to her tender flesh. She goes over to the explosives, picks them up, and pushes the detcord into the spongy end-cap—her gaze still riveted on the walkers. She sits the bundle of dynamite on the floor in front of them as though setting down a food dish for a family pet.

"There ya go," she murmurs, her voice sounding foreign to her ears. It sounds thick and coarse with fury, the voice of a gladiator about to enter the ring. "Chew on that for a while."

She turns and starts on her way eastward, carefully unfurling the fifty feet or so of safety fuse as she goes along, hastening toward the sewer manhole under Riggins Ferry Road.

Soaked in sweat, heart racing, Jeremiah breathes in and out through his mouth, the stench so thick it threatens to strangle him. He lies prone on the cold ground beneath the greasy chassis of the RV, still holding his 9mm pistol. Chaos surrounds the vehicle. All his followers are gone. Bodies are strewn across the lot like driftwood. But the Good Lord is still with Jeremiah. Fate always wins out, and it will prevail today if the preacher can just manage to get out of this mess.

He looks to his immediate left and sees through the reeds of wild grass and stiff-legged walkers brushing against the camper a small swarm still hovering over Chester Gleason's body, sucking the marrow from what's left of him.

Jeremiah lets out a pained sigh, his breath blowing dust off the ground next to his lips. He looks to his right and sees countless ragged legs, some of them sticking out of dresses, looking spindly and cadaverous as they trundle aimlessly back and forth. Intermittently, the preacher catches glimpses of his other disciples—half of Reese Lee Hawthorn over here, his remains spilling its purple, glistening delicacies for the swarm; Stephen Pembry over there, reduced to a pile of partially clothed guts—and the sight of such carnage makes Jeremiah twitch with cognitive dissonance. Is this what God wants? Is this what awaits *Jeremiah* himself in this everlasting darkness of the Rapture?

He manages to twist around and gaze down the length of the Winnebago's undercarriage toward its tail end.

He blinks. Is he hallucinating? He starts crawling toward the daylight at the rear of the RV, his gaze locked on a gap in the throng. He reaches the rear phalanx of exhaust pipes and trailer hitch and looks out beyond the adjacent switchyard of petrified train tracks and ancient directional signage. He sees a clear opening—an empty corridor of space between two halves of the multitude—where the mob of walkers has randomly separated.

On the far side of this opening sits a small building that looks relatively secure, its windows boarded or barred. If Jeremiah can slip unnoticed through the momentary break in the herd, he might be able to get to that building and gain entrance before he too is reduced to bloody fodder. His heart speeds up. He sucks in a searing hot breath.

Then he crawls out from under the RV, springs to his feet, and charges as fast as he can toward the stationhouse, where the children secretly huddle in the shadows, trying so desperately to be quiet.

TWENTY-ONE

Barbara Stern sits on the floor behind the dusty shelving units at the northeast corner of the litter-strewn stationhouse, bracing herself on the shelf legs as though waiting out a tornado. The kids sit on each of her flanks, trying to concentrate on their coloring books and sketch pads and Little Golden Books like *The Poky Little Puppy* and *The Little Red Hen* while the world is turned upside down outside their boarded windows.

Every time a burst of gunfire crackles in the distance, or a sonic boom from a shotgun lights up the sky, or a cluster of walkers brushes up against the wood-frame outer walls, the older kids twitch and flinch, while the younger ones whimper under their breaths as though they've been kicked in the gut. Barbara keeps whispering for them to relax, it's going to be okay, they have a good plan and Lilly and Bob know what they're doing, but her nerves are as raw and exposed as those of the children. She grips those shelf legs with white-knuckle pressure at the boom of each salvo, holding on so tightly that the molded steel has begun to make bloody indentations on her palms.

She keeps thinking she can identify the make and model of each gun as she hears its blast, and that she doesn't hear the blat of David's Tec-9, and this is driving her crazy. The machine pistol that they found a few weeks ago in the storage rooms of the Meriwether

County National Guard Depot has a distinctive sound: a sort of shrill metallic rattle, like a baby howitzer. She hasn't heard that noise for many minutes, and her brain keeps going to the worst-case scenario, flashing on images of David lying bullet-riddled and torn apart by walkers, and this makes her grip the shelf legs even tighter.

In fact, she's trying to drive these very images from her brain when she hears a noise coming from across the room that sets her teeth on edge and makes her flesh rash with goose bumps.

"Don't move!" she hisses at the children, pulling herself up and switching off the safety on her .44 Bulldog. The gun is extremely heavy for a snub-nosed revolver, and it seems to have gotten heavier over the last few hours. In addition, the trigger action is stiff, hard to pull. But at the moment, Barbara feels as though she could crack the grip in half with her bare hand.

The noise of someone trying to force the knob on the side door rattles again across the room, and Barbara assumes the shooting position as she approaches, gun in both hands, finger on the trigger pad, shoulders squared while she blows a long tendril of gray hair from her face. She makes sure to hold her zaftig body at an angle to the door so her right shoulder will absorb much of the recoil from the massive handgun.

She reaches the door, and puts her ear against the wooden frame, holding the Bulldog's muzzle up at the ceiling. She hears a frantic shuffling, someone huffing and puffing.

She's about to call out when the door suddenly explodes inward, bursting open with the force of a battering ram. The jamb smacks Barbara straight on, knocking her senseless, driving her backward, and sending her to floor. She lands on her ass, the Bulldog spinning off across the parquet tile. Her vision wavers, her ears ringing as she tries to crawl toward the gun.

At the corner of Dogwood and Jones Mill, in a curtain of cordite, smoke, dust, and death-stench as thick as gauze, Miles Littleton goes through an entire ten-round magazine, momentarily keeping the leading edge of the walker horde at bay while David and Norma attempt to drag Harold Staubach out of harm's way. Harold is having none of it.

"Forget it!" Lying on his side, sucking in raspy breaths, he pushes them away, kicking feebly, his shoulder in shreds, the front of his tunic a deep crimson red, drenched in arterial blood, which soaks the pavement. "Just go—GO!" He flinches as another walker drops to the cobblestones mere inches away from his right foot, half its head blown asunder by the dumdums from David's Glock.

"Shut up!—Shut the fuck up!—We're not leaving you and that's all there is to it!" David barks his words at him, refusing to let go, dragging the older man another ten feet or so toward the barricade. Norma tries to take Harold's feet and lift him up, but Harold kicks her off with his last drops of energy.

"Y'all are gonna get yourselves killed!" Harold screams at them, his voice breaking, his strength draining away. He tries to push David Stern off him. David's hands are slimy with blood, and Harold slips from his grasp. Collapsing back to the pavement, Harold lets out a gasp, his beautiful singing voice finally starting to crumble. "I'm done for—I'm gone—You've gotta get yourselves *inside*!"

Miles fires another burst into the column of biters pressing toward them. More and more of the creatures—drawn to the noise and commotion—surround them, closing in like a fist. In a few seconds it will be too late—their ammunition is dwindling to nothing. A few more bursts from the AK and that will be it.

The young car thief fires a short salvo, hitting the three closest walkers.

One of the putrid heads explodes in a cloud of black fluids, and another snaps back so far it almost rips free. The owner of the third head keeps coming, the blast only grazing its temple. "TOO MANY OF 'EM!" Miles screams. He is trying to fire another controlled burst, but now the gun only clicks impotently. "FUCK!— SHIT!—*SHIT!!*"

The walkers engulf them. Miles pulls a machete from a sheath on his leg, Norma grabs a garden spade strapped to her pack, and David is grunting and huffing as he drags Harold farther and farther away from the throngs. Harold wavers in and out of consciousness as more of the creatures press in from the west, cutting off their escape route. The persistent din of guttural growling rises up all around them now, as loud as a jet engine, the stench unbearable, the hooked fingers of outstretched arms clawing at the air. Harold finally passes out, and David shakes him, feeling for a pulse.

Miles and Norma put up a valiant last-ditch effort to fight the creatures off, flailing madly at them, lashing out at one dead pasty face after another, striking some in the eye socket, others in the forehead, still others up through the mandible, but it's futile. There are far too many of them now—so many that David's view of the barricade is cut off, blocked by the mob. He lets out a howl of rage. Harold is dead weight now. David collapses next to the older man, heaving pained breaths.

Norma trips over them and falls to the paving stones. Miles flails and flails, until he stumbles over his own feet and sprawls to the pavers next to the others. And in that horrible moment of anguish—that single frozen instant before they are engulfed and devoured—David shares a feverish glance with the others. It's as though they all realize the same thing at precisely the same moment: They are all going to die, and worse than that, they are going to die at the ravenous hands of the dead, torn apart, eviscerated, though they're a stone's throw of safety.

Only so much can be communicated in a single look—especially in a moment of suspended time such as this—but somehow, David Stern manages to gaze so deeply into Norma Sutters' sweaty, maternal, old-soul face right at that moment that he sees his last fleeting thought returned from her in a wordless response: *At least we'll go down together, as one—here in this desolate situation; we'll perish in each other's arms.* Norma nods at David, and then puts her plump arms around him.

David looks away from the fish-belly faces and shoe-button eyes as the creatures descend en masse upon them, and he has just closed his eyes and clasped onto the matronly Norma Sutters when he suddenly hears a noise that rises above the jet-engine rasp of the dead. And the noise is such a welcome surprise, David Stern silently begins to cry.

At first it sounds like a teakettle on the boil, a thin, shrill whistle. But when it swells into a shriek. David realizes the whistle is the sound of a young boy screaming. This is followed by the roar of a diesel engine, which farts a plume of black, acrid smoke into the air behind the adjacent barricade. David's heart leaps, his breath seizing up in the back of his throat.

A thunderous explosion shatters the morning air, piercing the droning chorus of growls, and David Stern recoils with a start as the makeshift barrier of wooden siding and drywall fifty feet away suddenly collapses, the boards slamming down to the ground with a resounding series of thuds, and in a storm cloud of dust a gargantuan contraption emerges from behind the fallen barricade.

David recognizes the massive front blades of the International Harvester combine.

The kid is early—God bless his little snot-nosed soul—the kid never could keep track of time—that beautiful, perfect little man!

Like a tidal wave of gleaming metal, the thirty-foot-wide mouth—filled with rows of razor-sharp blades—churns toward the swarm, kicking up waves of debris and particles of prairie grass. A stream of detritus pours out the top of the vent stack as the enormous machine chugs and whirs toward the closest moving corpses.

Up in the high cab, encased in glass like a tiny emperor, Tommy Dupree sits at the controls. The kid learned to operate the showroom-new harvester by reading the owner's manual, and the jerky way he's steering the thing reveals how green his skills are. But the livid, furrowed face behind the tinted glass of the pilot cubicle also shows his determination, which triggers another thought in the back of David Stern's traumatized mind.

Thank God for plan B.

On the floor, dazed and breathless from the pain shooting down her spine, Barbara Stern can see only blurry impressions of the huge man who has lunged into the stationhouse after kicking the door open. Tall, middle-aged, dressed in an ashy black funereal suit coat, bald as a billiard ball, face all broken out, blotchy, and livid, eyes crazy, he slams the door shut, then registers the fact that his entrance has knocked a sixty-something woman dressed in a floral-print muumuu over onto her fulsome ass. He's still hyperventilating from the terror and fatigue of sprinting across 150 yards of walker-infested real estate as he scans the dusty, cluttered stationhouse. The thud of a dozen biters hitting the door outside vibrates the air.

"Whoa, Nelly!" He lets out a deep, husky exclamation when he sees Barbara crawling toward her gun. He leaps across the room and reaches her at the precise moment she gets her hand around the Bulldog. "Hold on there, sis!"

He kicks the gun out of her sweaty grasp, the Bulldog spinning in the other direction.

Barbara Stern tries to roll away. The Slocum twins squeal in horrified unison as the preacher kicks the woman hard in the kidney with his big Wellington. Barbara gasps and rolls across the floor and tries to see where her gun went. Her vision blurs. Her nose gushes from the impact of the door, and she may or may not have bit her tongue, her mouth filling with the coppery warmth of blood as she tries to crawl toward the Bulldog. She senses the huge presence of the intruder looming over her.

"Calm down!" his voice booms, a deep, smoky, stentorian instrument trained in the sacristies and revival tents of charismatic religions. His face shines with exertion. He slams a boot down on Barbara Stern's dress. "It ain't like I'm gonna eat ya!"

"Okay!" Barbara breathlessly surrenders, flopping onto her side, bleeding profusely down the front of her muumuu. Her chin drips, the bridge of her nose throbbing, an occasional sharp stab behind her eyes. She blinks and holds up her trembling hands. "Okay . . ."

"Here." He digs in his breast pocket and pulls out a handkerchief. In the momentary lull, Barbara can hear the sound of the herd outside, an enormous, rusty, spinning turbine, surrounding the stationhouse; and she can hear something else, something in the distance, mingling with the din, vibrating the air, a low grinding noise that's as deep and raspy as the largest pipe on a church organ. Jeremiah throws the hankie and it lands on Barbara's legs. Then he goes over to the Bulldog, picks it up, checks the cylinder, and thrusts it down the back of his belt.

"Do whatever you need to do to me," Barbara murmurs, picking up the cloth and pressing it down on her nose. Her voice muted now by the fabric of the cloth and her congested airways, she says thickly, "But I'm asking you, please, I'm begging you, as a man of God, as a Christian, don't mess with these children. Don't hurt them. They have nothing to do with this."

He shoots a glance over at the cluster of kids hunkered and cowering behind the shelves. They look like scared animals in a cage. A soft continuous whimpering comes from the younger ones. The preacher smiles. He speaks without taking his eyes off the little ones. "Sorry to disagree with ya, sis, but they got *everything* to do with this."

He ambles over to the shelving unit, shoves it aside as though it were made of balsa wood, and gives the kids the once-over with gleaming eyes. The whimpering intensifies. The preacher's simian gaze settles on Bethany Dupree.

She appears to be the only child who isn't either hiding behind a sibling, crying, or gazing meekly down at the floor. She stands her ground, her hands on her hips as though she disapproves of the whole *concept* of this man. She meets his gaze with a withering sort of contempt.

The preacher grins. His face twitches. "You're a pistol, ain't ya?"

"Leave us alone," she says.

"You'll do nicely." He grabs her by the arm and pulls her out of hiding.

By this point, Barbara has managed to crawl across the floor, and now she struggles to her feet. The dizziness makes her head spin. She still can't see very well. She wavers slightly as she stands there holding the blood-soaked hankie to her nose, watching the preacher pull the little girl across the room toward the boarded window. "Don't do this, Jeremiah," Barbara says.

The preacher turns and faces the older woman in the blood-spattered muumuu. He draws his Glock and casually presses the barrel against the side of Bethany Dupree's head. All the fight goes out of the little girl's face. Her eyes moisten, and she swallows a big gulp of air, and her lips curl downward as she tries her hardest not to cry. The preacher's voice is flat and cold. "The wheels are already in motion, sis, there's nothing any of us can do. This here's the Rapture. We all been left behind, and now we're all just playing what ya might call a big old board game." The girl wriggles in his grasp, and Jeremiah tightens his grip on her collar, pressing the muzzle harder against her little pigtail. "The rivers are running red, sis." Jeremiah burns his gaze into Barbara. "Birds falling out of the sky, and the living wants me dead. This here tot, she's my little insurance policy."

Without any warning, a small child darts out from behind the shelf. Barbara whirls to see Lucas Dupree, his little five-year-old face furrowed with rage, his tiny fists clenched white-knuckle tight, racing toward the preacher screaming, "LET HER BE!"

Barbara drops the bloody cloth and deftly lunges toward the boy, snatching him up before he can cross the room, lifting him off his feet. The boy's feet continue to run in place in the air in a cartoonish pantomime. He's already beginning to sob as Barbara hugs him to her bosom and strokes the back of his hair. "Okay, bruiser, that's far enough, she's gonna be fine. It's okay. Easy now." Barbara caresses the boy's head and speaks softly but never takes her eyes off the preacher. "This man is *not* going to hurt your sister, he's just going to *borrow* her for a second." Barbara's eyes narrow almost to slits, fixing themselves on the preacher. "And if anything happens to her, even if a single hair on her head is mussed, the people who survive here today, whoever they may be, they're going to dedicate the remainder of their lives, however long *that* might be, to finding this man, this minister, this man of God, and making him sorry that he was ever born. Do you understand?"

Two individuals have listened closely to this soliloquy: the boy with his head buried in Barbara's chest, nodding slightly, and the preacher, who has gone very still through all this, regarding the woman with a strange mixture of malice and admiration. At last, with the gun still pressed to the little girl's head, he gives the woman a respectful nod. "Message received, sis. I think we could have very well done business together in another life." He drags the little girl to the door. She keeps her tears tamped down. The preacher gives Barbara one last glimpse over his shoulder. "Keep your powder dry, sis."

Then he turns, grasps the doorknob, and opens the door a few centimeters.

He peers out and sees an opening. The biters have drifted away from the door.

He pulls Bethany out into the pale light of day and makes an awkward run for it.

TWENTY-TWO

Jeremiah doesn't get more than twenty paces from the doorway of the derelict stationhouse when he staggers to an abrupt halt. The girl nearly falls over, the stop is so sudden, and for a moment, in that hideous ashen sunlight washing the switchyard, Jeremiah thinks he's seeing a ghost. He stands there, still clutching the little girl's collar, thunderstruck by what stands before him. The deep, sepulchral rumble of a giant combine—incongruously harvesting some unidentified crop where there are no crops—echoes from the northwest corner of town, accompanying Jeremiah's confusion with a contramelody of gnawing, grating, shredding noises. But the preacher barely notices the surreal, nonsensical sounds, nor does he register the unrelenting drone of the swarm, close enough to see through the neighboring trees and the wreckage-strewn gaps between buildings.

The figure that stands directly in front of Jeremiah doesn't move, and doesn't say anything at first, just stands there with her shoulders squared off and her gaze fixed on the preacher and the little girl. The breeze tosses the woman's dishwater auburn hair, which is pulled back in a tight French braid, though many tendrils had come loose over the past few hours of exertion, struggle, and trauma underground. Her fashionably ripped jeans and camo-jacket are now in shreds, her face and arms scourged with grit, cuts, and bruises. The look in her eyes penetrates Jeremiah's soul, reaching down into a dark place inside him and strumming some dissonant, unexpected chord of fear. Then, Jeremiah notices the enormous revolver with the four-inch barrel gripped in her right hand, which at the moment hangs at rest at her side, the muzzle pointed down at the ground.

"Look at you," the preacher finally says to her. "All pleased with yourself."

"Let her go." Lilly Caul's voice is so brittle with rage, so cold, it sounds almost like a recording of a voice played a scintilla too slow.

Jeremiah presses the barrel harder against Bethany Dupree's head. "I don't know how you did it but it don't matter one whit no more. Nothin' does."

"I don't think you heard me."

Jeremiah lets out a dry chuckle. "Acts of heroism, sacrifice, things done for the better good . . . none of it means high holy hell anymore."

"Excuse me. You're gonna die today." Lilly augers her gaze into his. "You might as well do something good beforehand to shore things up a little."

Jeremiah feels the hate rise up and fill his mouth with the bitter taste of odium. "Get out of my way, missy."

Lilly calmly raises the gun, aims it at him, and holds up a watch in her free hand. It looks cheap, shopworn, like an old Timex on a faded leather strap. "You know what this is?"

"No more games." Jeremiah presses the barrel so hard against the head of the little girl, her whimpers intensify to outright sobbing, her head bending over with the pressure of the muzzle. Jeremiah practically growls the words: "The death of this precious little girl will be on your eternal soul."

"It's a watch," Lilly casually informs him, ignoring his threats, indicating with a nod the importance of the used timepiece. "Belonged to Bob Stookey, a man whose death is on *your* worthless fucking soul." She glances at the second hand. "And if my calculations are correct, we should have about ten sec—"

The muffled explosion from below cuts off her words with the abruptness of a jump cut in a film.

Lilly's estimate was ten seconds off.

The ground seems to shudder slightly as the heat wave rams into the back of Lilly's neck. The noise is enormous and ear-shattering, cracking open the humid air and breaking windows as far as Canyon Road. Deafened by the boom, Lilly staggers forward and then sprawls to the ground in the aftershock. The sky behind her cleaves apart in a fountain of dirt, the particles of orange Georgia clay spewing upward in a vast smoke cloud that scrapes the clouds before dissipating.

The preacher stumbles backward, trips over his feet, and falls on his ass. The little girl staggers and goes down as well. Granules of dirt, litter, and unidentified shards of the underground rain down on them. The aftershocks tremble across the switchyard as the tunnels give way below and bury human and undead alike for eternity.

Lilly tries to rise to her feet but can only lift herself up to her hands and knees. Her head spins. She can't hear a thing, and she can barely see. Blinking frantically, she tries to focus on where her gun went. She sees it lying about five feet away. She lunges toward it, grabs it, and swings it up as she springs to her feet. She quickly assumes an offensive stance, but everything has gone all hazy and slow in the aftermath of the explosion.

Ears ringing, Lilly sees the preacher running away, his lanky arms pumping, his tattered waistcoat flapping in the wind as he charges as fast as he can toward the vacant lot to the east. With her gun still gripped in both hands, Lilly shuffles toward the girl. Little Bethany slowly rises, holding her ears, looking up at the sky.

"You okay, sweetie?" Lilly kneels by her, quickly giving her a once-over, looking for wounds. Lilly can barely hear, the ringing in her ears like a drill buzzing in her skull. She sees no injuries. "Talk to me."

"I can't hear anything!" The little girl holds her ears, opening her mouth as though trying to make them pop back into service.

"It's okay, sweetie. It's temporary. It's the noise of the explosion."

"How did you do that?"

Lilly glances over her shoulder. "We'll talk about it later, honey. Right now we gotta get you back inside and I gotta get to the safe zone."

In that single feverish moment, Lilly sees several things that quicken her pulse.

About a hundred yards away, the preacher is weaving through a cluster of walkers, slashing at them left and right with his Buck knife, apparently trying to work his way back to the vacant lot east of the switchyard—the same vacant lot across which all the gunfire had been exchanged. Adrenaline trickles through Lilly. She realizes the son of bitch is heading toward the enormous tow truck rig that sits about fifty yards south of the lot, still idling, sending intermittent puffs of inky black smoke out of its exhaust stack.

The second thing that Lilly sees triggers an even *bigger* spurt of panic: Three sides of the switchyard are now cut off by dense groups of dead shambling this way, drawn to all the tumult and yelling, their arms like divining rods, stiffly reaching, seeking fresh human meat. Lilly spins in a 360-degree pivot, searching for a way out, but seeing none. Even the stationhouse building is engulfed with the things now. Countless decomposing faces close in, pressing inward from all directions, face after face after face, each one featuring the same empty frosted-glass eyes, the same slimy lips curling away from blackened teeth. The noise and the odor of them rises to unbearable levels, and Lilly finds herself going blank again, as though her brain has just crashed.

Somehow, right then, in that fog bank of rot and decay, under that unforgiving pale sun, her ears still ringing, her heart palpitating, the flood of walkers engulfing her and the child, Lilly Caul realizes she has only one viable option—once again, the simplest solution proving

to be the best solution. She sees a grand total of a half dozen creatures between her and the front door of the stationhouse, which
lies about fifty feet away.

"Stay right by my side, sweetie," she says to the girl, and then aims
her gun at the two cadavers blocking their path to the door.

The first shot punches a divot in the top of the closest one's skull,
the thing folding in a cascade of black fluids and rancid blood. The
second shot rips through the center of the other one's face, sending
a cloud of dirty gray fluids out the exit wound.

Edging her way toward the building, Lilly multitasks now—
dumping the empty cylinder, tipping the speed-loader into the
chamber, injecting her last six bullets, while simultaneously yanking
Bethany toward the door.

They get within three feet of the entrance when a pair of male
biters—each one once a teenage farm kid, now clad in tattered,
blood-soaked long underwear—lunge single file, one after the
other, at the two living humans. The little girl squeals an involuntary shriek as Lilly instinctively points the gun at the closest assailant. The biter inadvertently gets caught on the barrel as it pounces,
its mouth gaping, the muzzle going down its throat like a tracheal
intubation. Lilly instantly squeezes off two shots. The first one blows
the back of the thing's skull off, and the second strikes the walker
coming up behind it. Both males collapse in showers of putrid
blood.

Lilly throws the door open and shoves the girl inside the shadows of the stationhouse, then follows her inside, slamming the door
behind them.

For a moment, Lilly bends down and catches her breath as the
little girl races over to Barbara Stern. Lilly takes in great, heaving
breaths, her hands on her knees, the rage crackling behind her eyes,
as bracing as smelling salts. The image of the preacher racing off
toward that tow truck has burned itself into her mind's eye. The
thought of him getting away makes her spine tingle with hate.
More than just the desire to wreak vengeance, more than the mere
satisfaction of evening a score, she needs to *end* this man.

"You're a sight for sore eyes," a voice says next to her, making her jump.

Lilly looks up at Barbara Stern, who stands nearby holding Bethany Dupree against her midriff. The girl softly cries into the folds of Barbara's muumuu. The older woman breathes through her mouth, her face severely swollen, both her eyes rimmed in swelling bruises, her nose enflamed to twice its size, blood crusted around her nostrils. Lilly stares. "Speaking of sore eyes . . . what the hell happened to you?"

"The preacher happened to me." Barbara takes a deep breath. "I'll live."

Lilly looks at her for a long time. "Yeah . . . but I promise you *he* won't."

"What?—What are you talking about?—You're not going after him!"

Lilly doesn't answer, simply checks her gun, flipping open the cylinder and seeing she has four rounds left. The children watch her from behind the shelves. She snaps the cylinder shut and hurries across to the room to the back window. Barbara follows her.

"Lilly, answer me. You're not thinking of going after him, are you?"

Lilly is too busy to answer, as she peers out a thin slat of daylight along the edge of the boarded window, gazing at the Woodbury town limits in the middle distance. At first, all she can see is the enormous combine mowing through columns of dead along Dogwood Street—a surreal sight, even from this great distance, like some kind of insanely elaborate irrigation system. Dark matter spews out a tall chimney stack, arcing up at least fifty feet in the air and then diffusing into a rainbow of wet tissue that sleets down and soaks the ground and the sides of buildings over half a block away.

Lilly gawks. Upon further scrutiny, it has become clear that the tall stack is actually the vertical vent on the huge farm machine that Tommy Dupree discovered only a few days ago in that gleaming showroom a few miles south of here. Originally designed for the laborious job of separating grain from chaff across wide expanses of land, it's now being repurposed—just as Lilly and Tommy had devised—for the task of mowing down row after row of shambling cadavers. And for a brief moment, seeing that thirty-foot-long mouth of rotating teeth gobbling the roiling masses of dead with the furious efficiency of a macabre assembly line fills Lilly with a sense of inevitability, fate, and maybe even a higher purpose. The sight of that putrescent geyser of gore soaring out through the air behind the harvester synchronizes with her rage. She wants to feed the preacher into the great steel oblivion of those circular teeth.

The preacher!

Lilly scans the outer limits of the town, sweeping her gaze across the adjacent switchyard, past the grove of sickly pecan trees, and into the vacant lot where the grisly remains of the battlefield still lie in mangled unidentified heaps like forgotten piles of kindling. In the far distance, beyond the dry creek bed, a lanky, tall figure in black hurriedly climbs up into the cab of a huge, heavy-duty tow truck. The back of the truck, including the massive tow crane, still drips with carnage, the top portion of a prisoner still lashed to the gantry, the bottom half of his torso ripped clean off by the horde, leaving entrails to dangle and dry in the sun. Lilly jerks away from the window. She turns and looks around the room as though she's lost something.

"Answer me, Lilly." Barbara gazes skeptically at the younger woman.

Lilly looks up. "Where's the walkie-talkie? You had one with you, right?"

"Don't do this, Lilly."

"Where is it?! C'mon, Barbara!"

"All right, all right!" Barbara sighs, gently moves the little girl aside, and quickly pads across the room. "It's right here." She digs through her pack, which sits on a peach crate near the shelving units. The children remain huddled in the shadows behind the adjacent shelves, peering through the gaps like stray puppies held captive in a pound, their eyes huge and bright with terror as they look on.

Barbara finds the device and brings it to Lilly, who has nervously returned to the window to peer back out at the edges of the vacant lot. The tow truck hasn't moved, the preacher still visible inside the cab, hunched over the wheel. It looks as though the thing won't start. Maybe it's out of gas.

"Here." Barbara hands her the two-way. "But please don't do this."

Lilly ignores her. She turns the power on and thumbs the Send button. "This is Lilly. Miles, are you there? Can you hear me? Over!"

Barbara lets out another anguished sigh. "The preacher is gone, Lilly—you'll never see him again, And good riddance, I say."

Lilly waves her back. "Sssssshhhhhhh!"

The walkie crackles, a voice on the other end of the line breaking though the static: *". . . Lilly . . . ?"*

Lilly presses the switch. "Miles, is that you?"

Through the speaker: *". . . Yes ma'am!"*

Barbara clutches Lilly's arm. "Lilly, don't go and get yourself killed over this—it's not worth it."

Lilly yanks her arm away and then barks into the walkie's mike as she stares through the slat of daylight at the far edge of the vacant lot. She can see a black cloud belch out of the tow truck's exhaust pipe as the preacher finally gets the engine started. "Miles, where are you? Are you with the others?"

Through the static: *". . . In the safe zone, with Norma, David, and Harold, just like we planned. . . . "*

Lilly squeezes the button. "Miles, can you get to your car?"

Another splash of static sizzles from the tiny speaker, and then, after a beat: *". . . I guess so, yeah, she's parked out behind the willow. . . . "*

Lilly says into the mike: "By the river, you mean? East of the tunnel entrance?"

". . . That's right. . . . "

"How fast can you get there?"

". . . You mean like now . . . ?"

"Yes! Fuck yes! Now, Miles! How soon can you meet me there?!"

Another beat of staticky silence, then the voice of the car thief sounding skeptical:

". . . Lotta walkers between us and the river, Lilly. . . . "

"Just do it!" Her voice slices through the interference like a bolt of lightning. "Everything depends on us getting to your car ASAP! You understand? Tell me you understand, Miles."

Through the speaker: *". . . I understand. . . . "*

"Good!" Lilly looks at Barbara, then back out the window at the tow truck pulling away in a cloud of exhaust and dust. "Get moving, Miles. And bring some firepower, whatever's left. And some extra ammo. I'll meet you there in five minutes, maybe less if I get lucky. The preacher's got a head start but those wheels of yours oughtta do the trick."

A burst of static, and then Miles's voice: *". . . What are we doing, Lilly . . . ?"*

Lilly licks her lips and looks at Barbara. She squeezes the switch. "Tying up a loose end."

TWENTY-THREE

Miraculously, they both make it to the small clearing east of town, at approximately the same time—Lilly circumnavigating the herd by taking the long way around the switchyard, avoiding the thickest pockets of dead, Miles getting there by exiting the safe zone along Flat Shoals Road and then circling around the northeast corner of town. Once they get there, things start moving very quickly, far too quickly for them to notice any signs of tampering, such as fluid dripping from the convolutions of the Challenger's undercarriage.

By the time they reach the car, they are each far too winded and pumped up with adrenaline to see the broken boughs and branches on the west edge of the clearing or the freshly formed tire tracks angling across the ground. Sheltered by the shaggy boughs of willow trees, surrounded by thickets of ironweed, the area is bordered on one side by the Flint River and barely large enough to accommodate a full-sized sedan. The neon purple Dodge Challenger sits in the center of the clearing, gleaming in the pale daylight filtering down through the skeletal branches of black oaks.

They don't say much to each other at first, communicating mostly through gestures and nods and quick hand signals. They're in a big hurry. Lilly figures the preacher has a ten-minute head start. If they're lucky, they can locate him by the wake of dust and exhaust kicked up by the massive tow truck. But luck will also have to play a part.

The preacher could easily take an unexpected turn and be off the grid in the blink of an eye.

Miles fires up the 426 cubic inches as Lilly climbs in through the passenger door. The gargantuan V8 gargles to life, emitting a belch of black exhaust and the roar of a mint-condition hemi cold block with zero catalytic converters to slow things down. Neither of them notice the recently formed imprint of a body in the dirt beneath the car, nor do they see the oily puddle of crimson brake fluid just beginning to form beneath the front end.

The car lurches backward.

Miles yanks the wheel, then rams the shift lever forward and steps on it, sending the Challenger into a fishtailing rush across greasy weeds, then blasting out through the south end of the clearing, where a dirt road wends along the Flint for about a mile and a half before giving way to the Crest Highway. If Miles had been less engaged with the mission and paying closer attention to the function of the brake pedal, he might have noticed the squishiness in the brakes when he brought the car to a stop in order to throw it into drive. But things are too chaotic now to detect such nuances, and besides, the line was only partially cut minutes earlier, and is still functioning. The intention of the saboteur, apparently, is for it to blow out under pressure.

Lilly glances over her shoulder at the walker-riddled landscape around the little town as it recedes into the distance behind them. She can see the gore shooting into the air a mile away, the vertical stack of Tommy's harvester spewing like a Texas gusher. The sight of the combine mowing down rows of walking dead while the beleaguered town sits in a miasma of smoke puts a crimp in her heart.

She shakes it off and turns back to gaze out the steeply angled windshield at the overcast sunlight beating down on the weathered pavement of the two-lane rushing under their car. Miles has already hit sixty miles an hour, a lot faster than the state police would recommend on an access road such as this, and now the kid has his hoodie up and over his head. Lilly can see only the front of his narrow nose, a few strands of his dreadlocks, and his boyish chin with

its little peach-fuzz goatee jutting out as he concentrates with practiced intensity, scanning and not staring, steering with his left
hand, his right on the shift knob. Lilly figures the hood is an affec-
tation, an obsessive-compulsive habit donned whenever the young
man is on the job, and that's fine with her. She needs this kid at the
peak of his game if they're going to catch up with the preacher's tow
truck—a vehicle that can't hope to match the Challenger for speed,
agility, and handling. In fact, the preacher is about the only thing
Lilly can think about right now.

The need for closure—for the termination of this madman's
reign—burns as bright as magnesium behind Lilly's eyes. This bloodlust so preoccupies her thoughts that she's completely oblivious to
the fact that the car is starting to exhibit obvious signs of tampering.

Of course, Lilly has no idea that Jeremiah Garlitz was once employed as a service station attendant when he was in his teens, and
that he knows all the tricks, especially the ones employed to quickly
and discreetly sabotage cars. Mechanics talk about this kind of stuff
all the time. They have chat lines on the Internet and they share inside information about how this kind of thing is not like it's shown
in the movies. How would Lilly ever know this? How would she ever
guess in a million years that Jeremiah would try such a thing in
order to ensure that nobody pursued him? How would she ever know
that his scouts had found the Challenger's secret parking place?

The truth is, even if Lilly had known all these things, she probably would have still gone after the preacher. Rage is pulling her
strings now, narrowing her thoughts into a tunnel, crackling in her
brain like an overloading circuit. She can taste the man's death on
her tongue.

But all this is about to change as soon as they hit their first big
downgrade.

Tommy Dupree loses his voice after nearly twenty minutes of sustained howling—his triumphant howls accompanied by the collective
din of hundreds and hundreds of walkers turned to pulp under

the churning devastation of the combine's massive cutting skid. Over the rumbling of the engine and the clatter of the whirling blades, the wet, garbled, crunching noise of cadavers being ground to pieces is tremendous, addictive, surreal.

Tommy's voice finally crumbles into a hoarse hissing noise as he cries out for his dead parents, for his lost childhood, for his ruined world.

The black geyser of tissues continues to leap up and wash across his machine, wave after wave, sluicing down the window glass, pulsing and streaking in the wipers, feeding Tommy's psychotic state. He has turned half of the super-herd into paste, cutting a swath of annihilation from the edge of the safe zone all the way east to Kendricks Road, and he keeps going, and he will keep going until he runs out of gas or dies—whichever comes first—because he was born to do this. All those summer landscaping jobs, commandeering the riding mower until his neck blistered in the sun and his arms seized up with cramps, all to help his parents dig their way out of bankruptcy, and maybe to also thumb his nose at the kids at Rolling Acres grade school who made fun of him because he was poor and he had to wear those Kmart tennis shoes all the time—all of it has led to this: his destiny, his true calling.

He is covered with a fine layer of gore the color of stomach bile, the suction of the wind blowing a mist of the walkers' tissue through the vents of the pilothouse. Tommy doesn't care. He also doesn't notice that the fuel gauge is on "E" and that the engine is starting to sputter.

Fiddling with the gearbox, increasing the speed of the windshield wipers, he steers the machine toward the next wave of walkers coming toward him from the parking lot of the derelict grocery store on Millard Road. Through the slime-coated glass, he sees them reaching for the blades as though deliverance awaits in the rushing metal teeth, and then go down in a chain reaction, faces furrowed and vexed, eyes popping out of their skulls.

The engine dies.

The great revolving shredder in front slowly jangles to a rusty, creaking stop.

Tommy leans forward with a jerk, the silence terrifying. Entrails drip down into the works of the reaper. Tommy looks at the gauge to his right, taps it, sees the needle resting on the pin below "E," and starts to panic. He unbuckles his safety harness and is climbing out of his bucket seat when the first impact shudders through the cabin, as though the earth itself has buckled under the machine. Something is pushing on the side of the combine. Tommy climbs across the cab to the side window and looks down.

Scores of biters, all shapes and sizes, all whipped into frenzies, push up against the side of the machine. Tommy grabs hold of the seat-back as another shudder passes through the interior. The right side of the machine levitates a few inches and then bangs back down as more and more walkers swarm the combine. Tommy holds on tightly, fingers digging into the upholstery.

The machine begins to list, leaning to the left on its enormous wheels, as the collective pressure of hundreds of the dead press in on the right side.

Tommy lets out a scream—his voice gone, only a hoarse rasp coming out—as the combine begins to tip over.

"Check that shit out! Down in the northbound fucking lane! There's that motherfucker!"

As the Challenger roars along the plateau overlooking Elkins Creek, Miles Littleton sees the distant bloom of dust about a quarter mile away on Highway 74. He points down at the valley of tobacco fields spreading off to their right like a vast patchwork quilt in the washed out sunlight. The tow truck roars eastward, burning oil, sending up gouts of black smoke into the atmosphere.

"Take the next turnoff!" Lilly indicates an intersection up ahead, a narrow dirt road snaking down the side of the hill toward the farmland.

"Fuck!—FUCK!" All at once Miles is looking down at the dashboard. "FUCK!!"

"What's the matter?" Lilly sees the intersection coming up fast, the turnoff on the right marked by reflectors on sticks. "Slow the fuck down!"

"The brakes are fucked!"

"WHAT?!"

"The brakes ain't working!"

"Turn here, goddamnit—TURN!" Lilly grabs the steering wheel and yanks it at the last possible moment, sending the Challenger into a skid, eliciting an angry cry from Miles as he wrestles the wheel back in line.

The car careens around the corner and plunges down the slope.

For a brief instant, Lilly feels the weightless sensation of a roller coaster, as though she might levitate out of her seat. The trees blur by them on either side, the wind whipping across their open windows, whistling above the engine. The car squeals around a series of curves and then the road straightens out.

The Challenger picks up speed.

"We. Got. No. Fucking. Brakes!" Miles restates this fact as though it is an imponderable cosmological formula that only a handful of astrophysicists might truly grasp. He struggles with the wheel, keeping a white-knuckle grip, teeth clenched inside the shadow of his hoodie. The speedometer inches past eighty, past eighty-five. "Motherfucker must have cut our lines, if you believe that shit!"

"Just keep it steady!" On the straightaway Lilly can now get a clear line of sight on the tow truck in the distance, a little over a quarter mile ahead of them, a watery image in the heat rays of the highway.

The Challenger reaches the bottom of the hill, their speed exceeding ninety miles an hour now, and the gravitational forces suck Lilly into her seat. Miles lets out an angry grunt and steers the car onto a forking entrance ramp. The wheels drum and complain on the weathered pavement as they roar onto the highway. The wind buffets them, pounding against the open window.

"AIN'T EVEN GIVING IT ANY GAS!" Miles marvels at this new development above the noise. "ABOUT TO HIT THE CENTURY MARK, AIN'T EVEN TOUCHING THE FOOT-FEED!—MOTHERFUCKER FUCKED WITH THE ENGINE!"

As Lilly checks the two pistols wedged behind her belt, their speed holds at around the 100-mph mark—a surprisingly bumpy ride on the original shocks and pinions. The distance between the two vehicles is closing fast. Apparently, Jeremiah has the tow truck opened up, running at top speed, judging by the way the thing is weaving from lane to lane and smoking profusely. This section of the highway is relatively free of wreckage, but every now and then, Miles is forced to swerve to avoid the carcass of an abandoned car or the fossilized remnants of a camper lying on its side.

"Shit!" Lilly drops the speed-loader, and it rolls under the seat.

Up ahead, the preacher's truck looms closer and closer. At this distance—a little less than a hundred yards—the human remains hanging off the tow crane are visible, a grisly simulacrum of something that used to be a man, the arms and legs long gone, the object now resembling a side of beef hanging in a meatpacking plant. The strobe, evidently connected to the truck's battery, still flickers at odd Pavlovian intervals.

Lilly stops looking for the bullets and stares at that blinking strobe.

Something breaks loose inside her—something unseen and deeply buried—triggered by that silver beacon flashing its cryptic signal. Looming closer and closer, the Challenger draws to within a hundred feet of the fishtailing, smoking, gore-draped heap of a truck, and Lilly feels the tide of rage inside her crash up against the wall of something far darker.

A psychologist might call this "hypomania." Active-duty soldiers call it a "kill frenzy."

"What the fuck are you doing now?!" Miles demands to know when Lilly tosses the gun into the backseat, her focus still locked on to that flickering signal light. He alternates his gaze from her to the front of the vehicle, which is closing in on the rear of the tow truck, the carnage-festooned crane close enough now to reach out and touch. "Hold on, girlfriend! Gonna ram it!"

The wide grille of the Challenger smashes into the truck's trailer hitch.

This shoves both Miles and Lilly forward, smashing them into the dash, sending shards of pain up the bridge of Lilly's nose, galvanizing her, electrifying her as the pale silver light goes on flashing like some out-of-kilter disco ball. In the cab of the tow truck, Jeremiah ducks down for a moment, flinching at the impact.

Miles holds the car steady as a large fragment of the tow truck's bumper tears away and clatters to the road, bouncing off into an adjacent field.

Lilly pushes herself up and out the open passenger window. The noise of the slipstream drowns out Miles's bellowing shouts of anger and confusion. All Lilly can hear now are the gusts of wind and the dissonant harmony of the two power plants roaring in unison as she climbs out onto the window frame, grasping the side mirror for purchase. Then she clambers onto the hood.

The car swerves slightly.

She braces herself on the air injector, rises up, coils herself, bending her knees and fixing her gaze on the rear deck of the massive tow truck, and leaps.

TWENTY-FOUR

Lilly lands on the rear edge of the truck's deck, her combat boots slipping off the ledge. She slides a few feet, clawing for a handhold. The toes of her boots brushing the pavement. Lilly grabs the tow arm. The metal is greasy with the blood of the dangling corpse.

For one terrible moment, she hangs there. Her feet drag along behind the truck on the rushing highway, causing the toes of her boots to heat up to the point of smoking. The truck swerves. Lilly flops to the right. The human remains break off the crane and tumble across the oncoming lanes and into a ditch. The truck jerks the other way.

Lilly nearly falls off, but now she finds the strength—probably through the sheer force of her hatred—to haul herself back up.

The wind buffets her. The gusts threaten to blow her off the truck as she climbs onto the blood-slick cargo area. She crouches down. The wind burns her eyes. She peers through the cab's rear window and sees the back of the preacher's head as he wrestles with the wheel and reaches for something on the seat—probably his gun. She quickly surveys the contents of the cargo hold. She sees small cable spools and railroad spikes and empty bottles rolling around. She sees an iron pry bar. She grabs it.

She glances back at the cab window.

Jeremiah is aiming his Glock 9mm at her. Before he can shoot, she swings the pry bar. The hooked end bangs against the glass but doesn't break it. The preacher flinches, the truck swerving again. Lilly stumbles and falls. The pry bar goes flying. Jeremiah sees an obstruction coming up fast in the left lane.

He swerves the other way to avoid it and sends Lilly tumbling back against the opposite side of the bulwark. Behind the truck, the wide, grimacing front grille of the Challenger hovers mere feet off the back of the tow arm. Miles refuses to abandon Lilly, bad brakes be damned. He'll stay with this truck forever.

Lilly gets back on her feet and grabs the iron bar and swings it harder at the window—once, twice, three times, the third impact shattering the safety glass into a sheet of diamonds.

The glass implodes. Glittering particles swirl into the cab. The truck swerves wildly. Lilly can hear the preacher's scream. Jeremiah's Glock goes spinning across the seat. Lilly lifts herself up on the edge of the broken window. Her hands impale themselves on the jagged glass. The pain drives her into the cab.

She grabs Jeremiah's arm. Half her body hangs out the broken window as she tugs on him. Jeremiah writhes and curses. Lilly yanks on his arm. The steering wheel jerks. The tow truck swerves across the two lanes toward the gravel shoulder. The tires squeal. The roar of the engine intensifies. The truck skirts along the edge of the ditch at seventy-five miles an hour. The wheels drum wildly over craggy, rutted sections of bare earth. The vibrations turn the cab into pandemonium.

Jeremiah tries to strangle Lilly. He gets one huge gnarled hand around her throat. Lilly pulls away. She falls the rest of the way into the cab. Jeremiah takes a wild swing at her and connects. The impact of his gigantic fist makes her see sparks and gasp.

Lilly has short fingernails but she slashes at the side of his face as the truck weaves and fishtails on the dirt slope. The truck leans at a forty-five-degree angle. Lilly's nails rake across the preacher's right eye and cheek. Jeremiah bellows in pain. He loses control of the truck. It starts to tip.

The preacher slams on the brakes. The rear tires dig in. Lilly bangs into the dash as the truck goes into a skid. Jeremiah tries to steer into it. The truck slides sideways for a moment.

Then Lilly screams as the whole world seems to turn on its axis and throw her against the ceiling.

Miles lets out a wail. He sees the truck tipping. He swerves. The tow truck slams down on its side. In a cloud of dust, the Challenger roars past the site. It has no brakes but Miles angrily stomps on the useless brake pedal.

In the rearview mirror, he can see the tow truck violently sliding along on its side. It slides and slides for almost a hundred yards, digging a grove out of the ground. Then it comes to a dusty stop in a ditch.

Miles frantically tries everything he can think of to stop. He stands on the brake pedal with both feet. He puts the car in low gear. The engine groans and revs but only slows the car down incrementally. The Challenger keeps barreling along—a mile, two miles past the wrecked truck.

He tries putting the car in neutral and letting it coast along the shoulder. This starts to work. But when a pile of wreckage looms, he has to shift back into drive and swerve around the obstruction.

Then, an instant later, he makes a critical error. He looks back up into the rearview. He just wants to see if there's any sign of the tow truck behind him. But his gaze lingers there too long. When he looks back at the road he lets out a yelp of shock.

Two large mobile homes lie wrecked across both lanes of the highway.

The Challenger crashes through the center of the wreckage, slamming Miles against the wheel, breaking a tooth, concussing his skull. The car barrels through another hundred feet of twisted metal and goes into a skid. Miles wrestles with the wheel. The Challenger spirals into a wild 360.

Miles blacks out as the car slides off the edge of a precipice and goes into a roll.

It rolls a total of five revolutions before landing in a dry river-bed.

Two figures crane their necks to see over the top of a makeshift barricade on the northeast corner of town.

"I'm going after him," the man mutters, peering through binoculars. In the oval field of vision, he can see the gigantic combine lying on its side in a gravel parking lot at the end of Kendricks Road.

"You think that's a good idea?" Norma Sutters stands next to David Stern, wiping her plump hands in a towel. Her face still has the stains of offal she'd smeared on herself to blend in with the horde. But her smock is now covered with the fresh blood shed by Harold Staubach. She'd been caring for him for the last hour now.

David looks at the woman. "We can't leave the poor kid out there."

"The boy might be gone, David. I'm sorry to be so damn harsh but—"

"Norma—"

"Listen, we don't want to be losing another one of us in order to save somebody who's already dead."

David wipes his gray goatee, thinks about it. "I'm going. That's all there is to it."

He climbs down the ladder and goes off in search of ammo for his Tec-9.

Lilly comes to in the smoky interior of the overturned truck. Blinking at first, squinting in the harsh glare of overcast daylight flooding down through the gaping driver's-side window—which is now the ceiling—she silently takes inventory of her injuries. Her back throbs, wrenched by the impact, and she tastes coppery blood where she bit her tongue, but she doesn't seem to have any broken bones.

She suddenly registers the fact that the preacher—still unconscious—is slumped over the steering wheel above her, his lanky limbs akimbo, tangled in his shoulder harness. She regards his limp form. She considers the possibility that he might already be dead. His flesh is gray and pallid. She watches his big barrel chest, and sees that it is slowly, subtly rising and falling—he's clearly alive—and Lilly is about to start looking for the gun when his eyes pop open and he pounces on her.

Lilly screams and the preacher responds by wrapping his big, callused hands around her throat.

He lowers the rest of his weight down upon her, the sound of tearing fabric coming from behind him as his waistcoat stays tangled in the steering wheel, the seams ripping apart. Lilly gasps, convulses—the common reactions to stage one of asphyxia—and tries to get air into her lungs, but the preacher's fingers tighten. She instinctively reaches up and tries to pry them from her neck, but this is easier to do in theory than in practice. His vise-grip lock on her throat is steadfast, immovable.

Jeremiah stares into her eyes with surprising calm, whispering something under his breath that sounds at first almost incantatory, as though he's putting a spell on her. Their faces are close enough for her to see the yellow tobacco stains between his teeth and the tiny capillaries of red lining the whites of his eyes, as well as the grain of the psoriatic skin patches on his cheeks. She enters stage two: the onslaught of hypoxia.

It feels to her as though he's been strangling her for hours. Her lungs catch fire, and her vision blurs, and she feels her entire body tingling as the tissues become oxygen-starved. She begins to involuntarily shudder in his grasp—a series of violent paroxysms resembling an epileptic fit. Her legs kick and tremble. Her boot heels bang off the floor. Her arms flail futilely, making feeble attempts to hit the man, when all at once her right hand brushes against something metallic and cold and familiar on the floor next to her, wedged between the mat and the door.

She is about to enter stage three—unconsciousness, a short jaunt to death—when it registers in her brain what she's touching: *the 9mm pistol.*

This revelation is the last blip of conscious thought that zips across Lilly's synapses before everything shuts down and she passes out.

Lilly Caul has experienced lost time on several occasions in her life—drunken binges at college, druggy parties with Megan Lafferty, the time she got in that terrible car wreck in Fort Lauderdale—but nothing even remotely compares with this. It's as though some cosmic film editor has cut a scene out of her time line.

She has no idea how the gun got picked up, how it got raised, how the trigger got pulled, or how the bullet found its way to such a critical part of the preacher's anatomy. The fact is, Lilly cannot for the life of her remember aiming it, let alone *firing* it.

All she remembers is awakening to the strangest noise, which at first sounded like a baby crying—a high, shrill whine that deteriorated into a rusty, creaking groan. Now she feels as though she's a deep-sea diver with the bends, frantically swimming up toward the surface of the ocean, toward sweet, sweet oxygen, toward release, toward life.

Bursting out of the black water, she gasps and breathes in great, heaving gulps of air.

Sensory overload assaults her. Her neck throbs as though rope-burned. She's holding the Glock, and it's as hot as a branding iron, and the air is thick with blue smoke, and Jeremiah lies in a fetal position on the other side the cab. He's holding his groin, which is soaked in blood, and he's caterwauling in agony, all of which explains the crying-baby sound.

All at once it comes rushing back to her. How they ended up in a sideways truck cab, and how he was strangling her, and how she felt the gun right before blacking out. Now she realizes she hit the bull's-eye.

She catches her breath, rubs her neck with her free hand, and tries to speak, but only a thin, wispy cough comes out. She swallows hard, and touches her windpipe. It feels as though it's intact. She takes in a few more breaths and manages to rise to a kneeling position in the upended cab. She ejects the ammo magazine, sees that it has plenty of rounds left, slams it back in, and points the gun at the preacher.

"Shut the fuck up." Her voice is hoarse and weak, but resolute, determined, cold. "And do what I say or the next one goes into your skull."

The preacher manages to sit up, swallowing thickly, breathing hard and fast. His bald head is stippled in blood. He winces. He holds his bloody crotch. He swallows again and finally utters, "Just get it over with."

"Get out." She indicates the door in the ceiling that used to be the driver's side. "Now!"

He cocks his bald head so that he can see the door directly above him. He looks at her. "You gotta be kidding."

She aims the gun at one of his knees, but before she can fire he struggles to his feet.

"I'm *going*," he moans, and with great, laborious effort rises up to his full height.

It takes forever for the wounded preacher to struggle out of the massive cab, lower himself down the front grille, and drop to the ground with an agonizing grunt. His pants are soaked with blood, his flesh is the color of wallpaper paste, his breathing is tacky with fluids.

Lilly climbs out of the cab behind him and hops to the ground. "Get on your knees," she says flatly, aiming the gun at him.

He takes a deep breath, stands up, faces her, and squares his shoulders as though prepared to fight. "No."

She shoots one knee.

Jeremiah screams. The blast takes a tuft out of his trousers, sends a gout of blood out the back of his leg, and tosses him staggering backward. He goes down in a heap, holding his knee, howling in pain. His face is a mask of agony. He looks up at her with tears in his eyes. "Why . . . ? Why are you doing this?"

She stands over him, expressionless, thinking of Bob and Woodbury. At last, she says, "Because the universe wants me to."

Covered in blood and tears and snot, he gazes up at her and begins to laugh. Nothing joyous. Just a dry, ironic, icy chuckle. "You think you're God?"

She stares unmercifully at him. "No, I'm not God." She aims at his shoulder. "And neither are you."

The gun barks.

This time the blast takes a chunk from his left pectoral and exits in a fog of red tissue out his trapezius, spinning him in an awkward arabesque and sending him sprawling to the ground. He gasps and tries to crawl away. He collapses. He huffs painfully into the dirt, rolls over, and stares at the sky.

She calmly walks over to him. She doesn't say anything at first, just gazes down at him.

"M-missy, p-please . . ." He's nearly hyperventilating now, his game-show-host face marbled with blood, his shaved pate looking almost comical. "P-please . . . f-finish it . . . p-put me outta my misery."

Then she smiles—perhaps one of the coldest smiles ever shared between two human beings—and says, "Nope . . . I got a better idea."

TWENTY-FIVE

It won't be long now.

Crouching in the tight quarters of the harvester's cab, out of ammo, out of options, David Stern *thinks* this, but he doesn't say it, not in the presence of this kid, this brave, heroic, badass twelve-year-old who took on the entire super-herd single-handedly in this giant monster that he barely knew how to operate—that he'd learned how to run by scanning the fucking manual, of all things.

Now the boy huddles next to David in the metal coffin, shivering, waiting to die.

The cab shudders once again, making creaking noises like a sinking ship as the swarm continues pressing in, harder and harder against all sides of the overturned harvester. Through the jagged opening of broken glass that used to be a windshield, three feet to his left, David can see the massive blade enclosure, still slimy with the entrails of countless dead, now bent into two pieces from the impact of the crash. He can also see the horde flocking to the wreckage, many more than when David first charged across those three blocks between the safe zone and the ruined machine with grandiose ideas of rescuing the boy.

You stupid, arrogant asshole, David thinks, *wallowing in your own hubris.*

Only fifteen minutes or so had passed since the moment David had run out of ammo and realized he had made a huge mistake, tossing his weapon aside and climbing into this battered crypt with the boy. Now hundreds, maybe thousands more biters have arrived to push inward on the crumpling steel shell of the combine without forethought, without purpose other than to feed; a thousand-plus pallid, mottled faces creased with torturous hunger, thousands of milky, cataract-crusted eyes fixed on the lone pair of humans hunkering in the tiny tomb that used to be a cab; thousands of blackened, clawlike fingers raking the metal skin of the machine like fingernails on a chalkboard.

"What if we go out the bottom!" The boy, with his bile-soaked sweatshirt and Little Rascal wheat-straw hair that's standing straight up as though electrocuted, is pointing at the single square foot of a corrugated metal trapdoor embedded in the bottom of the cab, which is now the wall to Tommy's immediate right. "We could—"

"No, it's no good." David sighs painfully. "Too many of them. We're safer in here for the time being."

The boy looks at him. "We can't just sit here forever—we gotta try something."

"I'm thinking."

The boy crawls to the trapdoor. He fiddles with the latch, which was damaged in the capsizing. "I think we could sneak out this—"

"Get away from it!" David Stern hisses his words at him. "They'll get in!"

"I don't think they—"

The trapdoor suddenly bursts inward with a metallic clang that sends the boy reeling backward, blinking convulsively, shuddering in shock. Dozens of hands reach into the enclosure, hooklike fingers with blackened nails clawing at the air, flailing for food. Tommy lets out a yelp. David lunges for the hatch and tries to kick the medusa knot of arms and hands back out the opening, when all at once a series of gigantic cracking noises spread through the infrastructure of the wreck, and David Stern turns just in time to see a nightmare unfurl before his very eyes.

The walls of the cab begin to bow outward under the pressure of a sudden surge of the dead, and the seams of the combine start to split apart down the middle. Rivets pop like firecrackers. Death-stench and the clamor of collective snarls fill the airless chamber. Tommy shrieks and backs up against the vertical floor.

David madly searches the cab for a weapon, but the shift in grav-ity as the machine tips and collapses into itself sends him to the floor.

Tommy falls on top of the older man, and the two of them hug each other almost instinctively as the last intact section of windshield breaks apart. Ragged figures tumble into the cab. David pushes Tommy into the corner and grabs a mangled four-foot section of window frame. The closest biter gets the pointed edge of the frame thrust through its eye, sending spurts of fluid down on top of Tommy Dupree. The boy howls with a primal mixture of rage, terror, and re-pulsion.

David swings at the next one, and the next, and the next, know-ing all along that it's just a show, a charade for the boy. David Stern has no hope of fighting off an endless clown car of monsters flood-ing the breached enclosure. But he keeps at them, slashing one across the temple, stabbing another through the eye socket, gouging yet an-other one through the roof of the mouth. Fluids and blood and tis-sue engulf the chamber, and soon the bodies collect on the floor of the cab inches away from where the boy struggles not to cry out loud. He just sits there, shoulders trembling, moist eyes taking it all in, tears tracking down his freckled face.

And when the older man is finally overcome, and he stumbles backward, tripping over his own feet and collapsing only inches away from the boy, the two living humans look away. They don't want to watch, they don't want to see the end come in its ghastly form of a feeding frenzy. They can sense the faces full of teeth looming over them, snarling, ravenous, teeth gnashing, lowering down to-ward them—and then *nothing*. No searing pain from the first bite, no convulsions of agony as more of them dig into the soft middle and the delicacies within.

David pops his eyes open. Dozens of dead hover motionless over him and the boy, as still as mannequins in a forgotten store window, each biter resembling a dog being summoned by an ultrasonic whistle. One by one, they twitch their empty gazes off to the south as though tracking the source of the silent whistle. David stares. The faintest clicking noise drifts on the wind; a flash of heat lightning flickers off the faces of the dead. The tableau is all very dreamlike at first, but with each passing second, it intensifies. An engine in the distance rises on the breeze.

Tommy starts to whisper something in a startled voice when the strangest thing happens: The monsters begin to retreat, backing slowly out of the enclosure, brushing against one another as they awkwardly withdraw and turn to seek out the source of that flashing light. They are wandering off en masse toward the sound of the engine, and the flickering silver light.

David sits up. He rubs his eyes as though awakening from a dream, and he looks at Tommy, who also levers himself up to a sitting position.

"What the *fuck*," Tommy says almost rhetorically as he watches the mass exodus of the dead.

Lilly keeps a close watch on the cracked side mirror of the battered tow truck as she pulls slowly past the ruins of Ingles Market. She moves along at less than five miles per hour—walking speed—in order to allow the greatest number of supplicants to follow along. The town is surprisingly quiet considering the population of dead currently filling the streets and lumbering along in the wake of the truck. The air smells of brimstone and scorched electrical terminals as the breeze wafts through the cab's broken window vent.

Lilly downshifts and turns south, heading toward the train yard.

In the reflection of her side mirror, she can see the preacher lashed to the massive tow arm at the back of the truck. Still clad in his stained shirtsleeves, black trousers, and boots, his gunshot wounds oozing now from under his clothes, he looks like a living figurehead on the prow of a ship, his arms dangling limply, his bald head lolling as he wavers in and out of consciousness.

The strobe light continues to blink above him, a beacon drawing the herd.

Every few seconds, Jeremiah lets out a garbled cry—a mishmash of words and nonsense syllables in which Lilly has absolutely no interest. She merely appreciates the Pavlovian effect the sound of his voice is having on the mass congregation following the tow truck. More and more of the dead are gathering—they're already at least fifty rows deep behind the preacher, and their number is growing.

Lilly drives slowly past the stationhouse, where the children still huddle with Barbara in the shadows, waiting for the all-clear signal.

From the train yard, Lilly turns west and makes a large, slow circle around the far corner of town. Lured by the eldritch noises of Jeremiah's voice, as well as by the flashing signal flare, walkers skulk out of speedway cloisters, out from behind abandoned semitrailers, out of ditches and culverts and nooks and crannies. The mob grows. In her hairline-fractured mirror, Lilly sees an ocean of dead trailing after the mumbled ravings of the madman.

From the top of Whitehouse Parkway, she turns east and heads back the way she came.

By the time she reaches the east side of town, the preacher is near death, and practically the entire herd is following along behind the truck, a vast field of walking dead spanning one and a half city blocks and at least two hundred yards deep. She marvels at the breadth and width of the throngs, visible in the funhouse reflection of her side mirror. The herd is so enormous that the seething masses in the rear, at the farthest point, are just a hazy blur in the overcast afternoon.

Lilly slowly passes the wreckage of Tommy Dupree's combine. She gazes over her shoulder as two figures climb out of the battered, overturned cab. Tommy comes first, lowering himself down the jagged length of windshield, looking like an animal coming out of hibernation. David comes next. The older man struggles out and squints into the steel gray sky, taking a deep breath of life-affirming air.

Tommy gapes at the receding multitude, robotically following the blinking light. He stares, and stares, his mouth hanging open. David stands next to him. The older man just shakes his head in awe as he watches.

Lilly makes a slight turn at Riggins Ferry Road and heads toward the wide expanse of desolate lots and fallow fields along the Flint River Valley.

Her destination is eleven miles away—roughly two and a half hours, at this speed—so she settles back in her seat, and lets out a long sigh.

Her thoughts wander, the mythic drama going on at this very moment directly behind her the furthest thing from her mind.

The great and honorable Reverend Jeremiah Garlitz preaches his last sermon that day, lashed to a gantry twelve feet above the scabrous land that he thinks of as Zion. In his scrambled final thoughts, he speaks to his vast megachurch of lost souls, who shamble dutifully after him in the dust of the holy land. He speaks much of his homily in old Latin, floating in midair, surrounded by angels. He spreads his arms and smiles beatifically at the great assembly of the faithful following him—his Christian soldiers, his righteous disciples—their dark, dirty, impoverished faces full of noble savagery. God bless his congregants.

This goes on for hours, Jeremiah recalling all the great chapters and verses, all the best sermons he delivered over his life in sweaty tents and backwater churches. The flicker of the votive candle above him illuminates his altar as the ragged parishioners follow him for miles and miles, many of them barefoot, bleeding, crippled, leprous, sick, old and infirm. Toward the end of the journey, Jeremiah feels a loosening of his soul, a shade coming down on his field of vision, and he rejoices. He feels his chariot speeding up, his wings spreading, catching the wind, the angels lifting him up through the stratosphere to paradise.

His last act is a singing out of joyous testimony in an ancient language.

While the heavens embrace him.

It happens almost too quickly for Lilly to notice the sound. She opens the driver's-side door a hundred feet from the edge of the precipice, on the south side of Emory Hill—the place where she used to gaze longingly upon her walker-riddled town—and now she wedges the crowbar between the seat and the accelerator pedal.

The tow truck lurches as Lilly leaps out onto the rocky earth, the thunder of wind and the revving engine drowning out all other sounds, except for the voice.

Even as she's running for the trees of the adjacent forest, hurrying to avoid contact with the herd, and the tow truck is careening over the edge of the precipice, Lilly can hear the faint sound of the preacher's voice. As the truck soars over the ledge and plummets seventy-five feet to the boulder-strewn river's edge below, Lilly hears the bizarre vocalizations of someone speaking in tongues.

Then the sound is drowned out by the collective growls of hundreds of walking cadavers dragging themselves over the edge— lemminglike, faithful to the last—as the light flickers all the way down into oblivion. From behind a thick grove of trees, breathless after the sprint, Lilly watches the mass migration over the precipice, a magnificent cascade of the dead as row after row plunges off the ledge.

Just before turning away, Lilly realizes an excoriating irony: At last, Jeremiah gets to partake in the mass suicide he'd always dreamed of experiencing.

TWENTY-SIX

David Stern is about to give up on his watch for the night. Lowering the binoculars, he lets out a pained breath, shaking his head. He has no idea what time it is, or how long it's been since he's slept, or how many hours he's been perched on the roof of this godforsaken semi-trailer, gazing over the top of the barricade, ceaselessly scanning the distant woods and hills of the neighboring tobacco country, hoping he might see a ghostly figure returning, beating the impossible odds of the previous day's climactic series of events. He stretches his sore, arthritic joints.

"And how long are you gonna keep waiting for her to magically appear?" a voice says from below.

David jumps with a start. "Jesus, Babs!" He looks down at his wife. "How long have you been standing down there?"

"About a year and half."

"Very funny." He starts climbing down a ladder that leans against the trailer. "Did the kids finally nod off?" he asks as he hops down to the street.

The safe zone, which encompasses four square blocks of Wood-bury, includes several merchants whose shelves haven't been completely picked clean, as well as a small bed-and-breakfast formerly called The Green Veranda, whose rooms are currently occupied by the six children. Earlier that night, they set up a makeshift infirmary in the front room of the inn, where Norma Sutters, if she's still awake, is continuing to look after Harold.

On the whole, though, compared with the hardships of living underground, the place is an oasis of luxury.

"All except Tommy," Barbara says with a weary shrug. Her face is bandaged, and her voice has gone a little nasal due to the swollen bridge of her nose. But to David, in the moonless dark, illuminated only by a torch burning in front of the inn, she is the most beautiful woman on earth. "The boy insists on staying on at his sister's bedside with a shotgun across his knees."

"Good for him," David says, and looks around the zone. "I'm still trying to get used to the quiet." He jerks a thumb at the wall. "There's a few stragglers out there."

"Yeah, there's a few creepers around—must be either atheists or Jews."

David looks askance at her. "Huh?"

"They didn't follow the preacher. Weren't interested. Can't say I blame them, either, even though, according to your mom, I'll always be a shiksa."

Too tired to laugh, David just grins and shakes his head and touches her cheek. "Whaddaya say we go and try to get some of that sleep people have been talking about?"

She's about to answer when they hear an incongruous noise outside the wall on the wind.

They look at each other.

Barbara finally says, "They may be Jews, but since when do they drive?"

David turns and hurries back up the ladder, grabbing the binoculars, peering through the lenses at the darkness beyond the outskirts. He sees the headlights first, and then recognizes the car.

"I'll be a son of a bitch!" he mutters, and hastens back down the ladder. "C'mon!" He trots over to the truck cab blocking a ten-foot-wide gap between barricades. Barbara follows.

David hands her his pistol, then climbs up into the cab, fires up the engine, and backs away from the entrance. Barbara holds the gun on the opening. She thumbs the hammer back when she hears the rumble of a big engine closing in.

David sits in the truck cab, poised to roll it back across the gap.

Miles Littleton's purple Dodge Challenger, now as battered as a demolition derby car, booms through the opening and skids to a stop. David revs the semicab's engine, then pulls back across the opening. He hurriedly climbs down the sideboard with a smile on his face.

"Thank God!" Barbara says, lowering the gun, putting a hand to her mouth. Her eyes moisten. When the Challenger's dented driver's door squeaks open, she says, "Miles, we thought for sure we lost you out there!"

A battered and bruised Miles Littleton climbs out of the muscle car. "Nope! Still kickin'." He gives her a sideways smirk. Barbara hugs the young man, and David furiously shakes his hand, and Miles says, "And look who I found." He indicates the backseat. "Wandering alone out there, dehydrated as fuck, totally messed up."

David and Barbara lean in and see the figure curled up on the backseat, unmoving and silent. Barbara can barely breathe. "Is she—?"

"Sawing logs, y'all," Miles informs them, "snoring like a motherfucking bull moose." He pauses. "I guess she was pretty worn out."

"Thank God she's okay," Barbara mutters, wiping tears from her black-rimmed, bruised eyes.

David carefully opens the rear door, reaches down to Lilly's dusty hair, and strokes it gently. She has a furrowed brow, a strange expression on her face. David wonders if she's having a nightmare. "Maybe we should let her sleep a while," he says, backing away from her, gently closing the door. He looks at Barbara. "I think she's earned it."

"I don't know." Miles leans against the front quarter panel. "After she drifted off, I kept noticing her in the rearview, tossing and turning and shit. I think she might be having a major fucking dream."

David thinks about it for a moment, and finally says, "Let's let her sleep." He shares another glance with Barbara, and then turns to Miles. "Everybody deserves a chance to dream."

The three of them gather at the front end of car, leaning against the hood, idly chatting. David and Barbara give Miles some water, and check his wounds. Miles waxes poetically about the benefits of an old-school roll bar and shoulder harness in a 1972 production-line car made in America. They talk some more about the events of the past few days, and they wait patiently for their friend to navigate her nightmare.

And they will wait patiently, and they will guard that car with their lives, and they will continue to wait in the flickering darkness that night for as long as it takes for Lilly to work through the thickets and problems of her epic dream.

extracts reading groups
competitions books new
discounts extracts
extracts
competitions
books
new
events books
new extracts
books new reading groups
interviews
events extracts
discounts events
new books events
events new
discounts extracts discounts
www.panmacmillan.com
extracts events reading groups
competitions books extracts new
reading groups
events
reading groups
discounts
reading groups
books
interviews
new
books
extracts
books